Know SHIPS

Guide to Boatwatching on the Great Lakes & St. Lawrence Seaway, 1997

38th Edition - Updated Annually

ISBN No. 0-9626930-8-1

Copyright, 1997

Marine Publishing Co. Inc.

Box 68, Sault Ste. Marie, MI 49783

E-mail: rlkysbook @ aol.com

Founder: Tom Manse, 1915-1994

Editor & Publisher: Roger LeLievre

Researchers: Philip A. Clayton, Angela S. Clayton, Neil Schultheiss and John Vournakis

On the front cover: Oglebay Norton's **Columbia Star** approaching Duluth harbor.
(Michael R. Sipper)

On the back cover: Canadian bulk carriers **Algosound** and **Algogulf** in temporary lay-up at Sarnia.
(Roger LeLievre)

CONTENTS

Laker Mapleglen passes the saltie Ziemia Gnieznienska near Sault Ste. Marie 10 July, 1996. (Roger LeLievre)

Downbound meets upbound as the parade of commerce continues.
(Roger LeLievre)

The GREAT LAKES AREA

The Great Lakes area, bounded generally on the north by Canada and on the south by the United States, is home to one of the greatest industrial complexes in the world. Its steel plants call upon the iron, coal, petroleum and limestone resources of the continent, while agricultural areas produce vast grain harvests, transported by way of the lakes in uniquely designed ships during the 9-10 month navigation season. This commerce is as essential to the economic well-being of the nation and region as it is fascinating for those on shore to observe.

To handle Great Lakes traffic there has evolved a special type of vessel, the North American "laker." These vary in size, the largest lakers being 1,000 feet/304.8 meters long, capable of carrying up to 60,000 tons/60,966 tonnes of iron ore or 1,700,000 bushels/45,552.5 tonnes of grain. In addition, dozens of tugs, barges and excursion vessels add to the parade of maritime activity on the inland seas.

Many of the world's merchant ships also trade on the Great Lakes, entering via the St. Lawrence Seaway, which opened in 1959. Inbound, they may carry imported goods, heading home with grain or manufactured items. From the heartland of America to the heartland of the world, this book is dedicated!

GREAT LAKES LOADING PORTS

Iron Ore	Limestone	Coal	Grain	Cement
Duluth	Port Inland	Superior	Thunder Bay	Charlevoix
Superior	Cedarville	Thunder Bay	Duluth	Alpena
Two Harbors	Drummond	Chicago	Milwaukee	
Taconite	Island	Toledo	Chicago	**Gypsum**
Harbor	Calcite	Sandusky	Saginaw	
Marquette	Stoneport	Ashtabula	Sarnia	Port Gypsum
Escanaba	Marblehead	Conneaut	Toledo	Alabaster
			Huron	

Petroleum

Sarnia
East Chicago

UNLOADING PORTS

The primary iron ore and limestone receiving ports are Cleveland, Lorain, Chicago, Gary, Burns and Indiana Harbors, Detroit, Toledo, Ashtabula and Conneaut. Coal is carried to Milwaukee, Green Bay and a host of smaller ports in the U.S. and Canada. Most grain loaded on the lakes is destined for export via the St. Lawrence Seaway. Cement is delivered to terminals stretching from Duluth to Buffalo. Tankers bring petroleum products to cities as diverse in size as Cleveland and Detroit or Escanaba and Muskegon.

Tanker Turid Knutsen discharges petroleum products at Sarnia, ON.

(Roger LeLievre)

THE GREAT LAKES

Lake Superior

According to most references, the Seaway system begins at Duluth-Superior, at the western-most end of Lake Superior. Taconite ore pellets from the Minnesota

iron ranges, grain, and low-sulfur coal from Montana and Wyoming start their long trip to the lower lakes from the twin ports region, as well as from nearby Two Harbors, Taconite Harbor and Silver Bay. Iron ore is also shipped from the Marquette Range, while grain is exported from the Canadian lakehead at Thunder Bay. Lake Superior itself can boast of being the single largest body of freshwater in the world, measuring 383 miles (616.4 km) in length, 160 miles (257.5 km) at its widest point and 1,333 feet (406.3 m) at its deepest.

Lake Michigan

The second-largest of the Great Lakes is 321 miles (516.6 km) long, 118 miles (189 km) wide and 932 feet (281.3 m) at its deepest. Vessels calling at Escanaba load taconite consigned to Chicago-area steel mills, while grain and manufactured goods ship worldwide from Milwaukee, Green Bay and Chicago.

Lake Huron

Lake Huron, at 247 miles (397.5 km) long, 183 miles (294.5 km) wide and 750 feet (228.6 m) deep, is fed from Lake Superior by the St. Mary's River. Collingwood, on Georgian Bay, has a rich shipbuilding history, while Goderich enjoys an active grain and salt trade. On the U.S. side, Calcite specializes in the shipment of limestone while Alpena is a major cement port.

Lake Erie

The shallowest of the Great Lakes is 210 feet (64 m) deep, 241 miles (387.8 km) long and 57 miles (91.7 km) wide. Ore and coal shipped to Toledo, Cleveland, Ashtabula, Conneaut, Erie and Buffalo feed the industries of the region, while the same ports are major trans-shipment points for overseas cargos. The Welland Canal, near the Niagara Falls, connects lakes Erie and Ontario.

Lake Ontario

The most easterly of the Great Lakes is also the smallest, measuring 193 miles (310.6 km) in length and 53 miles (85.3 km) in width. The Canadian ports of Toronto and Hamilton enjoy brisk grain and ore trades, and host many saltwater vessels, while Ogdensburg, NY marks the start of the St. Lawrence River that runs into the Atlantic Ocean.

Detroit River, Lake St. Clair & St. Clair River

The **Detroit River**, from its mouth at the Detroit River Light in Lake Erie to Windmill Point Light at its head in Lake St. Clair, divides the U. S. and Canada for 32 miles/51.5 km.

Passing **Bois Blanc Island** (pronounced Bob-Lo), the eight mile/12.9 km long **Grosse Ile** (the largest island in the river) and marshy **Grassy Island**, the lower part of the river is divided into the **Amherstburg Channel** (for upbound vessel traffic), the **Livingstone Channel** (for downbound traffic) and the **Trenton Channel**.

Crossing the St. Clair River at Detroit/Windsor and linking the United States and Canada are the Conrail rail tunnel, the Detroit - Windsor auto tunnel and the stately **Ambassador Bridge**. At Detroit, the **J. W. Westcott Co.** delivers mail, newspapers and other necessities of life to all up and downbound vessels from April to December via mail boat.

At the upper end of the river lies **Belle Isle**, home to the Dossin Great Lakes Museum and the annual Detroit Grand Prix auto race. The Canadian Coast Guard operates a mandatory Vessel Traffic Service known as Sarnia Traffic from Detroit River Light in Lake Erie to Lake St. Clair Light on Channel 12 (156.600 Mhz).

Lake St. Clair, at 26 miles/41.8 km long, is the smallest of the Great Lakes and, with a natural depth of only 21 feet/6.4 meters, the shallowest. A popular fishing and pleasure boating lake, Lake St. Clair can also be one of the most violent during summer thunderstorms and sudden fall gales.

The **St. Clair River**, which is about 39 miles/62.8 km long from its mouth at Lake St. Clair to its head at Port Huron, is one of the busiest waterways in the world. The lower third of the river is a vast delta through which numerous channels empty into Lake St. Clair, while the upper two-thirds of the river consists of a single deep channel.

At the upper end of the river lies **Port Huron**, boyhood home to Thomas Edison, and **Sarnia**, the petrochemical capital of the Midwest. Crossing the river at Port Huron/Sarnia is the Canadian National Railway tunnel and the newly-twinned **Blue Water Bridge**, the last international crossing between the United States and Canada until Sault Ste. Marie. Sarnia Traffic operates a mandatory Vessel Traffic Service from Lake St. Clair Light to just above the Blue Water Bridge on Channel 11 (156.550 Mhz).

ST. LAWRENCE SEAWAY

The St. Lawrence Seaway is a deep waterway extending some 2,300 miles (3,701.4 km) from the Atlantic Ocean to the head of the Great Lakes at Duluth, including Montreal harbor and the Welland Canal. More specifically, it is the system of locks and canals (both U.S. and Canadian), opened in 1959, that allow vessels to pass from Montreal to the Welland Canal at the western end of Lake Ontario. The vessel size limit within this system is 740 feet (225.6 meters) long, 78 feet (23.8 meters) wide and 26 feet (7.9 meters) draft.

Closest to the ocean is the **St. Lambert Lock,** which lifts ships some 15 feet (4.6 meters) from Montreal harbor to the level of the Laprairie Basin, through which the channel sweeps in a great arc 8.5 miles (13.7 km) long to the second lock. The **Cote St. Catherine Lock,** like the other six St. Lawrence Seaway locks, is built to the following standard dimensions:

Length - 766 feet (233.5 meters)
Width - 80 feet (24.4 meters)
Depth- 30 feet (9.1 meters)

The Cote St. Catherine requires 24 million gallons (90.9 million liters) to fill and can be filled or emptied in less than 10 minutes. It lifts ships from the level of the Laprairie Basin 30 feet (9.1 meters) to the level of Lake St. Louis, bypassing the Lachine Rapids. Beyond it, the channel runs 7.5 miles (12.1 km) before reaching Lake St. Louis.

The **Lower Beauharnois Lock,** bypassing the Beauharnois Power House, lifts ships 41 feet (12.5 meters) and sends them through a short canal to the **Upper Beauharnois Lock**, where they are again lifted 41 feet (12.5 meters) to reach the level of the Beauharnois Canal. After a 13 mile (20.9 km) trip in the canal, and a 30 mile (48.3 km) voyage through Lake St. Francis, vessels reach the U. S. border and the **Snell Lock,** which has a lift of 45 feet (13.7 meters) and empties into the 10-mile (16.1 km) long Wiley-Dondero Canal. After passing through Wiley-Dondero, ships are raised another 38 feet (11.6 meters) by the **Dwight D. Eisenhower Lock,** after which they enter Lake St. Lawrence, the pool upon which nearby HEPCO and PASNY power generating stations draw for their turbines located a mile to the north.

At the Western end of Lake St. Lawrence, the **Iroquois Lock** allows ships to bypass the Iroquois Control Dam. The lift here is only about one foot (.3 meters). Once in the waters west of Iroquois, the ship channel meanders through the scenic Thousand Islands to Lake Ontario, the Welland Canal and eventually Lake Erie.

A saltwater vessel has just passed a laker near St. Catharines, ON in the Welland Canal. The Garden City Skyway is in the background.

LOCKS and CANALS

The Soo Locks

MacArthur Lock

Named after World War II Gen. Douglas MacArthur, the MacArthur lock measures 800 feet (243.8 meters) long between inner gates, 80 feet (24.4 meters) wide and 31 feet (9.4 meters) deep over the sills. The lock was built by the United States in the years 1942-43 and opened to traffic 11 July, 1943. The maximum sized vessel that can transit the MacArthur Lock is 730 feet (222.5 meters) long by 75 feet (22.9 meters) wide. In emergencies, this limit may be exceeded for vessels up to 767 feet (233.8 meters) in length.

Poe Lock

The Poe Lock is 1,200 feet (365.8 meters) long, 110 feet (33.5 meters) wide and has a depth over the sills of 32 feet (9.8 meters). Named after Col. Orlando M. Poe, it was built by the United States in the years 1961-68. The lock's vessel limit is 1,100 feet (335.3 meters) long by 105 feet (32 meters) wide and is the only lock now capable of handling vessels of that size. There are currently 30 vessels sailing the lakes restricted by size to the Poe Lock.

Davis Lock

Named after Col. Charles E.L.B. Davis, the Davis Lock measures 1,350 feet (411.5 meters) long between inner gates, 80 feet (24.4 meters) wide and 23 feet (7 meters) deep over the sills. It was built by the United States in the years 1908-14 and now sees only limited use due to its shallow depth.

Sabin Lock

Measuring the same as the Davis Lock, the Sabin Lock was built from 1913-19. Named after L.C. Sabin, the lock is currently inactive.

The St. Mary's River

Connecting Lake Superior with Lake Huron, the 80 mile (128.7 km) long St. Mary's River is a beautiful waterway that includes breathtaking scenery, picturesque islands and more than its share of hazardous twists and turns.

Remote Isle Parisienne marks its beginning; the equally-lonely DeTour Reef light marks its end. In between, are two marvels of engineering, the West Neebish Cut, a channel literally dynamited out of solid rock, and the Soo Canal, which stands where Native Americans in their dugout canoes once challenged the St. Mary's Rapids.

Vessels in the St. Mary's River system are under control of the U.S. Coast Guard at Sault Ste. Marie, and are required to check in with Soo Control on VHF Ch.12 (156.600 Mhz) at various locations in the river. In the vicinity of the locks, they fall under jurisdiction of the Lockmaster, who must be contacted on VHF Ch. 14 (156.700 Mhz) for transit reports, lock assignments and other instructions.

All traffic through the Soo Locks is passed toll-free.

Looking northwest at the Soo Locks. Canada is at right.

The first lock was built on the Canadian side of the river by the Northwest Fur Co. in 1797-98. That lock was 38 feet (11.6 meters) long and barely 9 feet (2.7 meters) wide.

The first ship canal on the American side, known as the State Canal, was built from 1853-55 by engineer Charles T. Harvey. There were two tandem locks on masonry, each 350 feet (106.7 meters) long by 70 feet (21.3 meters) wide, with a lift of about 9 feet (2.7 meters).

The locks were destroyed in 1888 by workers making way for the canals of the present and future.

The Sault, ON Ship Canal

The present Canadian lock was constructed in 1887-95 through St. Mary's Island on the north side of the St. Mary's Rapids. It is the most westerly canal on the Seaway route. It was cut through red sandstone and is 7,294 feet (2,223.4 meters), or about 1.4 miles (2.2 km) long, from end to end of upper and lower piers.

The lock itself is 900 feet (274.3 meters) long, 60 feet (18.3 meters) wide and 21 feet (6.4 meters) deep. The approaches above and below the lock were dredged through boulder shoals.

Collapse of a lock wall in 1987 closed the Canadian canal, however preliminary repair work has begun that could see the historic waterway reopened for pleasure and tour boat traffic by 1998.

The Welland Canal

The 27-mile long (43,5 km) **Welland Canal** overcomes a difference in water level of 326 feet (99.4 meters) between lakes Erie and Ontario. **Locks 1-7** of the canal are lift locks, while **Lock 8** (at 1,380 feet (420.6 km) the longest lock in the world) is a guard lock. Locks 4, 5 and 6 are twinned and placed end to end, looking like giant stair-steps. All locks (except Lock 8) are 829 feet (261.8 meters) in length, 80 feet (24.4 meters) wide and 30 feet (9.1 meters) deep. The maximum sized vessel that may transit the canal is 740 feet (225.6 meters) in length, 78 feet (24.4 meters) wide and 26 feet (7.9 meters) of draft. Connecting channels are kept at a minimum of 27 feet (8.2 meters), allowing vessels drawing 26 feet (7.9 meters) fresh water draft to transit the canal.

Lock 1 is at Port Weller, 2 is between there and Homer, 3 is south of Homer. At Thorold, the

Vessels transiting the Welland Canal and St. Lawrence Seaway locks must pay tolls based on registered tonnage and cargo on-board.

twinned locks 4, 5 and 6, are controlled with an elaborate interlocking system for safety. The flight locks have an aggregate lift of 139.5 feet (42.5 meters) and are similar to the Gatun Locks on the Panama Canal. Just south of the flight locks is Lock 7, giving the final lift up to Lake Erie. The guard lock at Port Colborne completes the process.

All vessel traffic though the canal is regulated by a traffic control center. Upbound vessels must contact Seaway Welland off Port Weller on VHF Ch. 14 (156.700 Mhz), while downbound vessels must make contact off Port Colborne.

NO PUMPS NEEDED

All locks in the St Lawrence Seaway system operate on gravity ... water is merely allowed to seek its own level. Pumps may be used after the close of the navigation season to remove water from the locks. Considerable maintenance is done during the winter, when the waterways are still and most vessels are in layup.

LEFT PORTION IS MILES, RIGHT PORTION IS KILOMETERS

	Thunder Bay	Duluth	Marquette	Sault Ste. Marie	Escanaba	Milwaukee	Chicago	Gary	Alpena	Collingwood	Port Huron	Detroit	Toledo	Cleveland	Conneaut	Buffalo	Port Colborne	Toronto	Kingston	Montreal
Thunder Bay		313.8	275.2	439.3	791.8	999.4	1104.0	1124.9	659.8	854.5	872.2	972.0	1058.9	1144.2	1235.9	1390.4	1364.7	1453.2	1664.0	1950.5
Duluth	195		420.0	634.1	988.1	1195.7	1300.3	1319.6	856.1	889.9	1068.6	1168.3	1256.9	1340.5	1432.3	1506.3	1561.0	1649.5	1860.4	2146.8
Marquette	171	261		255.9	608.3	817.5	922.1	941.4	478.0	672.7	690.4	790.1	877.1	962.4	1054.1	1208.6	1182.8	1271.3	1482.2	1768.6
Sault Ste. Marie	273	394	159		352.4	561.6	666.3	685.6	220.5	416.8	432.9	532.7	619.6	704.9	796.6	952.7	925.3	1014.0	1224.7	1511.1
Escanaba	492	614	378	219		323.5	440.9	463.5	392.7	605.1	605.1	704.9	791.8	877.1	968.8	1124.9	1097.5	1186.1	1396.9	1683.3
Milwaukee	621	743	508	349	201		136.8	165.8	601.9	812.7	814.3	914.1	1001.0	1086.3	1178.0	1332.5	1306.8	1395.3	1606.1	1892.5
Chicago	686	808	573	414	274	85		40.2	706.5	917.3	918.9	1018.7	1107.2	1190.9	1282.6	1437.1	1411.4	1499.9	1710.7	1997.1
Gary	699	820	585	426	288	103	25		725.8	936.6	938.2	1038.0	1124.9	1210.2	1301.9	1456.4	1430.7	1519.2	1730.0	2016.5
Alpena	410	532	297	137	244	374	439	451		297.7	252.7	352.4	439.3	524.6	616.4	770.9	754.1	833.6	1044.4	1330.9
Collingwood	531	553	418	259	376	505	570	582	185		415.2	515.1	601.9	687.2	778.9	933.4	907.6	996.2	1207.0	1493.4
Port Huron	542	664	429	269	376	506	571	583	157	258		99.8	186.7	273.6	363.7	518.2	492.4	581.0	791.8	1078.2
Detroit	604	726	491	331	438	568	633	645	219	320	62		86.9	173.8	263.9	420.0	392.7	481.2	692.0	978.5
Toledo	658	781	545	385	492	622	688	699	273	374	116	54		154.5	252.7	408.8	381.4	469.9	680.7	967.2
Cleveland	711	833	598	438	545	675	740	752	326	427	170	108	96		115.9	283.2	257.5	346.0	556.8	843.3
Conneaut	768	890	655	495	602	732	797	809	383	484	226	164	157	72		172.2	148.1	236.6	447.4	733.8
Buffalo	864	936	751	592	699	828	893	905	479	580	322	261	254	176	107		35.4	123.9	334.7	621.2
Port Colborne	848	970	735	575	682	812	877	889	463	564	306	244	237	160	92	22		88.5	299.3	585.8
Toronto	903	1025	790	630	737	867	932	944	518	619	361	299	292	215	147	77	55		259.1	543.9
Kingston	1034	1156	921	761	868	998	1063	1075	649	750	492	430	423	346	278	208	186	161		292.9
Montreal	1212	1334	1099	939	1046	1176	1241	1253	827	928	670	608	601	524	456	386	364	338	182	

MEANINGS OF BOAT WHISTLES

1 SHORT: I am directing my course to starboard (right) for a port to port passing.

2 SHORT: I am directing my course to port (left) for a starboard to starboard passing.

5 OR MORE SHORT BLASTS SOUNDED RAPIDLY: Danger.

1 PROLONGED: Vessel leaving dock.

3 SHORT: Vessel moving astern.

1 PROLONGED, SOUNDED ONCE PER MINUTE: Vessel moving in fog.

1 SHORT, 1 PROLONGED, 1 SHORT: Vessel at anchor in fog.

3 PROLONGED and 2 SHORT: Salute.

1 PROLONGED and 2 SHORT: Master's salute.

Some of these signals are listed in the pilot rules, while others have been adopted through common use.

LAKES LORE

U.S.-flag carriers moved more than 117 million net tons of dry and liquid bulk cargo during the 1996 Great Lakes shipping season, a new record for the post-recession era. The previous peak was 115 million tons in 1994.

NAUTICAL MEASUREMENTS

Deadweight Tonnage: the actual carrying capacity of a vessel, equal to the difference between the Light displacement tonnage and the Heavy displacement tonnage, expressed in long tons (2,240 pounds or 1,016.1 kg).

Displacement Tonnage: the actual weight of the entire vessel and everything aboard her, measured in long tons. The displacement is equal to the weight of the water displaced by the vessel. Displacement tonnage may be qualified as Light, indicating the weight of the vessel without cargo, fuels, stores or Heavy, indicating the weight of the vessel loaded with cargo, fuel and stores.

Gross Tonnage: the internal capacity of a vessel, measured in units of 100 cubic feet (2.83 cubic cubic meters) = a gross ton.

Net Registered Tonnage: the internal capacity of a vessel, measured in units of 200 cubic feet (2.83 cubic meters) but does not include the space occupied by boilers, engines, shaft alleys, chain lockers, officers and crew's quarters. Net registered tonnage is usually referred to as registered tonnage or net tonnage and is used to figure taxes, canal tolls and port charges.

A knot: one nautical mile per hour. The international nautical mile equals 6,076 feet (1,852 meters). A land mile is 5,280 feet (1,609.3 meters). Miles or kilometers are generally used on the Great Lakes for measurement.

The GREAT LAKES SELF-UNLOADER

A self-unloader is just what its name implies - a vessel able to discharge its cargo using a system of conveyor belts and gates beneath the cargo holds and a movable boom, usually located on deck, that can be swung over either side of the ship. No dockside assistance is needed.

Self-unloaders first made an appearance in the 1920s, and became the mainstay of the coal, stone and cement trades shortly thereafter. But it was not until the 1970s, as older vessels became obsolete and newer ships were built, that the more versatile self-unloader began to edge out traditional "straight-deck" carriers for bulk cargos as well. At that time, many straight-deckers were converted to self-unloaders, while other vessels thought to have years of service ahead of them went to the scrapyard because they lacked self-unloading equipment.

As the Great Lakes shipping industry heads into the latter part of the 1990s, the only U.S.-flag, straight-deck bulk carriers in service are in the grain trade, but self-unloaders are making inroads there as well.

On the Canadian side, straight-deckers may backhaul ore after delivering a grain cargo, but it is probably only a matter of time before virtually all bulk cargo carried on lake boats will be carried on self-unloaders.

Armco extends its self-unloading boom to discharge a cargo of taconite pellets. (Roger LeLievre)

ICE JAM '96!

Water, water everywhere - and most of it was ice. After the shortest winter lay-up on record, 17 days, Great Lakes vessels resumed their runs in mid-March, urged on by high demand for iron ore at lower lakes steel mills. On Lake Superior, convoys quickly became the order of the day, with vessels following in tracks broken through the ice by the powerful U.S. Coast Guard icebreaker **Mackinaw**. *(See picture, Page 21)*

At the Soo Locks, brash ice pushed by northwesterly winds clogged the northwest approaches and lengthened the time required for passage by some vessels - especially 1,000-footers - to more than 15 hours. In the Mackinac Straits and on the St. Clair River, tightly-packed ice and strong winds created nearly-impassable conditions that lingered for weeks, with vessel after vessel requiring Coast Guard assistance.

When conditions returned to normal, nearly a dozen battle-weary ships limped into port for repairs to propellers, rudders, steering gear and hull damages. Among them, the **Joseph L. Block, Adam E. Cornelius, Wilfred Sykes, Columbia Star, Buckeye** and **Lee A. Tregurtha** suffered the most injury, with countless other vessels dented and scraped. The ice didn't move out of the Soo Locks area until May 18, and more of the white stuff was spotted offshore at Marquette in early June.

Canadian Coast Guard icebreaker Pierre Radisson in St. Clair River ice on 19 April, 1996.

U.S. Coast Guard icebreakers Neah Bay and Bristol Bay assist the James R. Barker, beset off Harsen's Island in the St. Clair River.
(David Maize)

Vessels

The rumor mill kicked into high gear late in 1996 with intense speculation over which fleet would operate the 1,000-footer **George A. Stinson** after Interlake Steamship Co.'s lease expired at the end of the year. After the dust settled, American Steamship Co. appeared to be the likely winner. No new name has been announced for '97.

Interlake is also converting the 1953-built bulk carrier **J.L. Mauthe**, idle since 1993, to a self-unloading barge at Bay Shipbuilding Co., Sturgeon Bay, WI. Work is expected to be completed by fall, 1997. When finished, she will be pushed by a tug via a notch cut in her stern. As such, the Mauthe joins a handful of other lakers now profitably employed after undergoing similar surgery. Her successful conversion may mean more of the same as older, self-powered lakers (with their large crews) become more uneconomical to run.

The long-idle Lake Michigan carferry **Viking** (renamed **Viking 1**), which had been refurbished and taken to Port Stanley, ON, to begin cross-Lake Erie service to Cleveland, is now at Erie, PA after the deal between Contessa Cruise Lines and the Port Stanley Cleveland Ferry Corp. fell through. Options that would see the ship in some kind of operation in 1997 are still being considered.

Two vessels resumed service in 1996 with new names - Pioneer Shipping's **Saskatchewan Pioneer** now sails as **Lady Hamilton** for

(Cont'd on Page 20)

(Roger LeLievre)

J.L. Mauthe returns to service in late 1997 as a self-unloading barge.

The new Lafarge barge Integrity, pushed by the tug Jacklyn M, calls on Green Bay during her maiden voyage, 10 August, 1996.

(G.J. Knuth)

Fednav, and **Sea Barge One** is now **Sarah Spencer**. The self-unloader **Atlantic Trader**, which has been under charter the past three years, returns to Algoma Central operation in 1997 under her original name, **Algobay**. Another familiar lake vessel that may enjoy a new lease on life is the 52-year-old icebreaker **Mackinaw**. If the U.S. Congress approves a plan now under development, modernization, which would include engine control automation and cutting her 75-member crew in half, could start in 1998.

Nicolet's final voyage. *(Jim Hoffman)*

The 1905-built self-unloader **Nicolet**, laid-up at Toledo since 1990, finally made the one way trip to scrappers at Port Maitland, ON, on 28 August, 1996. Her boom had been removed earlier in anticipation of the trip. The tug **Otis Wack** handled the towing chores.

On May 10, 1996, Algoma Central's motor vessel **Algosoo** had the honor of carrying the two billionth ton of cargo through the St. Lawrence Seaway, which opened in 1959. Algosoo was laden with 27,104 tons of iron ore from Pointe Noire, PQ to Lorain, OH.

Fleet News

When construction began last year on the Lafarge Corp's new, cement-carrying tug-barge **Jacklyn M/Integrity**, waterfront observers wondered what the impact would be on some of the older cement boats on the lakes operated for Lafarge by Inland Lakes Management Co. When the dust settled, not only had Inland Lakes lost it's bid to operate Integrity, it lost the contract to run the rest of the Lafarge fleet as well, which prompted a bitter strike by masters, engineers and other personnel last September. All vessels are now operated by Andrie Inc. of Muskegon. MI. Long-term impact has yet to be realized, however the **E.M. Ford**, built in 1898 and until recently, still in operation, has laid up, perhaps for good. The future of the steamer **S.T. Crapo** may also be in doubt. In related news, the Inland Lakes steamer **Lewis G. Harriman**, used lately for storage, is now owned by St. Mary's Cement.

The Canadian tanker fleet **Socanav** and it's sister company, **QMT Navigation Co**. have declared bankruptcy. Two of the firm's vessels, **Le Brave** and **A.G. Farquharson**, have been returned to Imperial Oil

(Cont'd on Page 22)

U.S. Coast Guard icebreaker Mackinaw assists the Kaye E. Barker at Marquette in April 1996. The tug Erika Kobasic is in the background.
(Mining Journal / Jerry Bilecki)

Ltd., while the future of **Le Chene No. 1, Le Saule No. 1, L'Orme No. 1** and **W.M. Vacy Ash** remains in doubt after a sales deal to another fleet collapsed. Reports in Canadian Sailor, the journal of the Seafarer's International Union, indicated that Socanav was unable to meet crew payroll, neglected essential vessel repairs, and may have even been unable to provision vessels with adequate food.

Construction and Conversions

Algoma Central's **Capt. Henry Jackman** re-entered service last June 21 after conversion to a self-unloader at Port Weller Drydocks. Algoma lost no time continuing its fleet upgrade, placing the **Algoville** in the same Port Weller dock for widening. The $6.5 million job increased the ship's beam by three feet, making her the widest Canadian laker in service. (Algoville returns to Port Weller for conversion to a self-unloader during the winter of 1977-'78.) Port Weller is also busy converting Upper Lakes Group's **Canadian Navigator** to a self-unloader, a job that should be completed in time for the vessel to return to work in 1997. U.S. Steel's 1,000-footer **Edwin H. Gott** also re-entered service in 1996 sporting a new, 280-foot self-unloading boom, replacing her original shuttle system.

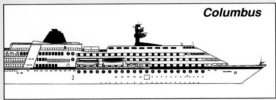

Columbus

If all goes according to plan, the Great Lakes should see overnight passenger cruises resume this fall with the advent of the new German liner **Columbus**. The 492-foot vessel, which carries 420 passengers and a crew of 169, will be operated by Hapag-Lloyd, based in Hamburg. A new passenger terminal is under construction in Toledo, which will be used by the new line, as well as any others that may eventually emerge.

Three new Fednav vessels entered service in 1996 - **Federal Calumet, Federal Saguenay** and **Federal St. Laurent**. Three more hulls are on order for Fednav from a Chinese shipyard, due for delivery this year. Meanwhile, Marinette Marine Corp. in Marinette, WI, continues to churn out new seagoing buoy tenders for the U.S. Coast Guard. **Juniper, Willow** and **Ida Lewis** were all completed in 1996.

Casualties - Close Calls

Tragedy was averted July 30, 1996 on Lake Superior after crewmembers of Canada Steamship Lines' **H.M. Griffith** discovered

(Cont'd on Page 24)

Algoma Central's newly-converted self-unloader Capt. Henry Jackman stops at Detroit on 23 June, 1996.   (Dave Marcoux)

part of the ship's coal cargo on fire. The vessel's crew was able to jettison 3,000 tons of burning coal overboard using its own self-unloading equipment. Permission for the emergency dump was first obtained from the U.S. Army Corps of Engineers and U.S. Coast Guard.

Another close call occurred October 2 when the downbound saltie *Ziemia Tarnowska* lost power and slammed into a pier at the Soo Locks, narrowly missing the upbound, gasoline-laden, tanker *Jade Star*. Considerable damage was done to the Tarnowska's bulbous bow below the waterline.

October 30 saw a dramatic rescue on stormy Lake Superior when two men were plucked from the drifting excursion boat *Grampa Woo*, which had broken it's moorings at Portage, MI. The downbound 1,000-footer *Walter J. McCarthy Jr.* and the tug *Glenada* took part in the rescue, which was carried out in 15-foot seas and 70 mph winds. Driven ashore at Passage Island, the Grampa Woo is a total loss.

The Great Lakes research vessel *Halcyon*, new to the lakes in 1996, sank at her dock near Muskegon, MI, December 3. Salvage operations were completed before winter set in, but the Halcycon may be too badly damaged for repair.

Carrying the Torch

The American Steamship Co. motor vessel *American Republic* became the first Great Lakes vessel to ever participate in the Olympic Games on 9 June, 1996, when the vessel proudly transported the Olympic flame across Lake Erie from Detroit to Cleveland. Festivities, and plenty of rain in both cities, marked the historic event.

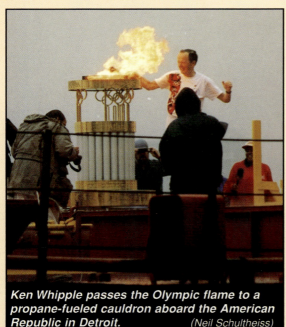

Ken Whipple passes the Olympic flame to a propane-fueled cauldron aboard the American Republic in Detroit. (Neil Schultheiss)

VESSEL INDEX

*Including current and former names
... turn to fleet number shown.*

Upper Lakes Group's self-unloader James Norris, downbound at the Soo.
(Mark Peabody)

Vessel Name	Fleet Number
A	
A-390	A-7
A-397	A-7
A-410	A-7
A. E. Clifford	S-11
A. G. Farquharson	II-1
A. S. Glossbrenner	A-3/S-5
A. T. Lowmaster	J-1
A.T.S. Tug No. 7	A-6
Abby	C-29
Abegweit	C-29
Abegweit	IM-4
Aburg	C-8
Acacia	U-3
Adam E. Cornelius {3}	C-1
Adam E. Cornelius {4}	I-2
Adanac	J-1
Adirondack	E-12
Admiral Ushakov	IM-12
Adrienne B.	K-4
Adventure	IP-6
Agawa Canyon	A-3/S-6
Aghia Marina	IA-4
Agios Georgios	IC-4
Agoming	T-4
Aivik	IT-13
Akadan Bulk	IP-6
Akti	IH-2
Al Battal	S-18
Al-Sayb-7	S-18
Alabama {2}	G-22
Alam Sejahtera	IP-2
Alam Sempurna	IP-2
Alam Senang	IP-2
Alam Tenteram	IP-2
Alam United	IP-2
Alan K. Luedtke	L-13
Alaska	G-22
Albany Bay	S-12
Alberni Carrier	B-15
Alcona	R-4
Alecto	IC-2
Alex D. Chisholm	C-10
Alexander Henry	M-9
Alexandria	IH-2
Alexis	IA-12
Alexis Simard	A-2
Alfred Needier	C-3
Algobay	A-3/S-6
Algocape {1}	P-1
Algocape {2}	A-3/S-5
Algocen {2}	A-3/S-5
Algogulf {1}	A-3
Algogulf {2}	A-3/S-5
Algoisle	A-3/S-5
Algolake	A-3/S-6
Algomah	A-11
Algomarine	A-3/S-6
Algonorth	A-3/S-5
Algontario	A-3/S-5
Algoport	A-3/S-6
Algorail {2}	A-3/S-6
Algoriver	A-3/S-5
Algosea	A-3
Algosoo {2}	A-3/S-6
Algosound	A-3/S-5
Algosteel {2}	A-3/S-6
Algoville	A-3/S-6
Algoway {2}	A-3/S-6
Algowest	A-3/S-5
Algowood	A-3/S-6
Alhajuela	M-16
Alice E.	E-6
Alidon	IH-1
Allegheny	M-4
Allegra	IS-3
Alpena {2}	A-7
Alpha	IS-11
Alphonse des Jarnins	L-1
Alsydon	IH-1
Altair	IH-6
Ambassador	U-11
Amelia Desgagnes	T-9
America {3}	G-22
American Eagle	G-7
American Girl	G-8
American Mariner	A-5
American Republic	A-5
American Viking	A-7
Americo Dean	D-3
Amherst Islander	O-2
Amilla	IA-7
Amitie	IG-3
Amoco	A-7
Amoco Great Lakes	C-28
Amoco Indiana	C-10
Amoco Michigan	C-28
Anangel Ares	IA-7
Anangel Atlas	IA-7
Anangel Endeavour	IA-7
Anangel Fidelity	IA-7
Anangel Honesty	IA-7
Anangel Honour	IA-7
Anangel Hope	IA-7
Anangel Horizon	IA-7
Anangel Liberty	IA-7
Anangel Might	IA-7
Anangel Prosperity	IA-7
Anangel Prudence	IA-7
Anangel Sky	IA-7
Anangel Spirit	IA-7
Anangel Triumph	IA-7
Anangel Victory	IA-7
Anax	IP-13
Anchor Bay	G-18
Andre H.	T-11
Andrea Marie I	D-1
Andrealon	IH-1
Andrew J.	E-4
Andrew Martin	A-7
Anemi	IP-13
Anemone	IP-13
Anglian Lady	J-1
Angus M.	S-14
Anita 1	IH-1
Ann Arbor No. 6	C-31
Ann Arbor No. 7	C-31
Anna	IP-12
Anna Desgagnes	T-9
Anna Sheridan	J-7
Annie M. Dean	D-3
Antalina	IT-4
Anthony	IA-13
Anthony J. Celebrezze	C-17
Antiquarian	G-21
Apex Chicago	A-8
APJ Angad	IS-26
APJ Anjli	IS-26
APJ Priti	IS-26
APJ Sushma	IS-26
Aptmariner	IC-9
Aquarama	E-7
Aquarius	IS-8
Arawanna Queen	J-3
Arctic	IF-3
Arctic Harvester	C-3
Arctic Ivik	IF-3
Arctic Nanook	IF-3
Arctic Nutsukpok	IF-3
Arctic Surveyor	M-16
Arctic Trader	S-8
Arctic Tuktu	M-16
Areito	IN-1
Argue Martin	M-16
Argut	IF-1
Arizona	G-22
Arkansas {2}	G-22
Arma	II-3
Armand Imbeau	L-1
Armco	O-1
Arosa	IT-10
Art Lapish	L-5
Arthur K. Atkinson	C-31
Arthur M. Anderson	U-13
Arundel	B-4
Asa W. Hughes	E-6
Asfamarine	E-9
Ashford	N-3
Ashtabula	J-7
ASL Sanderling	IF-3
Astra Lift	IC-3
Astral Ocean	IM-11
ATA-172	S-7
ATA-179	M-4
ATA-230	S-7
ATC 610	M-16
Athos	U-11
Atlantic	G-24
Atlantic Cedar	II-4
Atlantic Erie	C-1
Atlantic Fir	II-4
Atlantic Freighter	IM-4
Atlantic Hemlock	II-4
Atlantic Hickory	C-1
Atlantic Huron {1}	C-1
Atlantic Huron {2}	C-1
Atlantic Spruce	II-4
Atlantic Superior	C-1
Atlantic Trader	A-3
Atlantis Spirit	IA-14
Atlas	G-2
Atomic	M-16
Au Sable	D-13
Aurora Borealis	C-6
Aurora Topaz	IA-16
Aurum	IL-3
Avdeevka	IA-17
Avenger	J-1

Vessel Name / Fleet Number	
Avenger IV	J-1
Avondale	K-4

B

B-16	A-7
B-7	A-7
Badger {2}	L-4
Bagotville	C-4
Baldy B.	S-7
Balkan	IN-2
Balsambranch	J-1
Bantry Bay	G-2
Barbara Andrie	A-7
Barbara Ann	M-16
Barbara E.	IK-2
Barbara H	IB-8
Barbara Rita	A-7
Barge 252	M-16
Baronia	IT-7
Barry J	K-5
Bartlett	C-3
Bay Queen	J-3
Bayfield	U-2
Bayship	B-5
BD 1	G-2
Beam Beginner	G-14
Beatrice Ottinger	O-5
Beaver	U-6
Beaver D.	M-16
Beaver Islander	B-6
Beavercliffe Hall	N-1
Becky E.	E-6
Bee Jay	G-4
Belle River	A-5
Beluga	IL-5
Benjamin Ridgeway	K-3
Benson Ford {3}	I-3
Bergen Bay	IU-2
Bergen Luna	IU-2
Bergen Sea	IU-2
Bergon	IB-1
Bernard Oldendorff	C-1
Bert Reinauer II	IR-4
Beta Fortune	IO-2
Beta Luck	IO-2
Bethlake No. 1	G-2
Betsiamites	G-24
Betty D.	D-13
Betty Gale	H-6
BFT No. 50	IR-4
Bickersgracht	IS-17
Bide-A-Wee {3}	S-13
Bigorange XVI	S-18
Billie M.	M-16
Biscayne Bay	U-3
Black Bay	U-11
Black Carrier	M-16
Blackie B.	E-1
Blain McKeil	M-16
Blue Bill	IB-4
Blue Chip II	G-23
Blue Nose	IM-4
Bluewater Belle	M-22
Bonesey B.	K-4
Bonita {2}	E-1
Bonnie G. Selvick	S-7
Bontegracht	IS-17

Vessel Name & Fleet Number	
Bother Collins	L-5
Botic	IJ-1
Bounty	V-2
Bramble	U-3
Bremon	IB-1
Bristol Bay	U-3
Brochu	F-2
Brooklyn	H-6
Brooknes	A-3
Brunto	IJ-3
Buckeye {3}	O-1
Buckley	K-4
Buckthorn	U-3
Buffalo	U-2
Buffalo {1}	F-4
Buffalo {3}	A-5
Bulknes	A-3
Burns Harbor {1}	O-1
Burns Harbor {2}	B-9
Burro	M-6
Butterfield	A-7

C

C & O 452	M-13
C-11	K-3
C. E. "Ted" Smith	C-25
C. G. Richter	W-3
C. Martin	IS-10
C. West Pete	U-1
C.D. 110	DH
C.T.C. No.1	C-10
Cabot	U-11
Cabot	IF-3
Cadillac {5}	S-22
Calcite II	U-13
Caledonia	M-22
California	G-22
Calliroe Patronicola	IO-4
Camille Marcoux	L-1
Canada Marquis	IF3
Canadian	C-9
Canadian Ambassador	U-11
Canadian Century	U-11/S-6
Canadian Empress	S-16
Canadian Enterprise	U-11/S-6
Canadian Explorer	U-11/S-5
Canadian Franko	V-3
Canadian Leader	U-11/S-5
Canadian Mariner	U-11/S-5
Canadian Miner	U-11/S-5
Canadian Navigator	U-11/S-6
Canadian Olympic	U-11/S-6
Canadian Pioneer	U-11
Canadian Progress	U-11/S-5
Canadian Prospector	U-11/S-5
Canadian Provider	U-11/S-5
Canadian Ranger	U-11/S-5
Canadian Trader	U-11/S-5
Canadian Transport {2}	U-11/S-6
Canadian Venture	U-11/S-5
Canadian Voyager	U-11/S-5
Canadiana	F-5
Candice Andrie	A-7
Canmar Sea Eagle	S-18
Canmar Shuttle	S-18
Canmar Supplier VII	G-24
Cape Hurd	C-3

Vessel Name / Fleet Number	
Capitaine Simard	S-25
Capt. Charles T. Parker	G-14
Capt. Edward V. Smith	C-1
Capt. Henry Jackman	A-3/S-6
Capt. Ioannis S.	G-24
Capt. Matthew Flinders	M-12
Capt. Roy	B-14
Capt. Shepler	S-9
Captain Barnaby	L-5
Captain Bennie	R-2
Captain George	F-6
Captain Robbie	H-11
Caribou	IM-4
Caribou Isle	C-3
Carl Gorthon	T-9
Carl M.	C-9
Carl Metz	IF-5
Carl William Selvick	S-7
Carla Anne Selvick	S-7
Carlton	U-11
Carol Ann	K-5
Carol Lake	P-1
Carolyn Hoey	G-2
Carolyn Jo	M-16
Cartiercliffe Hall	A-3
Cartierdoc {2}	N-1
Cason J. Callaway	U-13
Caspian	E-6
Catherine Desgagnes	T-9
Catherine L.	IC-4
Catherine Le Gardeur	L-1
Cathy McAllister	M-14
Cavalier	M-16
Cavalier Maxim	C-32
Cavallo	IF-3
Cayuga II	N-3
Cecelia Desgagnes	T-9
Cecilia I	IH-1
Cemba	D-2
Chada Naree	IG-6
Challenge	G-19
Challenger {1}	S-19
Challenger {2}	H-6
Challenger {3}	D-13
Champion {1}	C-11
Champion {2}	D-4
Champion {3}	D-13
Charles Antoine	M-14
Charles E. Jackson	N-8
Charles E. Wilson	A-5
Charles L. Hutchinson {3}	K-6
Charles M. Beeghly	I-3
Charles W. Johnson	J-1
Charlevoix {1}	C-12
Charlevoix {2}	O-2
Charlie Mott	U-6
Charlie S.	M-14
Chas Asher	R-2
Chas E. Trout	E-6
Chennai Perumai	U-11
Cheraw	U-2
Cherokee {1}	E-6
Cherokee {2}	B-3
Chetek	U-2
Chi-Cheemaun	O-6
Chicago Harbor No. 4	K-5

Vessel Name / Fleet Number		Vessel Name / Fleet Number		Vessel Name / Fleet Number	
Chicago II	S-21	Curly B.	L-5	Drummond Islander II	M-17
Chicago's First Lady	M-19	Curtis Randolph	C-19	Drummond Islander III	E-2
Chief Shingwauk	L-12	Cuyahoga	B-11	Duc D' Orleans	D-10
Chief Wawatam	J-1	Cvijeta Zuzoric	IA-15	Duchess V	W-4
Chimo	U-11	Cygnus	IS-8	Duden	IS-13
Chippewa (6)	A-11			Dufresne	M-16
Chippewa (7)	G-22	**D**		Dufresne M-58	M-16
Chiwawa	I-3			Duga	T-11
Chris E. Luedtke	L-13	D. C. Everest	M-16	Duluth	U-2
Chris M.	N-3	D. L. Billmaier	U-2	Dumar Scout	R-2
Christopher Oldendorff	C-1	Dace Reinauer	IR-4	Dumit	C-3
Churchill	F-4	Dakota	E-6	Durrington	IS-21
Cicero	IF-3	Daldean	B-13	DXE 1640 OS	ID-6
Cindy Jo	H-6	Dana T. Bowen	J-1	DXE 1800	ID-6
Ciovo	IJ-1	Dandy	V-3	DXE 2401	ID-6
Cisco	U-4	Daniel E.	E-6	DXE 2805	ID-6
City of Algonac	W-2	Daniel McAllister	M-14		
City of Flint 32	M-13	Darya Kamal	IK-1	**E**	
City of Midland 41	L-4	Darya Ma	IK-1		
City of Milwaukee	C-21	Daryl C. Hannah (1)	S-7	E. A. Rockett	M-16
City of Sandusky	S-1	Daryl C. Hannah (2)	H-6	E. Bronson Ingram	S-18
Clara Andrie	A-7	Dauntless	M-18	E. C. Collins	A-7
Clarkson Carrier	S-18	David Boyd	G-21	E. James Fucik	S-7
Clipper	H-4	David J. Kadinger Jr.	K-1	E. M. Ford	A-7
Clipper Amaryllis	IP-13	David K. Gardiner	U-11	Earl Gray	C-3
Clipper Amethyst	IP-13	David Z. Norton (3)	O-1	Earl W. Oglebay	O-1
Clipper Majestic	IS-15	Dawn Light	C-8	Eber	IS-13
Coastal Cruiser	T-4	Day Peckinpaugh	E-10	Eclipse	N-5
Coastal Delegate	A-7	Dayliner	B-2	Ecosse	G-17
Cobia	W-8	DC 710	D-9	Edda	IH-6
Cod	G-16	DDS Salvager	J-1	Eddie B. (1)	K-5
Col. D. D. Gaillard	H-10	Debbie Lyn	M-1	Eddie B. (2)	K-4
Col. James M. Schoonmaker	C-23	Defiance	A-4	Edelweiss I	E-3
Colinette	W-4	Delaware (4)	G-22	Edelweiss II	E-3
Colorado	G-22	Demeterton	U-11	Edenfield	U-11
Columbia (2)	S-23	Denise E.	E-6	Edgar B. Speer	U-13
Columbia Star	O-1	Derek E.	E-6	Edith J.	E-4
Columbus	B-1	Des Groseilliers	C-3	Edmond J. Moran	A-7
Columbus	IH-3	Des Moines	C-18	Edna G.	L-3
Comeaudoc	N-1	Detroit (1)	N-8	Edouard Simard	IG-4
Commuter	N-6	Diamond Belle	D-5	Edward B. Greene	I-3
Comorant	F-1	Diamond Jack	D-5	Edward C. Whalen	J-1
Concorde	IS-9	Diamond Queen	D-5	Edward E. Gillen III	E-4
Condarrell	M-16	Diamond Star	IR-5	Edward L. Ryerson	I-2
Confederation	T-9	Diana	II-2	Edwin F. Holmes	A-7
Coniscliffe Hall (2)	U-1	Diligent	S-14	Edwin H. Gott	U-13
Connecticut	G-22	Dixie Avenger	ID-6	Edwin Link	IH-4
Connewango	G-2	Dixie Commander	ID-6	Edwin M. Cotter	C-14
Connie E.	M-16	Dixie Progress	ID-6	Edwin T. Douglas	M-14
Conny	IS-3	Dmitriy Donskoy	IM-12	Eemshorn	IC-1
Consensus Manitou	IF-3	Dmitriy Pozharskiy	IM-12	Eighth Sea	S-17
Constructor	D-7	Doan Transport	E-9	El Kef	IC-7
Coral	IS-20	Dobrush	IA-17	El Lobo Grande II	G-22
Corithian Trader	IT-3	Docegulf	IV-1	Elikon	IS-16
Corsair	A-11	Dolomite (1)	G-22	Ellie	IB-8
Courageous	ID-6	Dolphin	E-9	Elmglen (2)	G-24
Courtney Burton	O-1	Don-De-Dieu	A-3	Elmore M. Misener	M-16
Cove Isle	C-3	Donald Bert	M-1	Elton Hoyt II (1)	C-10
Credo	IR-3	Donald C. Hannah	H-6	Elton Hoyt 2nd (2)	I-3
Crestar	IT-2	Donald Mac	G-14	Emerald Empress	N-6
Crispin Oglebay (2)	U-11	Donald O' Toole	K-4	Emerald Isle (1)	D-5
Croaker	N-4	Donald P.	G-24	Emerald Isle (2)	B-6
CSL Atlas	C-1	Donegal	R-2	Emerald Star	IR-5
CSL Cabo	C-1	Donetskiy Komsomoltes	IB-2	Emma Willis	G-2
CSL Innovator	C-1	Doug McKeil	M-16	Emmet J. Carey	O-5
CSL Trillium	M-16	Douglas B. Mackie	L-5	Empire Sandy	N-3
CT-9	G-18	Dragonet	T-1	Empress of Canada	E-8
		Drummond Islander	E-2	Ems Ore	N-1

Vessel Name / Fleet Number		Vessel Name / Fleet Number		Vessel Name / Fleet Number	
Encouragement	IG-3	Feux - Follets	U-11	Georgia {3}	G-22
Endeavor	N-6	Finnfighter	IF-4	Georgian Queen	A-10
Enerchem Asphalt	E-9	Finnsnes	IJ-3	Georgian Storm	S-25
Enerchem Catalyst	E-9	Firefighter	C-14	Gerald D. Neville	D-4
Enerchem Dolphin	E-9	Fjordnes	IP-8	Giacinta	IS-3
Enerchem Refiner	E-9	Flo Cooper	P-5	Gladys Bea	A-7
Enerchem Travailleur	E-9	Flo-Mac	M-16	Glen Shore	L-6
English River	C-1	Florida	G-22	Glenada	T-4
Enterprise I	IG-3	Forney	U-2	Glenbrook	M-16
Epos	IG-3	Fort Dearborn	C-13	Glenevis	M-16
Erich R. Luedtke	L-13	Fort Hoskins	M-16	Glenlivet II	V-3
Erie Isle	K-2	Fort William	C-1	Glenmont	J-6
Erika Kobasic	B-4	Fossnes	IP-8	Glenora	O-2
Erikousa Wave	IT-4	Foster M. Ford	E-6	Glenside	M-16
Erna Oldendorff	IE-2	Foundation Valiant	T-11	GLMA Barge	G-18
Ernest Lapointe	B-8	Foundation Valour	T-5	Gobelet D' Argent	C-32
Ernest R. Breech	K-6	Foundation Venture	T-1	Goki	J-1
Ernest T. Weir {2}	O-1	Foundation Victor	M-16	Golden Hope 8	IH-7
Escort	S-7	Fourth Coast	S-17	Golden Shield	IA-5
Escort II	B-4	Frank Palladino Jr.	K-3	Golden Sky	IC-5
Escorte	M-21	Frank Purnell {1}	C-10	Gonio	IM-5
Eskimo	T-9	Frank Rockefeller	H-10	Goodtime I	G-10
Esperance III	B-1	Frankcliffe Hall {2}	C-1	Goodtime III	G-11
Ethel	M-16	Frankie D.	E-1	Gopher State	H-6
Ethel E.	E-6	Franklin Reinauer	IR-4	Gordon C. Leitch {2}	U-11/S-5
Europegasus	IP-5	Fred A. Busse	C-15	Gosforth	T-9
Euroreefer	IG-3	Fred R. White Jr.	O-1	Grace L.	IC-4
Evans McKeil	M-16	Fred Scandrett	C-25	Grand Island {1}	O-5
Evening Star	M-8	Frederick T. Kellers	A-6	Grand Island {2}	P-4
Eyrarbakki	W-3	Freja Nordic	IF-9	Grande Baie	A-2
		Freja Scandic	IF-9	Grande Hermine	U-11
F		French River {2}	G-14	Grande Prince	IA-6
F. A. Johnson	G-14	Frines	IJ-3	Grande Ronde	U-11
F. M. Osborne {2}	O-5	Frontenac {5}	C-1	Grayling	U-4
Fairchild	U-2	Frontenac II	O-2	Grazia	IS-3
Fastov	IM-12	Frotabrasil	U-11	Great Laker	IB-6
Fatezh	IA-17	Frotacanada	U-11	Great Lakes {2}	C-28
Federal Aalesund	IF-3	Fugaku Maru	C-1	Green Bay	G-22
Federal Agno	IF-3	Fuji Braves	IT-1	Greenstone	U-6
Federal Baffin	IF-3	Fujisan Maru	IG-6	Gregory J. Busch	B-17
Federal Bergen	IF-3	Fullnes	IJ-3	Greta V	M-16
Federal Calliope	IF-3	Fulton	IR-4	Gretchen B.	L-13
Federal Calumet	IF-3	Furunes	IJ-3	Griffon	C-3
Federal Dora	IF-3			Grues Des Iles	L-1
Federal Franklin	IF-3	**G**		Gulf Challenger	H-6
Federal Fraser	IF-3	G. W. Codrington	S-7	Gulfoil	O-1
Federal Fuji	IF-3	G. W. Falcon	L-5	Gull Isle	C-3
Federal Huron	IF-3	G.L.B. No. 2	J-1	Gunay-A	ID-3
Federal Kumano	IF-3	G.T.B. No. 1	G-2	Gur Master	IS-18
Federal Maas	IF-3	Gaelic Challenge	E-1	Guy M. No. 1	J-1
Federal Mackenzie	IF-3	Gajah Borneo	IG-1		
Federal Matane	IF-3	Galactica 001	G-3	**H**	
Federal Nord	IF-3	Galassia	IS-8	H. A. Smith	H-9
Federal Oslo	IF-3	Galway Bay	G-22	H. J. Schwartz	U-2
Federal Pescadores	IF-3	Gary {1}	G-22	H. Lee White {2}	A-5
Federal Pioneer	T-9	Gemini	C-27	H. M. Griffith	C-1
Federal Polaris	IF-3	Gemini	IS-8	H. R. Schemn	A-7
Federal Richelieu	IF-3	General	D-13	Hagieni	IN-3
Federal Saguenay	IF-3	General Blazhevich	IA-17	Haida	G-13
Federal St. Clair	IF-3	General Cabal	IJ-3	Haight	IS-11
Federal St. Laurent	IF-3	Genmar 132	B-15	Halifax	C-1
Federal St. Louis	IF-3	Genmar 252	M-16	Halton	C-4
Federal Vibeke	IF-3	George A. Sloan	U-13	Hamilton	G-12
Federal Vigra	IF-3	George A. Stinson	A-5	Hamilton Energy	U-11
Federal Wear	U-11	George L.	IC-4	Hamilton Transfer	U-11
Felicity	S-9	George Morris	IR-4	Hammond Bay	L-11
Ferbec	C-1	George N. Carleton	G-14	Hammond Bay	U-2

Vessel Name / Fleet Number		Vessel Name / Fleet Number		Vessel Name / Fleet Number	
Hamtun	J-1	Illinois {2}	G-22	J. G. II	M-6
Handy Laker	IF-3	Imperial Acadia	II-1	J. G. Langton	C-25
Handymariner	IF-3	Imperial Bedford	II-1	J. H. Hillman Jr.	U-11
Hannah 1801	H-6	Imperial Dartmouth	II-1	J. L. Mauthe	I-3
Hannah 1802	H-6	Imperial Kingston	J-1	J. N. McWatters {2}	A-3
Hannah 2801	H-6	Imperial Lachine {1}	M-16	J. S. St. John	E-11
Hannah 2901	H-6	Imperial Lachine {2}	II-1	J. W. McGiffin	C-1
Hannah 2902	H-6	Imperial Sarnia {2}	U-11	J. W. Westcott II	J-2
Hannah 2903	H-6	Imperial St. Clair	II-1	Jacklyn M.	A-7
Hannah 3601	H-6	Imperial St. Lawrence	II-1	Jacques Cartier	C-34
Hannah 5101	H-6	Indian Express	ID-1	Jacques Desgagnes	T-9
Hannah D. Hannah	H-6	Indian Maiden	B-7	Jade Star	IR-5
Hans Leonhardt	IL-4	Indiana	G-22	Jadran	C-7
Harbor Ace	H-6	Indiana Harbor	A-5	Jaguar II	N-7
Harry Coulby {2}	K-6	Industrial Transport	E-9	Jalobert	H-5
Harsens Island	B-13	Inge	ID-2	James A. Hannah	H-6
Harvey	U-2	Inland Seas	I-1	James B. Lyons	O-5
Harvey D. Goulder {1}	A-6	Innisfree	C-13	James E. McGrath	U-11
Heavenbound	T-3	Integrity	A-7	James E. Skelly	U-10
Helen M. B.	M-14	Interwaterways	Line	James Harris	L-5
Helen M. McAllister	M-14	Incorporated 101	E-10	James J. Versluis	C-16
Helena	M-14	Invincible	ID-6	James M. Bray	U-2
Helena Oldendorff	IE-2	Iocolite	J-1	James Norris	U-11/S-6
Helio Ferraz	IV-1	Iowa	G-22	James R. Barker	I-3
Hellenic Confidence	IO-3	Ira	IA-10	James R. Elliot	P-9
Henry Foss	H-6	Iroquois {1}	I-4	James Transport	E-9
Henry Stokes	C-8	Iroquois {2}	G-22	James W. Rickey	D-7
Henry T.	L-9	Irving Beech	II-4	Jana	M-11
Herbert C. Jackson	I-3	Irving Birch	II-4	Jarmac 42	S-18
Hercegovina	IA-15	Irving Cedar	II-4	Jason	M-11
Hiawatha {1}	S-11	Irving Elm	II-4	Jason A. Kadinger	K-1
Hiawatha {2}	S-13	Irving Fir	II-4	Jean Parisien	C-1
Hickory Coll	A-7	Irving Hemlock	II-4	Jeannie	IF-3
Highway 16	W-7	Irving Maple	II-4	Jennifer George	G-22
Hilda Marjanne	U-11	Irving Miami	C-1	Jenny T. II	J-7
Hill Annex	U-13	Irving Nordic	II-4	Jere C.	L-13
Hillsboro	G-22	Irving Spruce	II-4	Jerry G.	M-14
Holck-Larson	IL-1	Irving Timber	II-4	Jerry Newberry	M-16
Holiday	S-13	Island Clipper {1}	G-7	Jet Express	T-2
Holiday Island	IM-4	Island Clipper {2}	V-2	Jet Express II	T-2
Holly Ann	H-11	Island Express	A-11	Jhulelal	IT-6
Hon. Paul Martin	C-1	Island Gem	IL-8	Jiggs	L-7
Hope I	IJ-1	Island Queen {1}	P-8	Jiimaan	O-6
Horizon Montreal	S-8	Island Queen {2}	M-2	Jimmy L.	S-7
Houghton	U-2	Island Queen V {2}	E-8	Jing Hong Hai	IC-9
Howard T. Hagen	M-11	Island Queen V {3}	T-13	Jo Palm	IJ-4
Hull 28	T-9	Island Skipper	IS-2	Joanne Reinauer III	IR-4
Hull No. 3	C-10	Island Sky	IS-2	Joasla	T-9
Humaconna	B-17	Islander {1}	R-3	Joe J. Hogan	J-2
Huron	U-2	Islander {2}	M-20	Joe Van	D-13
Huron {5}	A-11	Isle Royale Queen III	D-8	Joey Haden	J-9
Huron Lady	B-12	Itabira	IV-1	John A. France {2}	A-3
Hydra	IS-11	Ithaki	IA-3	John A. McGuire	H-11
		ITM No. 1	H-6	John B. Aird	A-3/S-6
I		Ivan Bogun	IM-12	John F. Cushing	U-10
I.L.I. 101	E-10	Ivi	IA-10	John G. Munson {2}	U-13
Ian Mac	M-1			John Hamilton Gray	IM-4
Ida M. II	R-1	**J**		John Henry	L-8
Idaho	G-22	J. A. Cornett	H-9	John J. Boland {3}	A-5
Ierland	M-14	J. A. W. Iglehart	A-7	John Kelderhouse	E-6
Ierlandia	M-14	J. A. Z. Desgagnes	T-9	John Kendall	F-3
Ikan Selayang	IP-1	J. B. Ford	A-7	John L. A. Galster	A-7
Ikan Sepat	IP-1	J. B. John {1}	A-7	John M. Selvick	S-7
Ikan Tamban	IP-1	J. Burton Ayers	B-11	John M. Truby	G-22
Ile Des Barques	C-3	J. E. Bernier	C-3	John McLean	J-1
Ile Ste. Ours	C-3	J. E. Colombe	U-6	John O. McKellar {2}	G-24
Illinois {1}	S-7	J. Edouard Simard	IG-4	John Purves	A-7

James R. Barker, upbound at the Ambassador Bridge at Detroit/Windsor, as seen from the mailboat J.W. Westcott II. (Roger LeLievre)

Vessel Name / Fleet Number	
John R. Asher	R-2
John R. Emery	E-10
John Reinauer	IR-4
John Roen	G-22
John Roen III	S-7
John Sherwin (2)	I-3
John Spence	M-16
John W. Boardman	S-19
Johnson	L-7
Johnson II	L-7
Johnson Sea-Link I	IH-4
Johnson Sea-Link II	IH-4
Joliet (3)	S-22
Jon Ramsoy	E-9
Jos. Deschenes	L-1
Jos. F. Bigane	B-10
Joseph & Clara Smallwood	IM-4
Joseph H. Callan	G-22
Joseph H. Frantz	O-1
Joseph H. Thompson	U-12
Joseph H. Thompson Jr.	U-12
Joseph L. Block	I-2
Joseph Medill (2)	C-15
Joseph Savard	L-1
Joseph X. Robert	G-9
Juanita D.	H-6
Judge McCombs	H-3
Judi C.	E-6
Julia	IG-2
Julie Dee	K-5
Julio	J-9
Juniata	H-4
Juris Avots	IL-2

K

Kaho	U-4
Kaleli Ana	IB-2
Kalisti	IF-3
Kalliopi L.	IC-4
Kalvik	IF-3
Kaministiquia (2)	A-7
Kansas	G-22
Kapitan Alekseyev	IN-8
Kapitan Bochek	IM-12
Kapitan Chukhchin	IM-12
Kapitan Kudley	IM-12
Kapitan Lazarev	IN-8
Kapitan Milovzorov	IF-1
Kapitan Zamyatin	IN-8
Kapitonas A. Lucka	IL-6
Kapitonas Andzejauskas	IL-6
Kapitonas Chromcov	IL-6
Kapitonas Domerika	IL-6
Kapitonas Duagirdis	IL-6
Kapitonas Kaminskas	IL-6
Kapitonas Marcinkus	IL-6
Kapitonas Sevcenko	IL-6
Kapitonas Stulov	IL-6
Kapitonas Stulpinas	IL-6
Karen Andrie (1)	B-4
Karen Andrie (2)	A-7
Karl E. Luedtke	L-13
Karlobag	IM-1
Katanni	S-12
Kate B.	M-16
Kate N. L.	U-11
Katherine L.	H-6

Vessel Name / Fleet Number	
Kathrin	IR-2
Kathrine Clewis	A-7
Kathy Lynn	R-4
Katie Ann	H-11
Katmai Bay	U-3
Kavo Alexandros	IG-5
Kavo Mangalia	IG-5
Kavo Sidero	IG-5
Kavo Yerakas	IG-5
Kaw	G-2
Kawartha Voyager	O-3
Kay Cole	M-16
Kaye E. Barker	I-3
Keewatin	P3A
Kelley Islander	N-6
Kellstone 1	K-3
Kenoki	C-3
Kenosha	U-2
Kentucky (2)	G-22
Keta Lagoon	IB-3
Keta V.	V-1
Kings Challenger	H-6
Kings Pointer	B-4
Kings Squire	H-6
Kinsman Enterprise (2)	K-6
Kinsman Independent (3)	K-6
Kobuleti	IM-5
Komsomolets	IA-17
Kostantis F.	IS-1
Kramatorsk	IA-17
Kreon	IM-8
Krissa	IG-3
Kristen D.	P-7
Kristen Lee	H-6
Kristen Lee Hannah	H-6
Krystal K.	B-4
Kurt Luedtke	L-13
Kurt R. Luetdke	F-6

L

L' Orme No. 1	IG-4
L. E. Block	B-4
L. L. Wright	E-6
L.S.C. 236	G-2
La Malbaie	M-16
La Salle (4)	S-22
Lac Como	M-16
Lac Erie	M-16
Lac Manitoba	M-16
Lac Ottawa	W-4
Lac Vancouver	M-16
Lady Belle II	O-4
Lady Elda	H-6
Lady Emily	IS-25
Lady Hamilton	IF-3
Lady Ida	K-3
Lady Midland	O-4
Lake Carling	IF-3
Lake Challenger	IR-6
Lake Champlain	IF-3
Lake Charles	IF-3
Lake Edward	E-11
Lake Erie	IF-3
Lake Guardian	U-5
Lake Manitoba	A-3
Lake Michigan	IF-3
Lake Nipigon	A-3

Vessel Name / Fleet Number	
Lake Ontario	IF-3
Lake Superior	D-11
Lake Superior	IF-3
Lake Tahoe	IF-3
Lake Wabush	A-3
Laketon (2)	A-3
Lamont	G-22
Langdon C. Hardwicke	H-11
Lansdowne	S-15
Larry L.	IC-4
LaSalle	M-5
Laserbeam	IP-9
Laura Lynn	H-11
Laurence C. Turner	G-22
Laurentian	U-8
Laval	G-24
Laviolette	M-22
Lawrencecliffe Hall (2)	U-11
Le Brave	II-1
Le Chene No. 1	IG-4
Le Draveur	C-34
Le Gobelet D' Argent	C-32
Le Maxim	C-32
Le Roy Brooks	C-8
Le Saule No. 1	IG-4
Le Survenant III	C-33
Lead Horse	H-6
Ledastern	IR-5
Lee A. Tregurtha	I-3
Lee Reuben	H-6
Lehigh (3)	G-9
Lemoyne (2)	U-11
Leon Fraser	A-7
Leon Simard	IG-4
Leonard W.	G-24
Lesco	O-5
LeVoyageur	S-13
Lewis G. Harriman	S-19
Lewis Wilson Foy	O-1
Liberty Sky	IS-7
Lida	IJ-2
Lievre Consol	T-9
Lillifred	E-2
Limestone	G-22
Limnos	C-5
Linda Brooks	K-4
Linnhurst	F-1
Lisa E.	E-6
Liski	IS-19
Little Rock	N-4
Lok Maheshwari	IT-6
Lok Prakash	IT-6
Lok Pratap	IT-6
Lok Rajeshwari	IT-6
Lomer Gouin	L-1
Lord Selkirk	IN-9
Lotila	IF-4
Louie S.	R-2
Louis Howland	ID-6
Louis Jolliet	C-32
Louis M. Lauzier	C-5
Louis R. Desmarais	C-1
Louis St. Laurent	C-3
Louis W. Hill	L-10
Louisiana	G-22
Loutre Consol	T-9
Lowell D.	W-2

Vessel Name / Fleet Number		Vessel Name / Fleet Number		Vessel Name / Fleet Number	
LST-393	W-7	Maple	J-5	Meredith Andrie	A-7
LST-987	B-1	Maple	ID-5	Mesabi	G-9
LT Argosy	IL-1	Maple City	C-25	Mesabi Miner	I-3
LT Odyssey	IL-1	Maplecliffe Hall	U-11	Messenger	G-22
LT-18	D-11	Mapleglen {2}	P-1	Meteor	H-10
LT-1944	U-2	Marblehead	K-2	Metis	C-1
LT-280	H-6	Marcey	M-6	Metro Sun	U-11
LT-5	H-1	Margaret Ann	H-11	Michael D. Misner	N-2
LT-643	E-1	Margaret John	IM-10	Michigan	U-2
LT-815	H-6	Margaret M.	H-6	Michigan {4}	E-6
LT-821	H-6	Margaret M. Hannah	H-6	Michigan {9}	G-22
LTI-2194	G-14	Margaret Yorke	M-16	Michigan {10}	C-28
Lucien L.	L-1	Mari Beth Andrie	A-7	Mickie Birdsall	ID-6
Lucien Paquin	IL-7	Maria G L	IC-4	Middletown	O-1
Luckyman	IT-12	Marilis T.	IT-4	Midstate I	S-4
Ludger Simard	IG-4	Marina	E-9	Midstate II	S-4
Ludington	K-5	Marine Angel	U-10	Midway	G-22
Luna Verde	IP-10	Marine Evangeline	IM-4	Mikhail Kutuzov	IM-12
Lynx	IB-2	Marine Robin	U-12	Milan Kamak	IN-2
Lyra	IF-7	Marine Star	E-7	Millard County	B-1
		Marine Trader	A-1	Milwaukee Clipper	H-4
M		Marinik G.	IP-11	Miners Castle	P-4
M-1	D-13	Mariposa Belle	M-12	Minn	H-11
M-211	K-3	Marjolaine II	C-35	Minnesota {1}	G-22
M. Hass	ID-5	Mark Hannah	H-6	Miseford	N-2
M. L. 105	D-10	Marka L.	IC-4	Mishe-Mokwa	M-5
M.F.D. No. 15	G-22	Marlyn	S-10	Miss Brockville	U-9
M.I.L. Balsam	J-1	Marquette	O-1	Miss Brockville IV	U-9
M.I.L. Venture	T-1	Marquette {5}	S-22	Miss Brockville V	U-9
Macassa {2}	H-5	Marquette {6}	C-13	Miss Brockville VI	U-9
Mackinac Express	A-11	Marsea Fourteen	U-5	Miss Brockville VII	U-9
Mackinac Islander	D-5	Martha C.	H-11	Miss Brockville VIII	U-9
Mackinaw	U-3	Martha L. Black	C-3	Miss Buffalo	B-16
Madeline	M-2	Martin	E-6	Miss Buffalo II	B-16
Magnetic	F-3	Martin E. Johnson	J-1	Miss Dott-O	ID-6
Magpie	J-1	Marul	IJ-1	Miss Edna	K-5
Maid of the Mist	M-3	Mary Ann	E-6	Miss Ivy Lea II	I-5
Maid of the Mist III	M-3	Mary B.	M-16	Miss Ivy Lea III	I-5
Maid of the Mist IV	M-3	Mary B. VI	M-16	Miss Midland	P-2
Maid of the Mist V	M-3	Mary Cecilia	ID-6	Miss Montreal	C-36
Maid of the Mist VI	M-3	Mary E. Hannah	H-6	Miss Munising	P-4
Maid of the Mist VII	M-3	Mary Louis	J-9	Miss Superior	P-4
Maine {1}	G-22	Mary Page Hannah {1}	S-7	Mississippi	G-22
Maisi	IR-1	Mary Page Hannah {2}	H-6	Missouri {1}	G-22
Maissoneuve	L-2	Mary T. Tracy	H-11	Missouri {2}	G-22
Majestic Star Casino	B-2	Maryland {2}	G-22	Mljet	IA-15
Major Elisha K. Henson	H-1	Marysville	G-2	Mobile Bay	U-3
Major Emil H. Block	D-11	Massachusetts	G-22	Mobiloil	I-3
Makeevka	IA-17	Mathilda Desgagnes	T-9	Mohawk	D-5
Malabar	T-10	Mayan Prince	IA-6	Montana	G-22
Malden	J-1	McAllister 132	B-15	Montcalm	C-3
Malinska	IM-1	McAllister 252	M-16	Montcliffe Hall	N-1
Mammoth	M-16	McAsphalt 401	M-15	Monte Castillo	O-6
Mana	IG-3	McCauley	U-2	Monte Cruceta	O-6
Manatra II	U-14	McIntyre	C-10	Montmagny	C-3
Mangal Desai	IL-1	McKee Sons	U-10	Montmorency	C-3
Manitoba	M-16	McKeller	J-1	Montrealais	U-11/S-5
Manitou {1}	T-10	McLane	U-14	Montrealer	U-11
Manitou {2}	M-4	Meagan Beth	D-13	Morgan	K-4
Manitou Island	M-5	Med Transporter	IS-13	Morgan Reinaver	IR-4
Manitoulin {5}	C-1	Medusa Challenger	C-10	Morton Salt 74	M-23
Manitowoc	M-13	Medusa Conquest	C-10	Mosdeep	IF-3
Manitowoc	U-2	Mekhanik Aniskin	IA-17	Mountain Blossom	IL-3
Manitowoc	U-3	Melissa Desgagnes	T-9	Mr. Micky	H-2
Mantadoc {2}	N-1	Melvin H. Baker II {2}	C-1	Murray Bay {2}	N-1
Manx	O-6	Menasha	M-21	Murray Bay {3}	U-11
Manx Viking	O-6	Menier Consol	T-7	Muskegon {1}	H-6

Joseph L. Block and H. Lee White load taconite pellets at Escanaba, MI on 20 June, 1996.   (Rod Burdick)

Vessel Name / Fleet Number		Vessel Name / Fleet Number		Vessel Name / Fleet Number	
Plitvice	IA-15	R. C. L. Tug No. 1	M-16	Roubini	IT-5
Point Carroll	IE-1	R. F. Grant	T-11	Rouge	U-2
Point Chebucto	IE-1	R. G. Cassidy	G-14	Rover	IU-2
Point Halifax	IE-1	R. Manic	M-14	Royalton {2}	U-11
Point Valiant	T-11	R.C. L. No. 11	C-4	Rubin Hawk	IM-3
Point Valour	T-5	Racine	U-2	Ruder Boskovic	IA-15
Point Vibert	IE-1	Radiant	J-7	Ruffy J. Kadinger	K-1
Point Victor	M-16	Radisson {1}	L-1	Ruhr Ore	A-3
Point Vigour	IE-1	Radisson {2}	S-22	Russell 8	R-2
Point Vim	IE-1	Ralph Misener	U-11		
Pointe Aux Basques	IE-1	Ranger	IT-3	**S**	
Pointe Comeau	IE-1	Ranger III	U-6	S. P. Renolds	G-14
Pointe Levy	M-15	Rantum	IT-8	S. T. Crapo	A-7
Pointe Sept Iles	IE-1	Rapid Cities	G-14	S.M.T.B. No. 7	M-16
Polana	H-5	Ras Maersk	IA-1	S.O. Co. No. 19	S-7
Polk	G-22	Rasmine Maersk	IA-1	S.T. Co. No. 19	S-7
Polor Shore	G-24	Ray Durocher	D-13	Sachem	E-6
Polydefkis	IS-5	Razboieni	IN-3	Sacre Bleu	S-9
Pomorze Zachodnie	IP-7	Rebecca Lynn	A-7	Sadan Kaptanoglu	IG-10
Pontokratis	IM-9	Red Crown	C-10	Sagittarius	IS-8
Pontoporos	IM-9	Redestos	IM-6	Saguenay {2}	C-1
Poolgracht	IS-17	Regina Oldendorff	IE-2	Saipan	G-22
Port Alfred II	S-14	Reid McAllister	R-2	Salty Dog No. 1	M-16
Port City Princess	P-8	Reiss	S-2	Salvage Monarch	M-14
Port Welcome	G-15	Reiss Marine	M-7	Sam Laud	A-5
Porthos	U-11	Reliance	ID-6	Sam McBride	C-26
Powell No. 1	B-15	Relief	M-4	Samoset	I-3
Prabhu Daya	IT-9	Renee Simard	S-25	Samson II	D-13
Prabhu Gopal	IT-9	Reserve	O-1	Samuel E. Bool	G-22
Prairie Harvest	C-1	Resolute	ID-6	Samuel Risley	C-3
Praxitelis	IS-5	Reuben Johnson	F-4	San Juan	C-2
President Casino V	B-2	Rhea	IF-8	Sand Pebble	K-7
Presque Isle {1}	A-7	Rhine Ore	N-1	Sandpiper	H-8
Presque Isle {2}	U-13	Rhode Island	G-22	Sandy Cape	G-24
Pride of Donegal	IA-9	Richard J. Barnes	E-10	Sanita	M-8
Pride of Michigan	U-7	Richard J. Reiss {2}	E-12	Sarah Hays	A-7
Pride of Toronto	M-12	Richard Reiss	E-12	Sarah Spencer	C-1
Prince Edward	IN-9	Richelieu {3}	A-3	Saskatchewan Pioneer	IF-3
Prince Nova	IN-9	Richmond	IR-4	Saturn {4}	C-27
Princess	J-7	Richmond Hill	U-11	Sault au Couchon	M-16
Princess No. 1	J-7	Rideaulite	M-16	Sauniere	A-3
Princess of Acadia	IM-4	Rio Orinoco	T-9	Says	S-18
Progress	N-2	Riomar	IS-24	Scotia II	M-16
Project Americas	IM-2	Rivershell {4}	S-8	Scotoil	T-9
Project Europa	IM-2	Rixta Oldendorff	IE-2	Scotsman	S-18
Propeller	G-2	Roanoke {2}	M-13	Scott Misener {4}	A-3
Protector	M-8	Robert B. No. 1	M-16	Scranton	M-14
Proussa	IM-6	Robert Charles	T-6	Sea Barge One	C-1
Provider	S-11	Robert H.	T-11	Sea Castle	A-7
Provmar Terminal	U-11	Robert John	G-14	Sea Diver	IH-4
Provmar Terminal II	U-11	Robert L. Torres	A-7	Sea Eagle	S-18
Provo Wallis	C-3	Robert Noble	W-3	Sea Eagle II	S-18
PTF-17	N-4	Robert Purcell	A-7	Sea Fox II	S-3
Punica	IS-3	Robert W.	T-4	Sea Hound	M-16
Put-In-Bay {2}	S-9	Robin E.	E-6	Sea Islander	R-4
Put-In-Bay {3}	M-20	Robinson Bay	S-17	Sea Laurel	ID-5
		Rocket	J-1	Sea Monarch	IT-7
Q		Rockland	IR-4	Sea Queen II	A-9
Q. A. Gillmore	S-2	Roger Blough	U-13	Seachampion	IT-7
Quebecois	U-11/S-5	Roger M. Kyes	I-2	Seadaniel	IC-9
Quedoc {3}	N-1	Roger R. Simons	J-5	Seaglory	IF-3
Queen City {2}	H-5	Rogers City {1}	G-22	Sealane II	IT-7
Queen of Andersonville	W-5	Romeo and Annette	O-6	Seapearl II	IN-4
		Romo Maersk	IA-1	Searanger II	IT-7
R		Rong Cheng	IC-9	Seaval	H-11
R. & L. No. 1	G-17	Rosalee D.	T-4	Seaward Johnson	IH-4
R. C. Co. Tug No.1	M-16	Rosemary	M-12	Seaway Queen	U-11/S-5

Vessel Name	Fleet Number
Segwun	M-25
Selkirk Settler	IF-3
Seneca Queen	K-5
Senneville	A-3
Sentosa	IG-7
Serenade	IP-3
Sevilla Wave	IT-4
Shamrock {1}	J-8
Shamrock {2}	C-26
Shannon	G-2
Sharon M. Selvick	S-7
Shell Scientist	U-11
Shelter Bay	U-2
Shenango II	I-3
Sherman H. Serre	S-7
Shiawassie	M-12
Shirley Irene	K-2
Shoreline	S-10
Showboat Royal Grace	M-12
Shuttler	H-6
Sidsel Knutsen	IK-3
Sila	IG-3
Sillery	M-16
Silver Isle	A-3
Silversides	U-14
Simcoe	C-3
Simon Fraser	C-3
Simonsen	U-2
Sinmac	M-14
Sioux	E-6
Sir Denys Lowson	N-1
Sir Humphrey Gilbert	C-3
Sir John Douglas	C-3
Sir John Franklin	C-3
Sir Richard	D-5
Sir Robert Bond	IM-4
Sir Wilfred Laurier	C-3
Sir William Alexander	C-3
Siscowet	U-4
Sissili River	IB-3
Sistella	G-24
Skudenes	O-6
Skyline Princess	M-19
Skyline Queen	M-19
Slapy	IC-10
Slavonija	IM-1
Snark	IM-7
Socofl Wave	IU-1
Solta	IJ-1
Soo Chief	M-8
Soodoc {2}	T-9
Soren Toubro	IL-1
Soulanges	V-3
South Bass	M-20
South Carolina	G-22
South Channel	C-11
South Haven	E-6
South Islands	IN-1
South Park	H-10
South Shore	B-6
Sparrows Point	O-1
Spartan {2}	L-4
Spirit of Rochester	G-7
Spirit Sky	M-14
Spirit Trader	IT-11
Spuds	R-2
ST-2013	L-8

Vessel Name	Fleet Number
ST-500	S-7
ST-693	R-4
ST-880	K-4
St. Clair {2}	M-16
St. Clair {3}	A-5
St. Clair Flats	C-11
St. Joseph	G-14
St. Lawrence Navigator	U-11
St. Lawrence Prospector	U-11
St. Mary's Cement	S-19
St. Mary's Cement II	S-18
St. Mary's Cement III	S-18
Stalvang	IB-5
Stanley	U-2
Star of Charlevoix {1}	S-21
Star of Chicago II	S-21
Star of Nautica	J-3
Star of Sandford	S-21
Star of Toronto	S-21
State of Haryana	IT-6
STC 2004	B-17
Ste. Claire	S-24
Ste. Marie I	E-6
Ste. Marie II	E-6
Steel Flower	IP-4
Steelcliffe Hall	N-1
Steelton {3}	C-10
Stella	IB-8
Stella Borealis	P-10
Stella Desgagnes	G-14
Stepan Razin	IM-12
Stephan Reinauer	IR-4
Stephan Scott	IR-4
Stephen B. Roman	C-1
Stephen M. Asher	R-2
Stevnsland	IS-22
Stewart J. Cort	B-9
Still Watch	T-3
Stolt Alliance	IS-23
Stolt Aspiration	IS-23
Stolt Taurus	IS-23
Stormont	M-16
Stormy Annie	IU-2
Storon	IB-1
Straits Express	A-11
Straits of Mackinac II	A-11
Stril Pilot	M-14
Su-Joy III	F-4
Sugar Islander	E-2
Sugar Islander II	E-2
Sumy	IA-17
Sundew	U-3
Sunny Blossom	IL-3
Superior {3}	G-22
Susan E.	E-6
Susan Hoey {1}	G-2
Susan Hoey {2}	E-1
Susan M. Selvick	M-8
Susan Michelle	D-1
Susan W. Hannah	H-6

T

Vessel Name	Fleet Number
T. C. Lutz {2}	G-22
T. R. McLagan	P-1
Taboga	S-7
Tadoussac {2}	C-1
Takis V.	G-24

Vessel Name	Fleet Number
Tano River	IB-3
Tarantau	C-1
Tarawa	G-22
Tartan Sea	T-9
Tatiana L.	IC-4
Taurus	E-1
Taverner	IM-4
Tawas Bay	U-2
Techno Balsam	J-1
Techno St-Laurent	T-1
Techno Venture	T-1
Tecumseh {2}	G-14
Telesis	U-1
Temple Bar	A-3
Tennessee	G-22
Texaco Brave {2}	II-1
Texaco Chief {2}	II-1
Texas	G-22
Thalassa Desgagnes	T-9
The Hope	S-9
The Howe Islander	H-13
The Quinte Loyalist	O-2
The St. Joseph Islander	O-2
The Straits of Mackinac	C-30
The Sullivans	N-4
The Welcome	S-9
Theriot Offshore IV	T-9
Thistle	U-3
Thomas A. Payette	N-2
Thomas Rennie	C-26
Thor I	IA-2
Thornhill	U-11
Thorold {4}	T-9
Thorscape	IA-2
Thousand Islander	G-5
Thousand Islander II	G-5
Thousand Islander III	G-5
Thousand Islander IV	G-5
Thunder Bay	E-2
Tiffin	J-7
Tim Buck	IN-4
Timmy B.	S-7
Titan Scan	IM-2
Tobermory	D-4
Todd Fraser	F-4
Tofton	IB-1
Toledo	M-16
Tommy Wiborg	U-11
Tonawanda	R-4
Tonawanda	U-2
Toni D.	P-6
Torill Knutsen	IK-3
Torontonian	M-12
Tracy	C-3
Trans Arctic	IS-6
Trenton {1}	E-10
Trias	IF-3
Trident Mariner	IC-8
Trillium	C-26
Trinidad	W-1
Triton {1}	E-6
Triton {2}	S-19
Trois Rivieres	L-1
Trojan	E-6
Trump Casino	T-12
Truskavets	T-9
Trust	IS-14

Vessel Name / Fleet Number	
Tubarao	IV-1
Tug Malcom	M-4
Tulagi	G-22
Tupper	C-3
Turid Knutsen	IK-3
Turkay B.	IB-7
Tuscarora	S-19
Two Rivers	L-13
Tyee Shell	S-8

U

U-505	M-24
Ucka	IU-2
Ulloa	IP-1
Undaunted	B-4
Ungava Transport	U-11
Unicorn of St. Helier	G-19
Union	IP-1
Upper Canada	O-6
Utah	G-22
Utviken	IV-2
Uznadze	IA-11

V

V. W. Scully	A-3
Vacationland	IM-4
Vachon	F-2
Valeria Barsova	IB-2
Valley Camp {2}	L-10
Valour	T-5
Vamand Wave	IT-4
Vandoc {2}	N-1
Varangnes	U-11
Varjakka	IF-4
Vasiliy Musinskiy	IN-8
Vector	C-3
Vekua	IA-11
Velasco	S-18
Veler	U-2
Venture	R-4
Venus	J-9
Verendrye	D-6
Verendrye	U-11
Vermont	G-22
Victor L. Schlaegar	C-15
Vigilant	ID-6
Viking {2}	C-31
Ville Marie	T-3
Ville Marie II	M-22
Virginia {2}	G-22
Vison Consol	T-9
Vista King	D-12
Vista Star	D-12
Volta River	IB-3
Voyager	W-3
Voyageur II	S-11

W

W. C. Harms	G-12
W. E. Ricker	C-3
W. I. Scott Purvis	J-1
W. J. Ivan Purvis	J-1
W. L. Mercereau	G-22
W. M. Edington	M-16
W. N. Twolan	B-15
W. S. Grattan	C-14
W.A.C. 1	G-14

Vessel Name / Fleet Number	
Wabash {2}	H-11
Walpole Islander	W-2
Walter A. Sterling	I-3
Walter J. McCarthy Jr.	A-5
Wana Naree	IG-6
Wanda III	M-25
Washington	U-2
Washington {1}	G-22
Washington {2}	W-3
Waverly	L-5
Wayne Dean	D-3
Wayward Princess	N-3
Welcome {2}	G-22
Welland	D-1
Wellington Kent	II-4
Wendella Clipper	W-5
Wendella Limited	W-5
Wendella Sunliner	W-5
Wenonah	S-11
West Shore {2}	M-20
West Wind	J-4
Westchester	IR-4
Westoil	A-7
Weston	IB-1
Whitby	C-9
Whitefish Bay	U-2
Wicklow	G-22
Wilfred M. Cohen	J-1
Wilfred Sykes	I-2
Wilfred Templeman	C-3
William A. Irvin	D-11
William A. Whitney	H-6
William C. Gaynor	L-5
William C. Selvick	S-7
William Clay Ford {2}	I-3
William Darrell	H-12
William G. Clyde	U-13
William G. Mather {2}	H-7
William H. Donner	U-12

Vessel Name / Fleet Number	
William Hoey	H-11
William Inglis	C-26
William J. DeLancey	I-3
William M. Miller	M-20
William P. Feeley {2}	S-7
William P. Snyder	C-10
William R. Roesch	O-1
William Rest	C-25
William S. Bell	H-11
William W. Stender	S-7
Willis B. Boyer	C-23
Willowglen	G-9
Wilmac	M-16
Wind	IA-8
Windmill Point	C-25
Windoc {2}	N-1
Windsor {2}	M-13
Winnebago	J-9
Winnipeg {2}	A-3
Winter Star	IH-5
Wisconsin {4}	G-22
Wislanes	IP-7
Witch	D-13
WLV 526	C-22
Wm. A. Lydon	H-11
Wm. Lyon Mackenzie	C-24
Wm. Market	M-20
Wolf River	G-14
Wolfe Islander III	O-2
Wolverine	G-18
Wolverine {4}	O-1
WSA 6	E-6
Wyandot	S-9
Wynken, Blynken and Nod	L-4
Wyoming	G-22

Y

Yale	G-22
Yankcanuck {2}	J-1
Yankee	H-11
Yankee Clipper	V-2
Yankee Lady	G-23
Yankee Lady II	G-23
Yick Hua	IC-9
YO-178	E-11
Yorktown Clipper	IC-6
YP-673	U-7

Z

Z Four	G-22
Z One	G-22
Z Three	G-22
Z Two	G-22
Zachery Reinauer	IR-4
Zarnesti	IN-3
Ziemia Bialostocka	IP-7
Ziemia Chelminska	IP-7
Ziemia Gnieznienska	IP-7
Ziemia Krakowska	IP-7
Ziemia Olsztynska	IP-7
Ziemia Suwalska	IP-7
Ziemia Tarnowska	IP-7
Ziemia Zamojska	IP-7

FLEET & SHIP LISTINGS

FLEET & SHIP LISTINGS

Listed after each vessel in order are Type of Vessel, Year Built, Type of Engine, Cargo Capacity (at mid-summer draft in long tons) or Gross Tonnage* (tanker capacities are listed in barrels), Overall Length, Breadth and Depth or Draft*. The figures given are as accurate as possible and are given for informational purposes only. Vessels and owners are listed alphabetically as per American Bureau of Shipping and Lloyd's of London format. Former names of vessels and years of operation under prior names appear beneath the vessel's name.

AC	Auto Carrier	**FB**	Fire Boat	**RR**	Roll On / Roll Off
BC	Bulk Carrier	**FD**	Floating Dry Dock	**RV**	Research Vessel
BR	Brigantine	**GC**	Gambling Casino	**SB**	Supply Boat
BT	Buoy Tender	**GL**	Gate Lifter	**SC**	Sand Carrier
CA	Heavy Cruiser	**GU**	Grain Self-unloader	**SR**	Search and Rescue
CC	Cement Carrier	**IB**	Ice Breaker	**SS**	Submarine
CF	Car Ferry	**LS**	Lightship	**SU**	Self-unloader
CLG	Guided Missile Cruiser	**MB**	Mail Boat	**SV**	Survey Vessel
CS	Crane Ship	**MS**	Minesweeper	**TB**	Tugboat
DB	Deck Barge	**PA**	Passenger Vessel	**TF**	Train Ferry
DD	Destroyer	**PC**	Passenger	**TK**	Tanker
DR	Dredge		Catamaran	**TT**	Tractor Tugboat
DV	Drilling Vessel	**PF**	Passenger Ferry	**TV**	Training Vessel
ER	Env. Response Ship	**PK**	Package Freighter	**WM**	Med. Endurance
ES	Excursion Ship	**PT**	Patrol Torpedo Boat		Cutter

PROPULSION

B	Barge	**Q Steam**	Quadruple Expansion
D	Diesel		Compound Engine
DC	Batteries	**R Steam**	Triple Expansion
Sail	Sailing Vessel		Compound Engine
L Steam	Quad. Expansion	**S Steam**	Skinner "Uniflow" Engine
	Double Compound	**T Steam**	Turbine
	Engine "Lentz Poppet"	**U Steam**	Uniflow Engine - "Skinner"

Fleet No. and Name Vessel Name	Type of Ship	Year Built	Type of Engine	Cargo Cap. or Gross*	Length	Beam	Depth or Draft*
A-1 — ACME TUG SERVICE, DULUTH, MN							
Marine Trader	SB	1939	D	67*	65' 00"	15' 00"	7' 06"
Oatka	TB	1934	D	12*	40' 00"	10' 00"	4' 00"
A-2 — ALCAN SMELTERS & CHEMICALS LTD., PORT ALFRED, PQ							
Alexis Simard	TT	1980	D	286*	92' 00"	34' 00"	13' 07"
Grande Baie	TT	1973	D	194*	86' 06"	30' 00"	12' 00"
A-3 — ALGOMA CENTRAL CORPORATION, SAULT STE. MARIE, ON							
Agawa Canyon	SU	1970	D	23,400	647' 00"	72' 00"	40' 00"
Algobay	SU	1978	D	34,900	730' 00"	75' 10"	46' 06"
(Algobay '78 - '94, Atlantic Trader '94 - '97)							
Algocape (2)	BC	1967	D	29,950	730' 00"	75' 00"	39' 08"
(Richelieu (3) '67 - '94)							
Algocen (2)	BC	1968	D	28,400	730' 00"	75' 00"	39' 08"

Fleet No. and Name Vessel Name	Type of Ship	Year Built	Type of Engine	Cargo Cap. or Gross*	Length	Beam	Depth or Draft*
Algogulf {2}	BC	1961	T	26,950	730' 00"	75' 00"	39' 00"
(J. N. McWatters {2} '61 - '91, Scott Misener {4} '91 - '94)							
Algoisle	BC	1963	D	26,700	730' 00"	75' 00"	39' 03"
(Silver Isle '63 - '94)							
Algolake	SU	1977	D	32,150	730' 00"	75' 00"	46' 06"
Algomarine	SU	1968	D	27,000	730' 00"	75' 00"	39' 08"
(Lake Manitoba '68 - '87)							
Algonorth	BC	1971	D	28,000	729' 09"	75' 02"	42' 11"
(Temple Bar '71 - '77, Lake Nipigon '77 - '84, Laketon {2} '84 - '86, Lake Nipigon '86 - '87)							
Algontario	BC	1960	D	29,100	730' 00"	75' 09"	40' 02"
(Ruhr Ore '60 - '76, Cartiercliffe Hall '76 - '88, Winnipeg {2} '88 - '94)							
Algoport	SU	1979	D	32,000	658' 00"	75' 10"	46' 06"
Algorail {2}	SU	1968	D	23,750	640' 05"	72' 03"	40' 00"
Algoriver	BC	1960	T	26,800	722' 06"	75' 00"	39' 00"
(John A. France {2} '60 - '94)							
Algosoo {2}	SU	1974	D	31,300	730' 00"	75' 00"	44' 06"
Algosound	BC	1965	T	27,700	730' 00"	75' 00"	39' 00"
(Don-De-Dieu '65 - '67, V. W. Scully '67 - '87)							
Algosteel {2}	SU	1966	D	27,000	730' 00"	75' 00"	39' 08"
(A. S. Glossbrenner '66 - '87, Algogulf {1} '87 - '90)							
Algoville	SU	1967	D	28,200	730' 00"	78' 00"	39' 08"
(Senneville '67 - '94)							
Algoway {2}	SU	1972	D	24,000	650' 00"	72' 00"	40' 00"
Algowest	BC	1982	D	33,300	730' 00"	75' 10"	42' 00"
Algowood	SU	1981	D	31,750	730' 00"	75' 10"	46' 06"
Capt. Henry Jackman	SU	1981	D	31,800	730' 00"	75' 10"	42' 00"
(Lake Wabush '81 - '87)							
John B. Aird	SU	1983	D	31,300	730' 00"	75' 10"	46' 06"
Sauniere	SU	1970	D	23,900	642' 10"	74' 10"	42' 00"
(Bulknes '70 - '70, Brooknes '70 - '76, Algosea '76 - '82)							

A-4 — AMERICAN MARINE CONSTRUCTORS, ST. JOSEPH, MI

Defiance	TB	1966	D	26*	44' 08"	18' 00"	6' 00"

A-5 — AMERICAN STEAMSHIP COMPANY, WILLIAMSVILLE, NY

American Mariner	SU	1980	D	37,200	730' 00"	78' 00"	45' 00"
American Republic	SU	1981	D	24,800	634' 10"	68' 00"	40' 00"
Buffalo {3}	SU	1978	D	23,800	634' 10"	68' 00"	40' 00"
Charles E. Wilson	SU	1973	D	33,800	680' 00"	78' 00"	45' 00"
H. Lee White {2}	SU	1974	D	35,200	704' 00"	78' 00"	45' 00"
Indiana Harbor	SU	1979	D	78,850	1,000' 00"	105' 00"	56' 00"
John J. Boland {3}	SU	1953	T	20,200	639' 03"	72' 00"	36' 00"
Sam Laud	SU	1975	D	23,800	634' 10"	68' 00"	40' 00"
St. Clair {3}	SU	1976	D	44,000	770' 00"	92' 00"	52' 00"
Walter J. McCarthy Jr.	SU	1977	D	78,850	1,000' 00"	105' 00"	56' 00"
(Belle River '77 - '90)							

STINSON, INC. - MANAGED BY AMERICAN STEAMSHIP CO.

George A. Stinson	SU	1978	D	59,700	1,004' 00"	105' 00"	50' 00"

A-6 — AMERICAN TRANSIT & TUG CO., BAY CITY, MI

Frederick T. Kellers	TB	1898	D	146*	85' 00"	23' 03"	13' 06"
(Harvey D. Goulder {1} 1898 -'20, US Army A.T.S. Tug No. 7 '20 - '22)							

A-7 — ANDRIE, INC., MUSKEGON, MI

A-390	TK	1982	B	39,000	310' 00"	60' 00"	19' 03"
A-397	TK	1962	B	39,700	270' 00"	60' 00"	25' 00"
A-410	TK	1955	B	41,000	335' 00"	54' 00"	26' 06"
B-7	DB	1976	B	1,350	165' 00"	42' 06"	12' 00"
B-16	DB	1976	B	1,350	165' 00"	42' 06"	12' 00"
Barbara Andrie	TB	1940	D	298*	121' 10"	29' 06"	16' 00"
(Edmond J. Moran '40 - '76)							
Barbara Rita	TB	1991	D	20*	36' 00"	14' 00"	6' 00"

Fleet No. and Name Vessel Name	Type of Ship	Year Built	Type of Engine	Cargo Cap. or Gross*	Length	Beam	Depth or Draft*
Candice Andrie	CS	1958	B	1,000	150' 00"	52' 00"	10' 00"
Clara Andrie	DR	1930	B	1,000	110' 00"	30' 00"	6' 10"
John Purves	TB	1919	D	436*	150' 00"	27' 07"	16' 00"
(Butterfield '19 - '42, US Army Butterfield (LT-145) '42 - '45, Butterfield '45 - '57)							
Karen Andrie {2}	TB	1965	D	433*	120' 00"	31' 06"	16' 00"
(Sarah Hays '65 - '93)							
Mari Beth Andrie	TB	1961	D	147*	87' 00"	24' 00"	11' 06"
(Gladys Bea '61 - '73, American Viking '73 - '83)							
Meredith Andrie	DR	1947	B	1,000	76' 00"	26' 02"	5' 06"
Rebecca Lynn	TB	1964	D	433*	120' 00"	31' 08"	18' 09"
(Kathrine Clewis '64 - '96)							
Robert Purcell	TB	1952	D	28*	45' 00"	12' 06"	7' 09"
Sea Castle	CC	1909	B	2,600	260' 00"	43' 00"	25' 03"
*(Kaministiquia {2} '09 - '16, Westoil '16 - '23, J. B. John {1} '23 - '51, John L. A. Galster 51 - '69 — **Currently laid up in Muskegon, MI)***							

INLAND LAKES MANAGEMENT - DIVISION OF ANDRIE, INC.

Alpena {2}	CC	1942	T	15,550	519' 06"	67' 00"	35' 00"
(Leon Fraser '42 - '91)							
E. M. Ford	CC	1898	Q	7,100	428' 00"	50' 00"	28' 00"
(Presque Isle {1} 1898 - '56)							
J. A. W. Iglehart	CC	1936	T	12,500	501' 06"	68' 03"	37' 00"
(Pan Amoco '36 - '55, Amoco '55 - '60, H. R. Schemn '60 - '65)							
J. B. Ford	CC	1904	R	8,000	440' 00"	50' 00"	28' 00"
(Edwin F. Holmes '04 - '16, E. C. Collins '16 - '59) **(Last operated 15 November, 1985 — 5 year survey expired November, 1989 — In use as a stationary cement storage / transfer vessel in South Chicago, IL)**							
Paul H. Townsend	CC	1945	D	8,400	447' 00"	50' 00"	29' 00"
(USNS Hickory Coll '45 - '46, USNS Coastal Delegate '46 - '52)							
S. T. Crapo	CC	1927	R	8,900	402' 06"	60' 03"	29' 00"

LAFARGE CORP. - MANAGED BY ANDRIE, INC.

Integrity	CC	1996	B	14,000	460' 00"	70' 00"	37' 00"
Jacklyn M.	TB	1976	D	198*	140' 02"	40' 01"	22' 03"
(Andrew Martin '76 - '90, Robert L. Torres '90 - '94)							
(Overall Dimensions Together)					543' 00"	70' 00"	37' 00"

A-8 — APEX OIL CO., FORESTVIEW, IL

Apex Chicago	TK	1981	B	35,000	288' 00"	60' 00"	19' 00"

A-9 — APOSTLE ISLAND CRUISE SERVICE, BAYFIELD, WI

Sea Queen II	ES	1971	D	12*	42' 00"	14' 00"	2' 07"

A-10 — ARGEE CRUISES, INC., PENETANGUISHENE, ON

Georgian Queen	ES	1918	D	249*	119' 00"	36' 00"	16' 06"

A-11 — ARNOLD TRANSIT COMPANY, MACKINAC ISLAND, MI

Algomah	PF	1961	D	81*	92' 00"	31' 00"	8' 00"
Chippewa {6}	PF	1962	D	81*	92' 00"	31' 00"	8' 00"
Corsair	CF	1955	D	98*	94' 06"	33' 00"	8' 06"
Huron {5}	PF	1955	D	99*	91' 06"	25' 00"	10' 01"
Island Express	PC	1988	D	90*	82' 07"	28' 06"	8' 05"
Mackinac Express	PC	1987	D	90*	82' 07"	28' 06"	8' 05"
Ottawa {2}	PF	1959	D	81*	92' 00"	31' 00"	8' 00"
Straits Express	PC	1995	D	99*	101' 00"	29' 11"	6' 08"
Straits of Mackinac II	PF	1969	D	89*	89' 11"	27' 00"	8' 08"

B-1 — B+B DREDGING CORP., CRYSTAL RIVER, FL

Columbus	DR	1944	D	2,923*	310' 02"	50' 00"	22' 01"
(USS LST-987 '44 - '55, USS Millard County (LST-987) '55 - '73, Esperance III '73 - '86)							

B-2 — BARDEN DEVELOPMENT, GARY, IN

Majestic Star Casino	GC	1971	D	2,136*	280' 06"	62' 06"	19' 07"
(Dayliner '71 - '72, New Yorker '72 - '90, President Casino V '90 - '96)							

Fleet No. and Name Vessel Name	Type of Ship	Year Built	Type of Engine	Cargo Cap. or Gross*	Length	Beam	Depth or Draft*
B-3 — BARGE TRANSPORTATION, INC., DETROIT, MI							
Cherokee {2}	DB	1943	B	1,200	155' 00"	50' 00"	13' 06"
B-4 — BASIC MARINE, ESCANABA, MI							
Erika Kobasic	TB	1939	D	226*	110' 00"	26' 05"	15' 01"
(USCG Arundel (WYTM-90) '39 - '84, Karen Andrie {1} '84 - '90)							
Escort II	TB	1969	D	28*	50' 00"	13' 00"	7' 00"
Krystal K.	TB	1944	D	860*	143' 00"	33' 01"	17' 00"
(USS Undaunted (ATR-126, ATA-199) '44 - '63, USMA Kings Pointer '63 - '93)							
L. E. Block	BC	1927	T	15,900	621' 00"	64' 00"	33' 00"
(Last operated 31 October, 1981 — Currently laid up in Escanaba, MI)							
B-5— BAY SHIPBUILDING CORP., STURGEON BAY, WI							
Bayship	TB	1943	D	19*	45' 00"	12' 06"	6' 00"
B-6 — BEAVER ISLAND BOAT COMPANY, CHARLEVOIX, MI							
Beaver Islander	PF	1963	D	95*	96' 03"	9' 09"	9' 09"
Emerald Isle {2}	PF	1996	D				
South Shore	PF	1945	D	67*	64' 10"	24' 00"	9' 06"
B-7 — BERNARD McCUE, CHRISTIAN ISLAND, ON							
Indian Maiden	PF	1987	D	128*	74' 00"	23' 00"	8' 00"
B-8 — BERNIER MARITIME MUSEUM, L'ISLET-SUR-MER, PQ							
Ernest Lapointe	IB	1940	R	1,675*	185' 00"	36' 00"	22' 06"
(Currently a museum vessel in L'Islet-Sur-Mer, PQ. See page 111)							
B-9 — BETHLEHEM STEEL CORPORATION, CHESTERTON, IN							
Burns Harbor {2}	SU	1980	D	78,850	1,000' 00"	105' 00"	56' 00"
Stewart J. Cort	SU	1972	D	58,000	1,000' 00"	105' 00"	49' 00"
B-10 — BIGANE VESSEL FUELING COMPANY OF CHICAGO, CHICAGO, IL							
Jos. F. Bigane	TK	1973	D	7,500	140' 00"	40' 00"	14' 00"
B-11 — BLACK CREEK SHIPPING CO. LTD., PORT DOVER, ON							
Cuyahoga	SU	1943	L	15,675	620' 00"	60' 00"	35' 00"
(J. Burton Ayers '43 - '95)							
B-12 — BLUE WATER EXCURSIONS, INC., PORT HURON, MI							
Huron Lady	ES	1961	D	55*	65' 00"	17' 00"	5' 00"
B-13 — BLUE WATER FERRY LTD., SOMBRA, ON							
Daldean	CF	1951	D	145*	75' 00"	35' 00"	7' 00"
Ontamich	CF	1939	D	55*	65' 00"	28' 10"	8' 06"
(Harsens Island '39 - '73)							
B-14 — BRIAN UTILITIES SERVICES, INC., MUSKEGON, MI							
Capt. Roy	TB	1987	D	27*	42' 06"	12' 08"	6' 06"
B-15 — BUCHANAN FOREST PRODUCTS LTD., THUNDER BAY, ON							
McAllister 132	DB	1954	B	7,000	343' 00"	63' 00"	19' 00"
(Powell No. 1 '54 - '61, Alberni Carrier '61 - '77, Genmar 132 '77 - '79)							
W. N. Twolan	TB	1962	D	299*	106' 00"	29' 00"	14' 00"
B-16 — BUFFALO CHARTERS, INC., BUFFALO, NY							
Miss Buffalo	ES	1964	D	88*	64' 10"	23' 05"	7' 04"
Miss Buffalo II	ES	1972	D	88*	86' 00"	24' 00"	6' 00"
B-17 — BUSCH MARINE, CARROLLTON, MI							
Gregory J. Busch	TB	1919	D	299*	151' 00"	28' 00"	16' 09"
(Humaconna '19 - '77)							
STC 2004	DB	1986	B	2,364	240' 00"	50' 00"	9' 05"
C-1 — CANADA STEAMSHIP LINES, INC., MONTREAL, PQ							
Atlantic Erie	SU	1985	D	38,200	736' 06"	75' 10"	50' 00"
(Hon. Paul Martin '85 - '88)							
Frontenac {5}	SU	1968	D	27,500	729' 07"	75' 03"	39' 08"

Fleet No. and Name Vessel Name	Type of Ship	Year Built	Type of Engine	Cargo Cap. or Gross*	Length	Beam	Depth or Draft*
Halifax	SU	1963	T	30,100	730' 00"	75' 00"	39' 03"
(Frankcliffe Hall {2} '63 - '88)							
H. M. Griffith	SU	1973	D	31,250	730' 00"	75' 00"	46' 06"
Jean Parisien	SU	1977	D	33,000	730' 00"	75' 00"	46' 06"
J. W. McGiffin	SU	1972	D	33,100	730' 00"	75' 00"	46' 06"
Louis R. Desmarais	SU	1977	D	33,000	730' 00"	75' 00"	46' 06"
Manitoulin {5}	SU	1966	D	28,100	730' 00"	75' 00"	41' 00"
Nanticoke	SU	1980	D	35,100	730' 00"	75' 08"	46' 06"
Saguenay {2}	SU	1964	D	30,500	730' 00"	75' 02"	44' 08"
(Last operated 30 November, 1992 — Currently laid up in Toronto, ON)							
Tadoussac {2}	SU	1969	D	29,700	730' 00"	75' 03"	42' 00"
Tarantau	SU	1965	T	27,600	730' 00"	75' 00"	46' 06"
CSL INTERNATIONAL - DIVISION OF CANADA STEAMSHIP LINES, INC.							
Atlantic Superior	SU	1982	D	38,900	730' 00"	75' 10"	50' 00"
Bahia Magdalena	BC		D				
Bernard Oldendorff	SU	1991	D	77,000	747' 00"	105' 00"	60' 00"
Christopher Oldendorff	SU	1982	D	63,000	747' 00"	105' 00"	60' 00"
(Pacific Peace '82 - '86, Atlantic Huron {1} '86 - '88, CSL Innovator '88 - '94)							
CSL Atlas	SU	1990	D	68,000	747' 05"	105' 00"	60' 00"
CSL Cabo	SU	1971	D				
(Cabo San Lucas '71 - '95)							
Ferbec	BC	1965	D	60,000	731' 08"	104' 00"	57' 09"
(Fugaku Maru '65 - '77)							
Melvin H. Baker II {2}	SU	1984	D	34,600	736' 06"	75' 10"	46' 06"
(Prairie Harvest '84 - '89, Atlantic Huron {2} '89 - '94)							
GREAT LAKES TRANSPORT LTD. - CHARTERED BY CANADA STEAMSHIP LINES, INC.							
Atlantic Hickory	TB	1973	D	912*	145' 00"	38' 09"	21' 02"
(Irving Miami '73 - '95)							
Sarah Spencer	SU	1959	B	23,200	611" 03"	72' 00"	40' 00"
(Adam E. Cornelius {3} '59 - '89, Capt. Edward V. Smith '89 - '91, Sea Barge One '91 - '96)							
ESSROC CANADA, INC. - MANAGED BY CANADA STEAMSHIP LINES, INC.							
Stephen B. Roman	CC	1965	D	7,600	488' 09"	56' 00"	35' 06"
(Fort William '65 - '83)							
Metis	CC	1956	B	5,800	331' 00"	43' 09"	26' 00"
(Last operated 19 August, 1993 — In use as a cement storage barge in Green Bay, WI)							
LAFARGE CORP. CANADA, INC. - MANAGED BY CANADA STEAMSHIP LINES, INC.							
English River	CC	1961	D	7,450	404' 03"	60' 00"	36' 06"

C-2 — CANADA WEST INDIES MOLASSES CO. LTD., MISSISSAUGA, ON

San Juan	TK	1962	B	913*	195' 00"	35' 00"	12' 06"

C-3 — CANADIAN COAST GUARD, GREAT LAKES FLEET, OTTAWA, ON

Alfred Needier	RV	1982	D	925*	165' 09"	36' 09"	22' 01"
Arctic Harvester	RV	1971	D	696*	116' 08"	31' 01"	15' 05"
Bartlett*	BT	1969	D	1,317*	189' 05"	42' 06"	16' 06"
Cape Hurd	SR	1982	D	57*	70' 10"	18' 00"	8' 09"
Caribou Isle	BT	1986	D	92*	75' 06"	19' 08"	7' 04"
Cove Isle	BT	1980	D	80*	65' 07"	19' 08"	7' 04"
Des Groseilliers	IB	1983	D	5,910*	322' 07"	64' 00"	35' 06"
Dumit	BT	1979	D	569*	160' 01"	40' 00"	9' 02"
Earl Gray	BT	1986	D	1,971*	230' 00"	46' 02"	22' 01"
Griffon	IB	1970	D	2,212*	234' 00"	49' 00"	21' 06"
Gull Isle	BT	1980	D	80*	65' 07"	19' 08"	7' 04"
Ile Des Barques	BT	1985	D	92*	75' 06"	19' 08"	7' 04"
Ile Ste. Ours	BT	1986	D	139*	75' 06"	19' 07"	4' 07"
J. E. Bernier	IB	1967	D	2,457*	231' 04"	49' 00"	16' 00"
Kenoki	BT	1964	D	275*	105' 07"	32' 02"	6' 03"
Louis St. Laurent	IB	1969	D	10,908*	366' 06"	80' 00"	43' 00"
Martha L. Black	IB	1986	D	3,812*	272' 04"	53' 02"	25' 05"
Montcalm	IB	1957	S	2,017*	220' 06"	48' 03"	16' 05"

Fleet No. and Name Vessel Name	Type of Ship	Year Built	Type of Engine	Cargo Cap. or Gross*	Length	Beam	Depth or Draft*
Montmagny	BT	1963	D	497*	148' 00"	28' 10"	8' 06"
Montmorency*	BT	1957	D	751*	164' 05"	32' 01"	15' 00"
Nahidik	BT	1974	D	856*	175' 05"	49' 11"	10' 05"
Narwhal*	BT	1963	D	2,064*	253' 01"	43' 02"	21' 07"
Pierre Radisson	IB	1978	D	5,910*	322' 07"	64' 00"	35' 06"
Provo Wallis*	BT	1969	D	1,317*	189' 05"	42' 06"	16' 06"
Samuel Risley	BT	1985	D	1,988*	228' 09"	47' 01"	21' 09"
Simcoe*	BT	1962	D	961*	179' 01"	38' 00"	15' 06"
Simon Fraser	IB	1960	D	1,353*	204' 06"	42' 00"	18' 03"
Sir Humphrey Gilbert	IB	1959	D	1,931*	220' 06"	48' 06"	16' 03"
Sir John Douglas	BT	1956	D	564*	151' 04"	31' 03"	13' 05"
Sir John Franklin	IB	1979	D	5,910*	322' 07"	64' 00"	35' 06"
Sir Wilfred Laurier	IB	1986	D	3,812*	272' 04"	53' 02"	25' 05"
Sir William Alexander	IB	1986	D	3,550*	272' 06"	45' 00"	17' 06"
Tracy*	BT	1968	D	963*	181' 01"	38' 00"	16' 00"
Tupper	IB	1959	D	1,353*	204' 06"	42' 00"	18' 03"
Vector	RV	1967	D	516*	130' 06"	32' 00"	14' 05"
W. E. Ricker	RV	1979	D	1,040*	191' 04"	31' 03"	21' 03"
Wilfred Templeman	RV	1981	D	925*	166' 00"	36' 09"	22' 01"

(* Strengthened for icebreaking.)

C-4 — CANADIAN DREDGE & DOCK, INC., DON MILLS, ON

Bagotville	TB	1964	D	65*	65' 00"	18' 06"	10' 00"
Halton	TB	1942	D	15*	42' 09"	14' 00"	7' 06"
Paula M.	TB	1959	D	12*	46' 06"	16' 01"	4' 10"
R.C. L. No. 11	TB	1958	D	20*	42' 09"	14' 03"	5' 09"

C-5 — CANADIAN GOVT., MINISTRY OF ENERGY, MINES, & RESOURCES, OTTAWA, ON

Limnos	RV	1968	D	460*	147' 00"	32' 00"	12' 00"
Louis M. Lauzier	RV	1977	D	195*	125' 00"	27' 00"	11' 06"

C-6 — CANAMAC CRUISES, TORONTO, ON

Aurora Borealis	ES	1983	D	277*	101' 00"	24' 00"	6' 00"

C-7 — CAPTAIN NORMAC'S RIVERBOAT INN LTD., TORONTO, ON

Jadran	BC	1957	D	2,520*	295' 06"	42' 08"	24' 08"

(Former Jadranska Plovidba vessel last operated in 1975 — Now a restaurant in Toronto)

C-8 — CAROL N. BAKER, PENETANGUISHENE, ON

Dawn Light	TB	1891	D	64*	75' 00"	24' 00"	12' 00"

(Le Roy Brooks 1891 - '25, Henry Stokes '25 - '54, Aburg '54 - '81)

C-9 — CARTIER CONSTRUCTION CO., BELLEVILLE, ON

Carl M.	TB	1957	D	21*	47' 00"	14' 06"	6' 00"
Oshawa	TB	1971	D	24*	45' 00"	14' 00"	5' 00"
Whitby	TB	1978	D	24*	45' 00"	14' 00"	5' 00"
Canadian	DR	1954	B	1,088*	174' 00"	50' 00"	14' 00"

C-10 — CEMENT TRANSIT CO., CLEVELAND, OH

Medusa Challenger	CC	1906	S	10,250	552' 01"	56' 00"	31' 00"

(William P. Snyder '06 - '26, Elton Hoyt II {1} '26 - '52, Alex D. Chisholm '52 - '66)

Medusa Conquest	CC	1937	B	8,500	437' 06"	55' 00"	28' 00"

(Red Crown '37 - '62, Amoco Indiana '62 - '87)

C.T.C. No.1	CC	1943	R	16,300	620' 06"	60' 00"	35' 00"

(McIntyre '43 - '43, Frank Purnell {1} '43 - '64, Steelton {3} '64 - '78, Hull No. 3 '78 - '79, Pioneer {3} '79 - '82) **(Last operated 12 November, 1981 — In use as a stationary cement storage / transfer vessel in South Chicago, IL)**

C-11 — CHAMPION AUTO FERRY, ALGONAC, MI

Champion {1}	CF	1941	D	65*	65' 00"	29' 00"	8' 06"
North Channel	CF	1967	D	67*	75' 00"	30' 00"	8' 00"
St. Clair Flats	CF	1946	D	65*	65' 00"	28' 10"	8' 06"
South Channel	CF	1973	D	94*	79' 00"	31' 00"	8' 03"

Fleet No. and Name / Vessel Name	Type of Ship	Year Built	Type of Engine	Cargo Cap. or Gross*	Length	Beam	Depth or Draft*

C-12 — CHARLEVOIX COUNTY ROAD COMMISSION, CHARLEVOIX, MI
Charlevoix {1}	CF	1926	D	43*	50' 00"	32' 00"	3' 09"

C-13 — CHICAGO FROM THE LAKE LTD., CHICAGO, IL
Fort Dearborn	ES	1985	D	62*	64' 10"	22' 00"	4' 06"
Innisfree	ES	1953	D	34*	61' 08"	16' 00"	4' 06"
Marquette {6}	ES	1957	D	29*	50' 07"	15' 00"	4' 00"

C-14 — CITY OF BUFFALO, DEPT. OF PUBLIC WORKS, BUFFALO, NY
Edwin M. Cotter	FB	1900	D	208*	118' 00"	24' 00"	11' 06"

(W. S. Grattan '00 - '53, Firefighter '53 - '54)

C-15 — CITY OF CHICAGO FIRE DEPARTMENT, CHICAGO, IL
Fred A. Busse	FB	1937	D	209*	92' 00"	23' 00"	8' 00"
Joseph Medill {2}	FB	1949	D	350*	92' 06"	24' 00"	11' 00"
Victor L. Schlaegar	FB	1949	D	350*	92' 06"	24' 00"	11' 00"

C-16 — CITY OF CHICAGO WATER PUMPING STATION, CHICAGO, IL
James J. Versluis	TB	1957	D	126*	83' 00"	22' 00"	11' 02"

C-17 — CITY OF CLEVELAND FIRE DEPARTMENT, CLEVELAND, OH
Anthony J. Celebrezze	FB	1961	D	74*	66' 00"	17' 00"	5' 00"

C-18 — CITY OF DETROIT, DETROIT, MI
Des Moines	CA	1948	T	21,500*	716' 06"	76' 04"	26' 00"*

(Former US Navy Des Moines class cruiser (CA-134) that was stricken 14 July, 1961. Tentatively planned to be brought to Detroit in 1997 and opened as a museum.)

C-19 — CITY OF DETROIT FIRE DEPARTMENT, DETROIT, MI
Curtis Randolph	FB	1979	D	85*	77' 10"	21' 06"	9' 03"

C-20 — CITY OF ERIE, ERIE, PA
Niagara {1}	SU	1897	D	1,860	257' 00"	42' 03"	19' 06"

(Former Erie Sand Steamship Co. vessel last operated 31 August, 1982. Currently laid up in Erie, PA awaiting conversion to a museum vessel. See page 108)

C-21 — CITY OF FRANKFORT, FRANKFORT, MI
City of Milwaukee	TF	1931	R	26 cars	360' 00"	56' 03"	21' 06"

(Former Ann Arbor Railroad vessel being converted to a marine museum in Elberta, MI. See Page 109)

C-22 — CITY OF PORT HURON MUSEUM OF ARTS & HISTORY, PORT HURON, MI
WLV 526 (HURON)	LS	1920	D	392*	96' 05"	24' 00"	10' 00"*

(Former US Coast Guard 96-Foot class lightship (LS-103, WAL / WLV-526) was stricken 25 August, 1970.) Currently a museum vessel in Port Huron, MI. See Page 111)

C-23 — CITY OF TOLEDO, TOLEDO, OH
Willis B. Boyer	BC	1911	T	15,000	617' 00"	64' 00"	33' 01"

(Col. James M. Schoonmaker '11 - '69)

(Former Cleveland Cliffs Steamship Co. vessel last operated 17 December, 1980. Currently a museum ship in Toledo, OH. See Page 111)

C-24 — CITY OF TORONTO FIRE DEPARTMENT, TORONTO, ON
Wm. Lyon Mackenzie	FB	1964	D	102*	81' 01"	20' 00"	10' 00"

C-25 — CITY OF TORONTO HARBOUR COMMISSIONERS, TORONTO, ON
Fred Scandrett	TB	1963	D	52*	62' 00"	17' 00"	8' 00"
(C. E. "Ted" Smith '63 - '70)							
J. G. Langton	TB	1934	D	15*	45' 00"	12' 00"	5' 00"
Maple City	CF	1951	D	135*	70' 06"	36' 04"	5' 11"
Ned Hanlan II	TB		D				
William Rest	TB	1961	D	62*	65' 00"	18' 06"	10' 06"
Windmill Point	CF	1954	D	118*	65' 00"	36' 00"	10' 00"

C-26 — CITY OF TORONTO METROPOLITAN PARK DEPARTMENT, TORONTO, ON
Ongiara	PF	1963	D	180*	78' 00"	36' 00"	9' 09"

Algowood heads east as the sun rises over the Straits of Mackinac. (Todd L. Davidson)

Fleet No. and Name Vessel Name	Type of Ship	Year Built	Type of Engine	Cargo Cap. or Gross*	Length	Beam	Depth or Draft*
Sam McBride	PF	1939	D	412*	129' 00"	34' 11"	6' 00"
Thomas Rennie	PF	1950	D	419*	129' 00"	32' 11"	6' 00"
Trillium	PF	1910	R	611*	150' 00"	30' 00"	8' 04"
William Inglis	PF	1935	D	238*	99' 00"	24' 10"	6' 00"

C-27 — CLEVELAND TANKERS (1991), INC., CLEVELAND, OH

Gemini	TK	1978	D	75,000	430' 00"	65' 00"	29' 04"
Saturn {4}	TK	1974	D	48,000	384' 01"	54' 06"	25' 00"

C-28 — COASTWISE TRADING CO., EAST CHICAGO, IN

Great Lakes {2}	TK	1982	B	75,000	414' 00"	60' 00"	30' 00"
(Amoco Great Lakes '82 - '85)							
Michigan {10}	TB	1982	D	293*	107' 08"	34' 00"	16' 00"
(Amoco Michigan '82 - '85)							
(Overall Dimensions Together)					454' 00"	60' 00"	30' 00"

C-29 — COLUMBIA YACHT CLUB, CHICAGO, IL

Abby	CF	1947	D	6,694*	372' 06"	61' 00"	24' 09"
(Abegweit '47 - '81)							

C-30 — CONSTANTINOS MAKAYDAKIS, ATHENS, GREECE

The Straits of Mackinac	CF	1928	R	736*	202' 11"	48' 00"	16' 07"

C-31 — CONTESSA CRUISE LINES, LAFAYETTE, LA

Arthur K. Atkinson	PA	1917	D	3,241*	384' 00"	56' 00"	20' 06"
(Ann Arbor No. 6 '17 - '59)							

(Last operated in 1984 — 5 year survey expired August, 1985 — Laid up in Ludington, MI)

Viking I	PA	1925	D	2,713*	360' 00"	56' 03"	21' 06"
(Ann Arbor No. 7 '25 - '64, Viking {2} '64 - '96)							

(Last operated 11 April, 1982 — 5 year survey expires May, 2001 — Laid up in Erie, PA)

C-32 — CROISIERES AML, INC., QUEBEC, PQ

Cavalier Maxim	ES	1962	D	752*			
(Osborne Castle '62 - '78, Le Gobelet D' Argent '78 - '88, Le Maxim '89 - '92)							
Louis Jolliet	ES	1938	R	2,428*	170' 01"	70' 00"	17' 00"

C-33 — CROISIERES DES ISLES DE SOREL, INC., STE. ANNE DE SOREL, PQ

Le Survenant III	ES	1974	D	105*	65' 00"	13' 00"	5' 00"

C-34 — CROISIERES M/S JACQUES CARTIER, TROIS RIVIERES, PQ

Jacques Cartier	ES	1924	D	441*	135' 00"	35' 00"	10' 00"
Le Draveur	ES	1992	D	79*			
(Normand '92 - '94)							

C-35 — CROISIERES MARJOLAINE, INC., CHICOUTIMI, PQ

Marjolaine II	ES	1904	D		92' 00"	27' 00"	9' 00"

C-36 — CROISIERES RICHELIEU, INC., ST. JEAN, PQ

Miss Montreal	ES	1973	D	64*	44' 00"	20' 00"	6' 00"

D-1 — DAN MINOR & SONS, INC., PORT COLBORNE, ON

Andrea Marie I	TB	1963	D	87*	75' 02"	24' 07"	7' 03"
Susan Michelle	TB	1995	D	89*	79' 10"	20' 11"	6' 02"
Welland	TB	1954	D	94*	86' 00"	20' 00"	8' 00"

D-2 — DAVID MALLOCH, SCUDDER, ON

Cemba	TK	1960	D	944	50' 00"	15' 06"	7' 06"

D-3 — DEAN CONSTRUCTION CO., BELLE RIVER, ON

Americo Dean	TB	1956	D	15*	45' 00"	15' 00"	5' 00"
Annie M. Dean	TB	1981	D	58*	50' 00"	19' 00"	5' 00"
Neptune III	TB	1939	D	23*	53' 10"	15' 06"	5' 00"
Wayne Dean	TB	1946	D	10*	45' 00"	13' 00"	5' 00"

D-4 — DENNIS DOUGHERTY, SAULT STE. MARIE, MI

Gerald D. Neville	TB	1924	D	29*	50' 00"	13' 00"	4' 06"
(Tobermory '24 - '41, Champion {2} '41 - '81)							

Fleet No. and Name Vessel Name	Type of Ship	Year Built	Type of Engine	Cargo Cap. or Gross*	Length	Beam	Depth or Draft*
D-5 — DIAMOND JACK'S RIVER TOURS, DETROIT, MI							
Diamond Belle	ES	1958	D	93*	93' 06"	25' 10"	10' 01"
(Mackinac Islander '58 - '90, Sir Richard '90 - '91)							
Diamond Jack	ES	1955	D	82*	72' 00"	25' 00"	8' 00"
(Emerald Isle {1} '55 - '91)							
Diamond Queen	ES	1956	D	94*	92' 00"	25' 00"	10' 00"
(Mohawk '56 - '96)							
D-6 — DIRK SPLILLMAKER, EAST LANSING, MI							
Verendrye	RV	1958	D	297*	167' 06"	34' 00"	16' 07"
(CCGS Verendrye '58 - '86, 500 '86 - '92)							
D-7 — DISSEN & JUHN CORP., MACEDON, NY							
Constructor	TB	1950	D	14*	39' 00"	11' 00"	5' 00"
James W. Rickey	TB	1935	D	24*	46' 00"	14' 00"	7' 00"
D-8 — DONALD KIPELA - ISLE ROYALE FERRY SERVICE, INC., COPPER HARBOR, MI							
Isle Royale Queen III	PF	1959	D	88*	85' 00"	18' 04"	9' 05"
D-9 — DOW CHEMICAL CO., MIDLAND, MI							
DC 710	TK	1969	B	25,500	260' 00"	50' 00"	9' 00"
D-10 — DUC D' ORLEANS CRUISE BOAT, SARNIA, ON							
Duc D' Orleans	ES	1943	D	112*	112' 00"	17' 10"	6' 03"
(HMCS M. L. 105 '43 - '48)							
D-11 — DULUTH & AREA CONVENTION CENTER, DULUTH, MN							
Lake Superior	TB	1943	D	248*	114' 00"	26' 00"	13' 08"
(Major Emil H. Block '43 - '47, US Army LT-18 '47 - '50)							
(Former US Corps of Engineers vessel last operated in 1995)							
William A. Irvin	BC	1938	T	14,050	610' 09"	60' 00"	32' 06"
(Former United States Steel Corp. vessel last operated 16 December, 1978)							
(Above two currently museum vessels in Duluth, MN. See page 111)							
D-12 — DULUTH - SUPERIOR EXCURSIONS, INC., DULUTH, MN							
Vista King	ES	1978	D	60*	78' 00"	28' 00"	5' 02"
Vista Star	ES	1987	D	95*	91' 00"	24' 09"	7' 08"
D-13 — DUROCHER DOCK & DREDGE, INC., CHEBOYGAN, MI							
Betty D.	TB	1953	D	14*	40' 00"	13' 00"	6' 00"
Champion {3}	TB	1974	D	125*	75' 00"	24' 00"	9' 06"
General	TB	1954	D	119*	71' 00"	19' 06"	9' 06"
(US Army ST-1999 '54 - '61, USCOE Au Sable '61 - '84, Challenger {3} '84 - '87)							
Joe Van	TB	1955	D	32*	57' 09"	16' 06"	9' 00"
Meagan Beth	TB	1982	D	94*	60' 00"	22' 00"	9' 00"
M-1	CS	1924	B	750	100' 00"	24' 11"	4' 11"
Nancy Anne	TB	1969	D	73*	60' 00"	20' 00"	6' 00"
Ray Durocher	TB	1943	D	20*	45' 06"	12' 05"	7' 06"
Samson II	CS	1959	B	700	90' 00"	50' 00"	7' 02"
Witch	TB	1950	D	14*	30' 08"	9' 05"	6' 00"
A variety of derrick barges are also available.							
E-1 — EAGLE MARINE TOWING, BURNS HARBOR, IN							
Blackie B.	TB	1952	D	146*	85' 00"	25' 00"	11' 00"
(Bonita {2} '52 - '85, Susan Hoey {2} '85 - '95)							
Frankie D.	TB	1943	D	196*	130' 00"	30' 00"	15' 01"
(US Army LT-643 '44 - '77, Taurus '77 - '90, Gaelic Challenge '90 - '95)							
E-2 — EASTERN UPPER PENINSULA TRANSIT AUTHORITY, KINCHELOE, MI							
Drummond Islander	CF	1947	D	99*	84' 00"	30' 00"	8' 03"
Drummond Islander III	CF	1989	D	96*	108' 00"	37' 00"	12' 03"
Neebish Islander	CF	1950	D	49*	55' 00"	20' 07"	6' 00"
(Lillifred '50 - '56)							
Neebish Islander II	CF	1946	D	90*	89' 00"	29' 06"	6' 09"
(Sugar Islander '46 - '95)							

Fleet No. and Name Vessel Name	Type of Ship	Year Built	Type of Engine	Cargo Cap. or Gross*	Length	Beam	Depth or Draft*
Sugar Islander II	CF	1995	D	223*	114' 00"	40' 00"	10' 00"
Thunder Bay	TB	1953	D	15*	45' 00"	13' 00"	7' 00"

E-3 — EDELWEISS CRUISE DINING, MILWAUKEE, WI

Edelweiss I	ES	1988	D	87*	64' 08"	18' 00"	6' 00"
Edelweiss II	ES	1989	D	89*	73' 08"	20' 00"	7' 00"

E-4 — EDWARD E. GILLEN CO., MILWAUKEE, WI

Andrew J.	TB	1950	D	25*	47' 00"	15' 07"	8' 00"
Edith J.	TB	1962	D	19*	45' 03"	13' 00"	8' 00"
Edward E. Gillen III	TB	1988	D	95*	75' 00"	26' 00"	9' 06"

E-5 — EDWIN M. ERICKSON, BAYFIELD, WI

Outer Island	PK	1942	D	300	112' 00"	32' 00"	8' 06"

E-6 — EGAN MARINE CORP., LEMONT, IL

Alice E.	TB	1950	D	183*	100' 00"	26' 00"	9' 00"

(L. L. Wright '50 - '55, Martin '55 - '74, Mary Ann '74 - '77, Judi C. '77 - '94)

Becky E.	TB	1943	D	146*	81' 01"	24' 00"	9' 10"

(WSA 6 '44 - '46, Chas E. Trout '46 - '78, Naomi Marie '78 - '80, South Haven '80 - '90)

Daniel E.	TB	1967	D	70*	70' 00"	18' 06"	6' 08"

(Foster M. Ford '67 - '84)

Denise E.	TB	1912	D	138*	80' 07"	21' 06"	10' 03"

(Caspian '12 - '49, Trojan '49 - '81, Cherokee {1} '81 - '92)

Derek E.	TB	1907	D	85*	72' 06"	20' 01"	10' 06"

(John Kelderhouse '07 - '25, Sachem '25 - '90)

Ethel E.	TB	1913	D	96*	81' 00"	20' 00"	12' 06"

(Michigan {4} '13 - '78, Ste. Marie II '78 - '81, Dakota '81 - '92)

Lisa E.	TB	1963	D	75*	65' 06"	20' 00"	8' 06"
Robin E.	TB	1889	D	123*	84' 09"	19' 00"	9' 00"

(Asa W. Hughes 1889 - '13, Triton {1} '13 - '81, Navajo {2} '81 - '92)

Susan E.	TB	1921	D	96*	81' 00"	20' 00"	12' 06"

(Oregon {1} '21 - '78, Ste. Marie I '78 - '81, Sioux '81 - '91)

E-7 — EMPIRE CRUISE LINES, U. S. A.

Marine Star	PA	1945	T	12,773*	520' 00"	71' 06"	43' 06"

(USNS Marine Star '45 - '55, Aquarama '55 - '94)

(Last operated in 1962 — 5 year survey expired May, 1965 — Laid up in Lackawanna, NY. See Page 106)

E-8 — EMPRESS OF CANADA ENTERPRISES LTD., TORONTO, ON

Empress of Canada	ES	1980	D	399*	112' 00"	28' 00"	6' 06"*

E-9 — ENERCHEM TRANSPORT, INC., MONTREAL, PQ

Dolphin	TK	1967	D	72,077	411' 05"	55' 02"	27' 06"

(James Transport '67 - '86, Enerchem Travailleur '86 - '95, Enerchem Dolphin '95 - '96)

Enerchem Asphalt	TK	1972	D	133,858	414' 00"	52' 06"	36' 01"

(Marina '72 - '82, OT Marine '82 - '87, Asfamarine '87 - '88)

Enerchem Catalyst	TK	1972	D	84,097	431' 00"	62' 04"	34' 05"

(Jon Ramsoy '72 - '74, Doan Transport '74 - '86)

Enerchem Refiner	TK	1969	D	69,327	391' 00"	55' 00"	27' 06"

(Industrial Transport '69 - '86)

E-10 — ERIE NAVIGATION CO., ERIE, PA

Day Peckinpaugh	CC	1921	D	1,490	254' 00"	36' 00"	14' 00"

(Interwaterways Line Incorporated 101 '21 - '32, I.L.I. 101 '32 - '36, Richard J. Barnes '36 - '58)

(Last operated 9 September, 1994 — 5 year survey expired August, 1995 — Currently laid up in Erie, PA)

John R. Emery	SC	1905	D	490	140' 00"	33' 00"	14' 00"

(Trenton {1} '05 - '25)

E-11 — ERIE SAND & GRAVEL CO., ERIE, PA

J. S. St. John	SC	1945	D	680	174' 00"	32' 02"	15' 00"

(USS YO-178 '45 - '51, Lake Edward '51 - '67)

Fleet No. and Name Vessel Name	Type of Ship	Year Built	Type of Engine	Cargo Cap. or Gross*	Length	Beam	Depth or Draft*

E-12 — ERIE SAND STEAMSHIP CO., ERIE, PA

Richard Reiss	SU	1943		14,900	620' 06"	60' 03"	35' 00"

(Adirondack '43 - '43, Richard J. Reiss {2} '43 - '86)

F-1 — FAUST CORP., GROSSE POINT FARMS, MI

Comorant	TB	1991	D	10*	25' 02"	14' 00"	4' 06"
Linnhurst	TB	1930	D	11*	37' 06"	10' 06"	4' 08"

F-2 — FEDERAL TERMINALS LTD., QUEBEC CARTIER MINING CO., PORT CARTIER, PQ

Brochu	TT	1972	D	390*	100' 00"	36' 06"	14' 06"
Vachon	TT	1973	D	390*	100' 00"	36' 06"	14' 06"

F-3 — FERRIS MARINE CONTRACTING CORP., DETROIT, MI

John Kendall	TB	1929	D	347*	135' 00"	29' 02"	13' 07"
Magnetic	TB	1925	D	30*	55' 00"	14' 00"	6' 06"
Norma B.	TB	1940	D	14*	43' 00"	15' 00"	4' 00"

F-4 — FRASER SHIPYARDS, INC., SUPERIOR, WI

Reuben Johnson	TB	1912	D	71*	78' 00"	17' 00"	11' 00"

(Buffalo {1} '12 - '28, USCOE Churchill '28 - '46, USCOE Buffalo '46 - '74, Todd Fraser '74 - '78)

Su-Joy III	TB	1941	D	12*	40' 00"	10' 00"	5' 03"

F-5 — FRIENDS OF THE CANADIANA, BUFFALO, NY

Canadiana	PA	1910	R		216' 00"	45' 00"	18' 10"

(Hull is in Port Colborne, ON awaiting conversion to a museum vessel. See Page 108)

F-6 — FROST ENGINEERING CO., LUDINGTON, MI

Captain George	TB	1929	D	61*	63' 00"	17' 00"	7' 08"

(USCOE Captain George '29 - '68, Captain George '68 - '73, Kurt R. Luetdke '73 - '91)

G-1 — G. J. TAYLOR, TORONTO, ON

Nelvana {1}	ES	1963	D	61*	55' 10"	16' 00"	5' 00"

G-2 — GAELIC TUG BOAT CO., GROSSE ILE, MI

Carolyn Hoey	TB	1951	D	146*	90' 00"	25' 00"	11' 00"

(Atlas '51 - '84 Susan Hoey {1} '84 - '85, Atlas '85 - '87)

G.T.B. No. 1	DB	1956	B	2,500	248' 00"	43' 00"	12' 00"

(Emma Willis '56 - '70, Bethlake No. 1 '70 - '74, BD 1 '74 - '89)

Kaw	TB	1944	D	148*	110' 00"	26' 05"	15' 00"

(USCG Kaw (WYT-61) '44 - '80)

L.S.C. 236	TK	1946	B	10,000	195' 00"	35' 00"	10' 06"
Marysville	TK	1973	B	16,000	200' 00"	50' 00"	12' 06"

(N.M.S. No. 102 '73 - '81)

Patricia Hoey {2}	TB	1949	D	146*	88' 06"	25' 00"	11' 00"

(Propeller '49 - '82, Bantry Bay '82 - '91)

Shannon	TB	1944	D	145*	101' 00"	28' 00"	13' 00"

(USS Connewango (YTB-338) '44 - '77)

G-3 — GALACTICA 001 ENTERPRISES LTD., TORONTO, ON

Galactica 001	ES	1957	D	67*	87' 00"	19' 00"	7' 00"

G-4 — GALLAGHER MARINE CONSTRUCTION CO., INC., ESCANABA, MI

Bee Jay	TB	1939	D	19*	45' 00"	13' 00"	7' 00"

G-5 — GANANOQUE BOAT LINE, GANANOQUE, ON

Thousand Islander	ES	1972	D	200*	99' 00"	22' 00"	5' 00"
Thousand Islander II	ES	1973	D	200*	100' 00"	22' 00"	5' 00"
Thousand Islander III	ES	1975	D	376*	115' 00"	28' 00"	6' 00"
Thousand Islander IV	ES	1976	D	347*	115' 00"	28' 00"	6' 00"

G-6 — GARY ZULAUF, OSHAWA, ON

Rhea	MS	1943	D	245*	136' 00"	24' 06"	10' 00"

G-7 — GENESEE MARINE, INC.,

Spirit of Rochester	ES	1975	D	80*	124' 03"	28' 06"	7' 03"

(American Eagle '75 - '83, Island Clipper {1} '83 - '94)

Fleet No. and Name Vessel Name	Type of Ship	Year Built	Type of Engine	Cargo Cap. or Gross*	Length	Beam	Depth or Draft*

G-8 — GILLESPIE OIL & TRANSIT, INC., ST. JAMES, MI

American Girl	PK	1922	D	40	64' 00"	14' 00"	8' 03"
Oil Queen	TK	1949	B	620	65' 00"	16' 00"	6' 00"

G-9 — GODERICH ELEVATORS LTD., GODERICH, ON

Willowglen	BC	1943	R	16,300	620' 06"	60' 00"	35' 00"

(Mesabi '43 - '43, Lehigh {3} '43 - '81, Joseph X. Robert '81 - '82)

(Last operated 21 December, 1992 — 5 year survey expires October, 1997 — Currently in use as a stationary grain storage vessel in Goderich, ON)

G-10 — GOODTIME ISLAND CRUISES, INC., SANDUSKY, OH

Goodtime I	ES	1960	D	81*	111' 00"	29' 08"	9' 05"

G-11 — GOODTIME TRANSIT BOATS, INC., CLEVELAND, OH

Goodtime III	ES	1990	D	95*	161' 00"	40' 00"	11' 00"

G-12 — GORDON WELDING, SARNIA, ON

W. C. Harms	TB	1949	D	147*	78' 00"	24' 00"	9' 08"

(W. C. Harms '49 - '56, Hamilton '56 - '89)

G-13 — GOVERNMENT OF ONTARIO, ONTARIO PLACE, TORONTO, ON

Haida	DD	1943	T	2,000*	377' 00"	37' 06"	11' 02"

(Former Royal Canadian Navy Tribal class destroyer (G63 / 215) was stricken 11 October, 1963. Currently a museum vessel in Toronto, ON. See Page 112)

G-14 — GRAVEL & LAKE SERVICES LTD., THUNDER BAY, ON

Donald Mac	TB	1914	D	69*	71' 00"	17' 00"	10' 00"
F. A. Johnson	TB	1953	D	439*	150' 00"	32' 00"	10' 00"
(Capt. Charles T. Parker '52 - '54, Rapid Cities '54 - '69, S. P. Renolds '69 - '70)							
French River {2}	TB	1953	D	286*	115' 01"	30' 00"	9' 08"
(US Army LTI-2194 '53 - '61, St. Joseph '61 - '70, R. G. Cassidy '70 - '96)							
George N. Carleton	TB	1943	D	97*	82' 00"	21' 00"	11' 00"
Peninsula	TB	1944	D	261*	104' 06"	26' 00"	12' 06"
(HMCS Norton '44 - '45, W.A.C. 1 '45 - '46)							
Robert John	TB	1945	D	98*	82' 00"	20' 01"	11' 00"
Wolf River	BC	1956	D	5,880	349' 02"	43' 07"	25' 04"
(Tecumseh {2} '56 - '67, New York News {3} '67 - '86, Stella Desgagnes '86 - '93, Beam Beginner '94 - '95)							

G-15 — GREAT LAKES CRUISES, INC., HARSENS ISLAND, MI

Port Welcome	PA	1959	D	463*	128' 01"	32' 06"	12' 01"

(Former Maryland Port Authority vessel last operated in 1988 — Laid up Algonac, MI)

G-16 — GREAT LAKES HISTORICAL SOCIETY, VERMILLION, OH

Cod	SS	1943	D/DC	1,500*	312' 00"	27' 00"	15' 00"

(Former US Navy Albacore (Gato) class submarine (SS / AGSS / IXSS-224) stricken 15 December, 1971. Currently a museum vessel in Cleveland, OH — See Page 112)

G-17 — GREAT LAKES INTERNATIONAL TOWING & SALVAGE, INC., BURLINGTON, ON

Ecosse	TB	1979	D	145*	91' 00"	26' 00"	8' 06"

(R. & L. No. 1 '79 - '96)

G-18 — GREAT LAKES MARITIME ACADEMY, TRAVERSE CITY, MI — 616-922-1200

Anchor Bay	TV	1953	D	23*	44' 00"	11' 06"	7' 00"
GLMA Barge	TV		B		80' 00"	20' 00"	7' 00"
Northwestern	TV	1960	D	77*	79' 00"	9' 00"	8' 00"
(USS CT-9 '60 - '94)							
Wolverine	TV	1954	D	12*	40' 00"	10' 00"	3' 00"

G-19 — GREAT LAKES SCHOONER CO., TORONTO, ON

Challenge	PA	1980	SAIL	76*	96' 00"	16' 06"	8' 00"
Unicorn of St. Helier	PA	1947	SAIL	95*	115' 00"	20' 00"	10' 06"

G-20 — GREAT LAKES SHIPWRECK HISTORICAL SOCIETY, SAULT STE. MARIE, MI

Antiquarian	RV		D		40' 00"	12' 00"	4' 00"
David Boyd	RV	1982	D		47' 00"	17' 00"	3' 00"

Fleet No. and Name Vessel Name	Type of Ship	Year Built	Type of Engine	Cargo Cap. or Gross*	Length	Beam	Depth or Draft*
G-21 — GREAT LAKES TOWING CO., CLEVELAND, OH							
Alabama {2}	TB	1916	D	98*	81' 00"	21' 03"	12' 05"
Alaska	TB	1912	D	71*	74' 00"	19' 06"	12' 00"
(Gary {1} '12 - '34, Green Bay '34 - '81, Oneida '81 - '87, Iroquois {2} '87 - '90)							
Arizona	TB	1931	D	98*	81' 00"	21' 03"	12' 05"
Arkansas {2}	TB	1909	D	98*	81' 00"	21' 03"	12' 05"
(Yale '09 - '48)							
California	TB	1926	D	98*	81' 00"	21' 03"	12' 05"
Colorado	TB	1928	D	98*	81' 00"	21' 03"	12' 05"
Connecticut	TB	1927	D	98*	81' 00"	21' 03"	12' 05"
Delaware {4}	TB	1924	D	98*	81' 00"	21' 03"	12' 05"
El Lobo Grande II	TB	1978	D	199*	136' 02"	36' 05"	18' 00"
Florida	TB	1926	D	98*	81' 00"	21' 03"	12' 05"
(Florida '26 - '83, Pinellas '83 - '84)							
Georgia {3}	TB	1895	D	199*	110' 00"	22' 00"	12' 00"
(USCOE Lamont 1895 - '36, John Roen '36 - '51, Samuel E. Bool '51 - '72)							
Idaho	TB	1931	D	98*	81' 00"	20' 00"	12' 06"
Illinois {2}	TB	1914	D	98*	81' 00"	20' 00"	12' 06"
Indiana	TB	1911	D	98*	81' 00"	20' 00"	12' 06"
Iowa	TB	1915	D	98*	81' 00"	20' 00"	12' 06"
Kansas	TB	1927	D	98*	81' 00"	20' 00"	12' 06"
Kentucky {2}	TB	1929	D	98*	81' 00"	20' 00"	12' 06"
Louisiana	TB	1917	D	97*	81' 00"	20' 00"	12' 06"
Maine {1}	TB	1921	D	98*	81' 00"	20' 00"	12' 06"
(Maine {1} '21 - '82, Saipan '82 - '83, Hillsboro '83 - '84)							
Maryland {2}	TB	1925	D	98*	81' 00"	21' 03"	12' 05"
(Maryland {2} '25 - '82, Tarawa '82 - '83, Pasco '83 - '84)							
Massachusetts	TB	1928	D	98*	84' 04"	20' 00"	12' 06"
Michigan {9}	TB	1915	D	99*	81' 00"	20' 00"	12' 06"
(Missouri {1} '15 - '83, Polk '83 - '84)							
Minnesota {1}	TB	1911	D	98*	81' 00"	20' 00"	12' 06"
Mississippi	TB	1916	D	97*	81' 00"	20' 00"	12' 06"
Missouri {2}	TB	1927	D	149*	95' 00"	24' 00"	13' 06"
(Rogers City {1} '27 - '56, Dolomite {1} '56 - '81, Chippewa {7} '81 - '90)							
Montana	TB	1929	D	98*	84' 04"	20' 00"	12' 06"
Nebraska	TB	1929	D	98*	84' 04"	20' 00"	12' 06"
Nevada {2}	TB	1930	D	98*	84' 04"	20' 00"	12' 06"
New Hampshire {2}	TB	1951	D	149*	88' 07"	24' 10"	10' 09"
(Messenger '51 - '84, Patricia Hoey {1} '84 - '90)							
New Jersey	TB	1924	D	98*	81' 00"	20' 00"	12' 06"
(New Jersey '24 - '52, Petco-21 '52 - '53)							
New Mexico	TB	1910	D	97*	81' 00"	20' 00"	12' 06"
(W. L. Mercereau '10 - '38)							
New York	TB	1913	D	98*	81' 00"	20' 00"	12' 06"
North Carolina {2}	TB	1952	D	145*	95' 06"	24' 00"	13' 06"
(Limestone '52 - '83, Wicklow '83 - '90)							
North Dakota	TB	1910	D	97*	81' 00"	20' 00"	12' 06"
(John M. Truby '10 - '38)							
Ohio {3}	TB	1903	D	194*	118' 00"	24' 00"	13' 06"
(M.F.D. No. 15 '03 - '52, Laurence C. Turner '52 - '73)							
Oklahoma	TB	1913	D	97*	81' 00"	20' 00"	12' 06"
(T. C. Lutz {2} '13 - '34)							
Oregon {2}	TB	1952	D	149*	88' 07"	24' 10"	10' 09"
(Jennifer George '52 - '82, Galway Bay '82 - '90)							
Pennsylvania {3}	TB	1911	D	98*	81' 00"	20' 00"	12' 06"
Rhode Island	TB	1930	D	98*	84' 04"	20' 00"	12' 06"
South Carolina	TB	1925	D	102*	86' 00"	21' 00"	11' 00"
(Welcome {2} '25 - '53, Joseph H. Callan '53 - '72 South Carolina '72 - '82, Tulagi '82 - '83)							

Fleet No. and Name Vessel Name	Type of Ship	Year Built	Type of Engine	Cargo Cap. or Gross*	Length	Beam	Depth or Draft*
Superior {3}	TB	1912	D	147*	97' 00"	22' 00"	12' 005"
Tennessee	TB	1917	D	98*	81' 00"	20' 00"	12' 06"
Texas	TB	1916	D	97*	81' 00"	20' 00"	12' 06"
Utah	TB	1909	D	97*	81' 00"	20' 00"	12' 06"
Vermont	TB	1914	D	98*	81' 00"	20' 00"	12' 06"
Virginia {2}	TB	1914	D	97*	81' 00"	20' 00"	12' 06"
Washington {1}	TB	1925	D	97*	81' 00"	20' 00"	12' 06"
Wisconsin {4}	TB	1897	D	106*	90' 03"	21' 00"	12' 03"
(America {3} 1897 - '82, Midway '82 - '83)							
Wyoming	TB	1929	D	98*	84' 04"	20' 00"	12' 06"

TUGZ INTERNATIONAL - DIVISION OF GREAT LAKES TOWING CO.

Z Four	TT	1997	D		95' 00"	32' 00"	11' 06"
Z One	TT	1996	D		95' 00"	32' 00"	11' 06"
Z Three	TT	1997	D		95' 00"	32' 00"	11' 06"
Z Two	TT	1996	D		95' 00"	32' 00"	11' 06"

G-22 — GREELY GOODTIME CHARTERS, INC., TORONTO, ON

Yankee Lady	ES	1965	D	56*	42' 10"	16' 06"	9' 02"
Yankee Lady II	ES	1980	D	68*	75' 00"	16' 00"	9' 08"
(Blue Chip II '80 - '89)							

G-23 — GROUPE OCEAN, INC., QUEBEC, PQ

Betsiamites	SU	1969	B	11,600	402' 00"	75' 00"	24' 00"
Capt. Ioannis S.	TB	1973	D	722*	136' 08"	35' 08"	22' 00"
(Sistella '73 - '78, Sandy Cape '78 - '80)							
Donald P.		1970	D	320*	110' 00"	28' 06"	17' 00"
(Takis V. '70 - '80, Donald P. '80 - '80, Nimue '80 - '83)							
Elmglen {2}	BC	1952	B	21,425	678' 00"	68' 03"	36' 03"
(John O. McKellar {2} '52 - '84)							
Leonard W.	TB	1973	D	448*	123' 02"	31' 06"	18' 09"
Nanook	CS	1946	B	1,198*	225' 00"	38' 00"	12' 06"
Ocean Echo II	TB	1969	D	438*	104' 08"	35' 05"	18' 00"
(Atlantic '69 - '75, Laval '75 - '96)							
Ocean Foxtrot	TB	1971	D	700*	184' 05"	38' 05"	16' 07"
(Polor Shore '71 - '77, Canmar Supplier VII '77 - '95)							

H-1 — H. LEE WHITE MARINE MUSEUM, OSWEGO, NY

LT-5	TB	1943	D	249*	114' 00"	26' 00"	14' 00"
(Major Elisha K. Henson '43 - '47, US Army LT-5 '47 - '47, Nash '47 - '95)							

(Former US Army Corps of Engineers vessel last operated in 1990. Currently in use as a museum vessel in Oswego, NY. See Page 112)

H-2 — HALCO BARGE LINES, GREEN BAY, WI

Mr. Micky	TK	1940	B	10,500	195' 00"	35' 00"	10' 00"

H-3 — HAMILTON HARBOUR COMMISSIONERS, HAMILTON, ON

Judge McCombs	TB	1948	D	10*	36' 00"	10' 03"	4' 00"

H-4 — HAMMOND PORT AUTHORITY, HAMMOND, IN

Clipper	PA	1904	Q	4,272	361' 00"	45' 00"	28' 00"
(Juniata '04 - '41, Milwaukee Clipper '41 - '70)							

(Former Wisconsin & Michigan Steamship Co. vessel last operated in 1970 — Currently laid up in South Chicago, IL. See Page 108)

H-5 — HANK VAN ASPERT, WINDSOR, ON

Queen City {2}	PA	1911	D	248*	116' 00"	23' 00"	12' 07"
(Polana '11 - '30, Jalobert '30 - '54, Macassa {2} '54 - '65)							

H-6 — HANNAH MARINE CORP., LEMONT, IL

Daryl C. Hannah {2}	TB	1956	D	268*	102' 00"	28' 00"	8' 00"
(Cindy Jo '56 - '66, Katherine L. '66 - '93)							
Donald C. Hannah	TB	1962	D	191*	91' 00"	29' 00"	11' 06"
Hannah D. Hannah	TB	1955	D	134*	86' 00"	24' 00"	10' 00"
(Harbor Ace '55 - '61, Gopher State '61 - '71, Betty Gale '71 - '93)							

Fleet No. and Name Vessel Name	Type of Ship	Year Built	Type of Engine	Cargo Cap. or Gross*	Length	Beam	Depth or Draft*
Hannah 1801	TK	1967	B	18,550	240' 00"	50' 00"	12' 00"
Hannah 1802	TK	1967	B	18,550	240' 00"	50' 00"	12' 00"
Hannah 2801	TK	1980	B	28,665	275' 00"	54' 00"	17' 06"
Hannah 2901	TK	1962	B	17,400	264' 00"	52' 06"	12' 06"
Hannah 2902	TK	1962	B	17,360	264' 00"	52' 06"	12' 06"
Hannah 2903	TK	1962	B	17,350	264' 00"	52' 06"	12' 06"
Hannah 3601	TK	1972	B	35,360	290' 00"	60' 00"	18' 03"
Hannah 5101	TK	1978	B	49,660	360' 00"	60' 00"	22' 06"
James A. Hannah	TB	1945	D	593*	149' 00"	33' 00"	16' 00"

(US Army LT-280 '45 - '65, Muskegon {1} '65 - '71)

| Kristen Lee Hannah | TB | 1945 | D | 602* | 149' 00" | 33' 00" | 16' 00" |

(US Army LT-815 '45 - '64, Henry Foss '64 - '84, Kristen Lee '84 - '93)

| Margaret M. | TB | 1956 | D | 167* | 89' 06" | 24' 00" | 10' 00" |

(Shuttler '56 - '60, Margaret M. Hannah '60 - '84)

| Mark Hannah | TB | 1969 | D | 191* | 127' 05" | 32' 01" | 14' 03" |

(Lead Horse '69 - '73, Gulf Challenger '73 - '80, Challenger {2} '80 - '93)

| Mary E. Hannah | TB | 1945 | D | 612* | 149' 00" | 33' 00" | 16' 00" |

(US Army LT-821 '45 - '47, Brooklyn '47 - '66, Lee Reuben '66 - '75)

| Mary Page Hannah {2} | TB | 1972 | D | 99* | 59' 08" | 24' 01" | 10' 03" |

(Kings Squire '72 - '78, Juanita D. '78 - '79 Katherine L. '79 - '93)

No. 25	TK	1949	B	19,500	254' 00"	54' 00"	11' 00"
No. 26	TK	1949	B	19,500	254' 00"	54' 00"	11' 00"
No. 28	TK	1957	B	20,725	240' 00"	50' 00"	12' 06"
No. 29	TK	1952	B	22,000	254' 00"	54' 00"	11' 06"
Peggy D. Hannah	TB	1920	D	145*	108' 00"	25' 00"	14' 00"

(William A. Whitney '20 - '92)

| Susan W. Hannah | TB | 1977 | D | 174* | 121' 06" | 34' 06" | 18' 02" |

(Lady Elda '77 - '78, Kings Challenger '78 - '78, ITM No. 1 '78 - '81, Kings Challenger '81 - '86)

H-7 — HARBOR HERITAGE SOCIETY, CLEVELAND, OH

| William G. Mather {2} | BC | 1925 | T | 13,950 | 618' 00" | 62' 00" | 32' 00" |

(Former Cleveland Cliffs Steamship Co. vessel last operated 21 December, 1980. Currently a museum vessel in Cleveland, OH. See Page 112)

H-8 — HARBOR LIGHT CRUISE LINES, INC., TOLEDO, OH

| Sandpiper | ES | 1984 | D | 19* | 65' 00" | 16' 00" | 4' 00" |

H-9 — HARRY GAMBLE SHIPYARDS, PORT DOVER, ON

| H. A. Smith | TB | 1944 | D | 24* | 55' 00" | 16' 00" | 5' 06" |
| J. A. Cornett | TB | 1937 | D | 60* | 65' 00" | 17' 00" | 9' 00" |

H-10 — HEAD OF THE LAKES MARITIME SOCIETY, SUPERIOR, WI

| Col. D. D. Gaillard | DR | 1916 | | | | | |
| Meteor | TK | 1896 | R | 4,635 | 380' 00" | 45' 00" | 26' 00" |

(Frank Rockefeller 1896 - '28, South Park '28 - '43)

(Former Cleveland Tankers, Inc. vessel last operated in 1969. Above two are currently museum vessels in Superior, WI, See Page 112)

H-11 — HOLLY MARINE TOWING, CHICAGO, IL

| Holly Ann | TB | 1926 | D | 220* | 108' 00" | 26' 06" | 15' 00" |

(Wm. A. Lydon '26 - '92)

| Katie Ann | TB | 1924 | D | 99* | 85' 00" | 21' 06" | 10' 09" |

(Martha C. '24 - '52, Langdon C. Hardwicke '52 - '82, Wabash {2} '82 - '93)

| Laura Lynn | TB | 1950 | D | 146* | 82' 00" | 25' 00" | 10' 07" |

(Navajo {1} '50 - '53, Seaval '53 - '64, Mary T. Tracy '64 - '69, Yankee '69 - '70, Minn '70 - '74, William S. Bell '74 - '83, Newcastle '83 - '93)

| Margaret Ann | TB | 1954 | D | 131* | 82' 00" | 24' 06" | 11' 06" |

(John A. McGuire '54 - '87, William Hoey '87 - '94)

| Philip M. Pearse | TB | 1982 | D | 45* | 51' 09" | 17' 00" | 6' 01" |

(Captain Robbie '82 - '90)

H-12 — HORNE'S FERRY, WOLFE ISLAND, ON

| William Darrell | CF | 1952 | D | 66* | 66' 00" | 28' 00" | 6' 00" |

Fleet No. and Name Vessel Name	Type of Ship	Year Built	Type of Engine	Cargo Cap. or Gross*	Length	Beam	Depth or Draft*
H-13 — H-13 — HOWE ISLAND TOWNSHIP, GANANOQUE, ON							
The Howe Islander	CF	1946	D	13*	53' 00"	12' 00"	3' 00"
H-14 — HYDROGRAPHIC SURVEY CO., CHICAGO, IL							
Neptune	RV	1970	D		67' 00"	18' 05"	5' 00"
I-1 — INLAND SEAS EDUCATION ASSOCIATION, SUTTONS BAY, MI							
Inland Seas	RV	1994	SAIL	41*	61' 06"	17' 00"	7' 00"
I-2 — INLAND STEEL CO., EAST CHICAGO, IN							
Edward L. Ryerson	BC	1960	T	27,500	730' 00"	75' 00"	39' 00"
(Last operated 24 January, 1994 — 5 year survey expires August, 2001 — Currently laid up in Sturgeon Bay, WI)							
Joseph L. Block	SU	1976	D	37,200	728' 00"	78' 00"	45' 00"
Wilfred Sykes	SU	1949	T	21,500	678' 00"	70' 00"	37' 00"
AMERICAN STEAMSHIP CO. - CHARTERED BY INLAND STEEL CO.							
Adam E. Cornelius {4}	SU	1973	D	28,200	680' 00"	78' 00"	42' 00"
(Roger M. Kyes '73 - '89)							
I-3 — INTERLAKE STEAMSHIP CO., CLEVELAND, OH							
Charles M. Beeghly	SU	1959	T	31,000	806' 00"	75' 00"	37' 06"
(Shenango II '59 - '67)							
Elton Hoyt 2nd {2}	SU	1952	T	22,300	698' 00"	70' 00"	37' 00"
Herbert C. Jackson	SU	1959	T	24,800	690' 00"	75' 00"	37' 06"
James R. Barker	SU	1976	D	63,300	1,004' 00"	105' 00"	50' 00"
J. L. Mauthe	SU	1953	B	21,400	647' 00"	70' 00"	36' 00"
(Last operated 5 July, 1993 — 5 year survey expires May, 1998 — Currently being converted to a barge in Sturgeon Bay, WI)							
Mesabi Miner	SU	1977	D	63,300	1,004' 00"	105' 00"	50' 00"
Paul R. Tregurtha	SU	1981	D	68,000	1,013' 06"	105' 00"	56' 00"
(William J. DeLancey '81 - '90)							
LAKES SHIPPING CO., INC. - DIVISION OF INTERLAKE STEAMSHIP CO.							
John Sherwin {2}	BC	1958	T	31,500	806' 00"	75' 00"	37' 06"
(Last operated 16 November, 1981 — 5 year survey expired May, 1984 — Currently laid up in Superior, WI)							
Kaye E. Barker	SU	1952	T	25,900	767' 00"	70' 00"	36' 00"
(Edward B. Greene '52 - '85, Benson Ford {3} '85 - '89)							
Lee A. Tregurtha	SU	1942	T	29,300	826' 00"	75' 00"	39' 00"
(Mobiloil '42 - '42, Samoset '42 - '42, USS Chiwawa (AO-68) '42 - '47, Chiwawa '47 - '61, Walter A. Sterling '61 - '85, William Clay Ford {2} '85 - '89)							
I-4 — IROQUOIS BOAT LINE CO., MILWAUKEE, WI							
Iroquois {1}	ES	1946	D		61' 09"	21' 00"	6' 04"
I-5 — IVY LEA 1000 ISLANDS BOAT TOURS, IVY LEA, ON							
Miss Ivy Lea II	ES		D		66' 00"	15' 00"	5' 00"
Miss Ivy Lea III	ES		D		48' 00"	12' 00"	5' 00"
J-1 — J. W. PURVIS MARINE LTD., SAULT STE. MARIE, ON							
Adanac	TB	1913	D	108*	80' 03"	19' 00"	10' 06"
(Edward C. Whalen '13 - '66, John McLean '66 - '95)							
Anglian Lady	TB	1953	D	398*	136' 06"	30' 00"	14' 01"
(Hamtun '53 - '72, Nathalie Letzer '72 - '88)							
Avenger IV	TB	1962	D	293*	120' 00"	30' 05"	17' 05"
(Avenger '62 - '85)							
Charles W. Johnson	DB	1916	B	1,685	245' 00"	43' 00"	14' 00"
(Iocolite '16 - '47, Imperial Kingston '47 - '61)							
Chief Wawatam	DB	1911	B	4,500	347' 00"	62' 03"	15' 00"
G.L.B. No. 2	DB	1953	B	3,215	290' 00"	50' 00"	12' 00"
Goki	TB	1940	D	24*	57' 00"	12' 08"	7' 00"

Fleet No. and Name Vessel Name	Type of Ship	Year Built	Type of Engine	Cargo Cap. or Gross*	Length	Beam	Depth or Draft*
Malden	DB	1946	B	1,075	150′ 00″	41′ 09″	10′ 03″
Martin E. Johnson	TB	1959	D	26*	46′ 00″	16′ 00″	5′ 09″
McKeller	DB	1935	B	200	90′ 00″	33′ 00″	8′ 00″
P.M.L. Alton	DB	1951	B	150	93′ 00″	30′ 00″	8′ 00″
P.M.L. Salvager	DB	1945	B	5,200	341′ 00″	54′ 00″	27′ 00″

((Unnamed) '45 - '55, Balsambranch '55 - '73, M.I.L. Balsam '73 - '77, Techno Balsam '77 - '77, DDS Salvager '77 - '88)

Rocket	TB	1901	D	39*	70′ 00″	15′ 00″	8′ 00″
Wilfred M. Cohen	TB	1948	D	284*	104′ 00″	28′ 00″	14′ 06″

(A. T. Lowmaster '48 - '75)

W. I. Scott Purvis	TB	1938	D	206*	96′ 06″	26′ 04″	10′ 04″

(Orient Bay '38 - '75, Guy M. No. 1 '75 - '90)

W. J. Ivan Purvis	TB	1938	D	191*	100′ 06″	25′ 06″	9′ 00″

(Magpie '38 - '66, Dana T. Bowen '66 - '75)

Yankcanuck {2}	CS	1963	D	4,760	324′ 03″	49′ 00″	26′ 00″

J-2 — J. W. WESTCOTT CO., DETROIT, MI

J. W. Westcott II	MB	1949	D	11*	46′ 01″	13′ 04″	4′ 06″
Joe J. Hogan	MB		D				

J-3 — JACOBS INVESTMENTS, INC., CLEVELAND, OH

Nautica Queen	ES	1981	D	95*	124′ 00″	31′ 02″	8′ 10″

(Bay Queen '81 - '85, Arawanna Queen '85 - '88, Star of Nautica '88 - '92)

J-4 — JAMES MAZUREK, MOUNT CLEMENS, MI

West Wind	TB	1941	D	54*	60′ 04″	17′ 01″	7′ 07″

J-5 — JOHN BLOSWICK

Maple	RV	1939	D	350*	122′ 03″	27′ 00″	7′ 06″*

(USCG Maple (WLI / WAGL-234) '39 - '73, Roger R. Simons '73 - '94)

(US Coast Guard 122-foot class lighthouse tender (WLI / WAGL-234) / EPA vessel last operated in 1991)

J-6 — JOHN G. JONES, TORONTO, ON

Glenmont	TB	1943	D	102*	82′ 00″	20′ 01″	9′ 00″

J-7 — JOSEPH GAYTON, HARROW, ON

Jenny T. II	TB	1915	D	66*	68′ 07″	17′ 00″	11′ 00″

(Ashtabula '15 - '55, Tiffin '55 - '69)

Princess No. 1	TB	1903	D	87*	77′ 00″	20′ 04″	7′ 11″

(Radiant '03 - '33, Anna Sheridan '33 - '62, Princess '62 - '77)

J-8 — JOSEPH MARTIN, ST. JAMES, MI

Shamrock {1}	TB	1933	D	60*	64′ 00″	18′ 00″	7′ 04″

J-9 — JULIO CONTRACTING CO., HANCOCK, MI

Julio	TB	1941	D	84*	71′ 00″	18′ 00″	9′ 06″

(Mary Louis '41 - '48, Venus '48 - '49, Joey Haden '49 - '72)

Winnebago	TB	1945	D	14*	40′ 00″	10′ 02″	4′ 06″

K-1 — KADINGER MARINE SERVICE, INC., MILWAUKEE, WI

David J. Kadinger Jr.	TB	1969	D	98*	65′ 06″	22′ 00″	8′ 06″
Jason A. Kadinger	TB	1963	D	60*	52′ 06″	19′ 01″	7′ 04″
Ruffy J. Kadinger	TB	1981	D	74*	55′ 00″	23′ 00″	7′ 02″

K-2 —KELLEY ISLAND FERRY BOAT LINES, MARBLEHEAD, OH

Erie Isle	CF	1951	D	59*	72′ 00″	24′ 00″	8′ 03″

(Erie Isle '51 - '92, Marblehead '92 - '93)

Shirley Irene	CF	1991	D	68*	160′ 00″	46′ 00″	9′ 00″

K-3 — KELLSTONE, INC., CLEVELAND, OH

Benjamin Ridgeway	TB	1969	D	51*	53′ 00″	18′ 05″	7′ 05″
Frank Palladino Jr.	TB	1980	D	89*	100′ 00″	32′ 00″	13′ 00″

(Lady Ida '80 - '92)

Kellstone 1	SU	1957	B	9,000	396′ 00″	71′ 00″	22′ 06″

Fleet No. and Name Vessel Name	Type of Ship	Year Built	Type of Engine	Cargo Cap. or Gross*	Length	Beam	Depth or Draft*

K-4 — KINDRA LAKE TOWING, CHICAGO, IL

Buckley	TB	1958	D	94*	95' 00"	26' 00"	11' 00"
(Linda Brooks '58 - '67, Eddie B. {2} '67 - '95)							
Morgan	TB	1974	D	134*	90' 00"	30' 00"	10' 06"
(Donald O' Toole '74 - '86, Bonesey B. '86 - '95)							
Old Colony	TB	1945	D	94*	85' 00"	23' 00"	10' 04"
(US Army ST-880 '45 - '47, USCOE Avondale '47 - '64, Adrienne B. '64 - '95)							

K-5 — KING COMPANY, INC., HOLLAND, MI

Barry J	TB	1943	D	42*	46' 00"	13' 00"	7' 00"
Carol Ann	TB	1981	D	115*	68' 00"	24' 00"	8' 07"
Julie Dee	TB	1903	D	59*	63' 03"	17' 05"	9' 00"
Ludington	TB	1903	D	58*	69' 03"	17' 05"	11' 05"
Chicago Harbor No. 4 '16 - '60, Eddie B. {1} '60 - '69, Seneca Queen '69 - '70)							
Miss Edna	TB	1935	D	29*	36' 08"	11' 02"	4' 08"
Muskegon {2}	TB	1973	D	138*	75' 00"	24' 00"	11' 06"

K-6 — KINSMAN LINES, INC., ROCKY RIVER, OH

Kinsman Enterprise {2}	BC	1927	T	16,000	631' 00"	65' 00"	33' 00"
(Harry Coulby {2} '27 - '89)							
Kinsman Independent {3}	BC	1952	T	18,800	642' 03"	67' 00"	35' 00"
(Charles L. Hutchinson {3} '52 - '62, Ernest R. Breech '62 - '88)							

K-7 — KUHLMAN CORP., TOLEDO, OH

Sand Pebble	TB	1969	D	30*	46' 00"	15' 00"	7' 07"

L-1 — LA SOCIETE DES TRAVERSIERS DU QUEBEC, QUEBEC, PQ

Alphonse des Jarnins	CF	1971	D	1,741*	214' 00"	71' 06"	20' 00"
Armand Imbeau	CF	1980	D		190' 00"	71' 00"	15' 00"
Camille Marcoux	CF	1974	D		310' 00"	60' 06"	16' 00"
Catherine Le Gardeur	CF	1974	D	6,122	312' 05"	63' 00"	39' 02"
Grues Des Iles	CF	1981	D		101' 02"	39' 06"	12' 05"
Jos. Deschenes	CF	1980	D		190' 00"	71' 00"	15' 00"
Joseph Savard	CF	1985	D	1,445	207' 02"	72' 02"	18' 00"
Lomer Gouin	CF	1971	D	1,741*	214' 00"	71' 06"	20' 00"
Lucien L.	CF	1967	D		222' 00"	62' 00"	15' 05"
Radisson {1}	CF	1954	D	1,043	164' 03"	72' 00"	10' 06"
Trois Rivieres	CF	1961	D	882*	200' 00"	70' 06"	10' 00"

L-2 — LA SOCIETE DU PORT DE MONTREAL, MONTREAL, PQ

Maissoneuve	TB	1972	D	103*	63' 10"	20' 07"	9' 03"

L-3 — LAKE COUNTY HISTORICAL SOCIETY, TWO HARBORS, MN

Edna G.	TB	1896	R	154*	102' 00"	23' 00"	14' 06"

(Former Duluth, Missabe & Iron Range Railroad vessel last operated in 1981. Currently a museum vessel in Two Harbors, MN. See Page 112)

L-4 — LAKE MICHIGAN CARFERRY SERVICE, INC., LUDINGTON, MI

Badger (43) {2}	CF	1953	S	4,244*	410' 06"	59' 06"	24' 00"
City of Midland 41	CF	1941	S	3,968*	406' 00"	58' 00"	23' 06"

(Last operated 18 November, 1988 — 5 year survey expired November, 1991. — Currently laid up in Ludington, MI)

Spartan (42) {2}	CF	1952	S	4,244*	410' 06"	59' 06"	24' 00"

(Last operated 20 January, 1979 — 5 year survey expired January, 1981. — Currently laid up in Ludington, MI)

Wynken, Blynken and Nod	CF	1957	D	73*	61' 01"	28' 10"	8' 06"

L-5 — LAKE MICHIGAN CONTRACTORS, INC., HOLLAND, MI

Art Lapish	TB	1954	D	15*	44' 03"	12' 08"	5' 04"
Captain Barnaby	TB	1956	D	146*	94' 00"	27' 00"	11' 09"
(William C. Gaynor '56 - '87)							
Curly B.	TB	1956	D	131*	84' 00"	26' 00"	9' 02"
(Waverly '56 - '74, Bother Collins '74 - '80)							

Arthur M. Anderson passes Detroit upbound on 20 January, 1996. (John Belliveau)

Fleet No. and Name Vessel Name	Type of Ship	Year Built	Type of Engine	Cargo Cap. or Gross*	Length	Beam	Depth or Draft*
Douglas B. Mackie	TB	1978	D	98*	72' 00"	26' 00"	7' 06"
G. W. Falcon	TB	1936	D	22*	49' 07"	13' 08"	6' 02"
James Harris	TB	1943	D	18*	41' 09"	12' 05"	5' 07"

L-6 — LAKE MICHIGAN HARDWARE CO., LELAND, MI

Glen Shore	PK	1957	D	105	68' 00"	21' 00"	6' 00"

L-7 — LAKE TOWING, INC., AVON, OH

Jiggs	TB	1911	D	45*	61' 00"	16' 00"	8' 00"
Johnson	TB	1976	D	287*	140' 06"	40' 00"	15' 06"
Johnson II	TB	1975	D	311*	194' 00"	40' 00"	17' 00"

L-8 — LAKESHORE CONTRACTORS, INC., HOLLAND, MI

John Henry	TB	1954	D	66*	70' 00"	20' 06"	9' 07"
(US Army ST-2013 '54 - '80)							

L-9 — LE BRUN CONSTRUCTORS LTD., THUNDER BAY, ON

Henry T.	DB	1932	B	1,000	120' 00"	44' 00"	11' 00"

L-10 — LE SAULT DE SAINTE MARIE HIST. SITES, INC., SAULT STE. MARIE, MI

Valley Camp {2}	BC	1917	R	12,000	550' 00"	58' 00"	31' 00"
(Louis W. Hill '17 - '55)							

(Former Republic Steel Corp. vessel last operated in 1968. Currently a museum vessel in Sault Ste. Marie, MI. See Page 114)

L-11 — LEE MARINE LTD., PORT LAMBTON, ON

Hammond Bay	ES	1992	D	43*	54' 00"	16' 00"	7' 00"
Nancy A. Lee	TB	1939	D	9*	40' 00"	12' 00"	3' 00"

L-12 — LOCK TOURS CANADA BOAT CRUISES, SAULT STE. MARIE, ON

Chief Shingwauk	ES	1965	D	109*	70' 00"	24' 00"	4' 06"

L-13 — LUEDTKE ENGINEERING CO., FRANKFORT, MI

Alan K. Luedtke	TB	1944	D	149*	86' 04"	23' 00"	10' 03"
(US Army ST-527 '44 - '55, USCOE Two Rivers '55 - '90)							
Chris E. Luedtke	TB	1936	D	18*	45' 00"	12' 03"	6' 00"
Erich R. Luedtke	TB	1939	D	18*	45' 00"	12' 03"	6' 00"
Gretchen B.	TB	1943	D	18*	45' 00"	12' 03"	6' 00"
Karl E. Luedtke	TB	1928	D	32*	59' 03"	14' 09"	8' 00"
Kurt Luedtke	TB	1956	D	96*	72' 00"	22' 06"	7' 06"
(Jere C. '56 - '90)							
Paul L. Luedtke	TB	1935	D	18*	42' 06"	11' 09"	6' 09"

M-1 — MACDONALD MARINE LTD., GODERICH, ON

Debbie Lyn	TB	1950	D	10*	45' 00"	14' 00"	10' 00"
Donald Bert	TB	1953	D	11*	45' 00"	14' 00"	10' 00"
Ian Mac	TB	1955	D	12*	45' 00"	14' 00"	10' 00"

M-2 — MADELINE ISLAND FERRY LINE, INC., LAPOINTE, WI

Island Queen {2}	CF	1966	D	90*	75' 00"	34' 09"	10' 00"
Madeline	CF	1984	D	97*	90' 00"	35' 00"	8' 00"
Nichevo II	CF	1962	D	89*	65' 00"	32' 00"	8'09"

M-3 — MAID OF THE MIST STEAMBOAT CO. LTD., NIAGARA FALLS, ON

Maid of the Mist	ES	1987	D	54*	65' 00"	16' 00"	7' 00"
Maid of the Mist III	ES	1972	D	54*	65' 00"	16' 00"	7' 00"
Maid of the Mist IV	ES	1976	D	74*	72' 00"	16' 00"	7' 00"
Maid of the Mist V	ES	1983	D	74*	72' 00"	16' 00"	7' 00"
Maid of the Mist VI	ES	1990	D	155*	78' 09"	29' 06"	7' 00"
Maid of the Mist VII	ES	1997	D	160*	80' 00"	30' 00"	7' 00"

M-4 — MALCOM MARINE, ST. CLAIR, MI

Manitou {2}	TB	1943	D	491*	110' 00"	26' 05"	11' 06"
(USCG Manitou (WYT-60) '43 - '84)							
Relief	CS	1924	B		159' 00"	40' 00"	9' 00"

Fleet No. and Name Vessel Name	Type of Ship	Year Built	Type of Engine	Cargo Cap. or Gross*	Length	Beam	Depth or Draft*
Tug Malcom	TB	1944	D	508*	143' 00"	33' 01"	14' 06"

(USS ATA-179 '44 - '48, USS Allegheny (ATA-179) '48 - '72, GLMA Allegheny '72 - '78)

M-5 — MANITOU ISLAND TRANSIT, LELAND, MI

Manitou Island	PF	1946	D	39*	52' 00"	14' 00"	8' 00"
Mishe-Mokwa	PF	1966	D	49*	65' 00"	17' 06"	8' 00"

(LaSalle '66 - '80)

M-6 — MANSON CONSTRUCTION CO., INC., NORTH TONAWANDA, NY

Burro	TB	1965	D	19*	36' 00"	13' 03"	5' 01"
J. G. II	TB	1944	D	16*	42' 03"	13' 00"	5' 06"
Marcey	TB	1966	D	22*	42' 00"	12' 06"	6' 10"

M-7 — MARINE FUELING CO., SUPERIOR, WI

Reiss Marine	TK	1978	D	8,000	149' 06"	39' 06"	14' 08'

M-8 — MARINE MANAGEMENT, INC., BRUSSELS, WI

Nathan S.	TB	1954	D	76*	66' 00"	19' 00"	9' 00"

(Sanita '54 - '77, Soo Chief '77 - '81, Susan M. Selvick '81 - '91)

Nicole S.	TB	1949	D	146*	88' 07"	24' 10"	10' 09"

(Evening Star '49 - '86, Protector '86 - '94)

M-9 — MARINE MUSEUM OF THE GREAT LAKES AT KINGSTON, KINGSTON, ON

Alexander Henry	IB	1959	D	1,674*	210' 00"	44' 00"	17' 09"

(Former Canadian Coast Guard vessel was stricken in 1985. Currently a museum vessel in Kingston, ON. See Page 114)

M-10 — MARINE MUSEUM OF UPPER CANADA, TORONTO, ON

Ned Hanlan	TB	1932	R	105*	79' 06"	19' 00"	9' 09"

(Municipality of Toronto vessel last operated in 1965. Currently a museum vessel in Toronto, ON. See Page 114)

M-11 — MARINE TECH OF DULUTH, INC., DULUTH, MN

Jana	TB	1954	D	15*	49' 06"	13' 00"	7' 00"
Jason	TB	1945	D	21*	48' 00"	12' 01"	7' 00"
Nancy Ann	TB	1910	D	51*	64' 03"	16' 09"	8' 06"

(Howard T. Hagen '10 - '96)

M-12 — MARIPOSA CRUISE LINE, TORONTO, ON

Capt. Matthew Flinders	ES	1984	D	746*	144' 00"	40' 00"	8' 06"
Mariposa Belle	ES	1970	D	195*	93' 00"	23' 00"	8' 00"

(Niagara Belle '70 - '73)

Northern Spirit I	ES	1983	D	489*	136' 00"	31' 00"	9' 00"

(New Spirit '83 - '89, Pride of Toronto "89 - '92)

Oriole	ES	1987	D	200*	75' 00"	23' 00"	9' 00"
Rosemary	ES	1960	D	52*	68' 00"	15' 06"	6' 08"
Showboat Royal Grace	ES	1988	D	135*	58' 00"	18' 00"	4' 00"
Torontonian	ES	1962	D	68*	68' 00"	18' 06"	6' 08"

(Shiawassie '62 - '82)

M-13 — MARITIME INVESTING LLC., NAPERVILLE, IL

Manitowoc	TF	1926	B27 rail cars		371' 03"	67' 03"	22' 06"
Roanoke (2)	TF	1930	B30 rail cars		381' 06"	58' 03"	22' 06"

(City of Flint 32 '30 - '70)

Windsor (2)	TF	1930	B28 rail cars		370' 05"	65' 00"	21' 06"

(Above three last operated 1 May, 1994 — Above three currently laid up in Toledo, OH)

C & O 452	TB	1957	D	239*	98' 00"	30' 00"	12' 00"
Pere Marquette 10	TF	1945	B27 rail cars		400' 00"	53' 00"	22' 00"

(Above two last operated 7 October, 1994 — Currently laid up in Port Huron, MI)

M-14 — McALLISTER TOWING & SALVAGE, INC., MONTREAL, PQ

Charles Antoine	TB	1976	D	448*	120' 00"	32' 00"	19' 00"

(Stril Pilot '76 - '81, Spirit Sky '81 - '86, Ierland '86 - '89, Ierlandia '89 - '95)

Cathy McAllister	TB	1954	D	225*	101' 10"	26' 00"	13' 08"

(Charlie S. '54 - '75)

Fleet No. and Name Vessel Name	Type of Ship	Year Built	Type of Engine	Cargo Cap. or Gross*	Length	Beam	Depth or Draft*
Daniel McAllister	TB	1907	D	268*	115' 00"	23' 02"	12' 00"
(Helena '07 - '57, Helen M. B. '57 - '66)							
Helen M. McAllister	TB	1959	D	152*	103' 00"	25' 10"	11' 09"
(Scranton '59 - '59)							
Jerry G.	TB	1960	D	202*	91' 06"	27' 03"	12' 06"
P. S. Barge No. 1	CS	1923	B	3,000	258' 06"	43' 01"	20' 00"
(Edwin T. Douglas '23 - '60)							
R. Manic	TB	1967	D	15*	35' 00"	11' 00"	4' 00"
Salvage Monarch	TB	1959	D	219*	97' 09"	28' 00"	14' 06"
Sinmac	TB	1958	D	224*	96' 00"	26' 00"	13' 00"

M-15 — McASPHALT INDUSTRIES LTD., SCARBOROUGH, ON

McAsphalt 401	TK	1966	B	43,000	300' 00"	60' 00"	23' 00"
(Pittson 200 '66 - '73, Pointe Levy '73 - '87)							

M-16 — McKEIL MARINE LTD., HAMILTON, ON

Argue Martin	TB	1895	D	71*	69' 00"	19' 06"	9' 00"
(Ethel 1895 - '38, R. C. Co. Tug No.1 '38 - '58, R. C. L. Tug No. 1 '58 - '62)							
Atomic	TB	1945	D	96*	82' 00"	20' 00"	10' 00"
Beaver D.	TB	1955	D	15*	36' 02"	14' 09"	4' 04"
Billie M.	TB	1897	D	34*	58' 00"	16' 00"	5' 06"
Black Carrier	DB		B		200' 11"		
Blain McKeil	TB	1978	D	736*	115' 00"	42' 00"	12' 00"
(Arctic Surveyor '78 - '96)							
Carolyn Jo	TB	1941	D	60*	65' 06"	17' 00"	7' 00"
((Unnamed) '41 - '56, Sea Hound '56 - '80)							
CSL Trillium	CC	1966	B	18,064	475' 00"	75' 00"	35' 00"
(Pacnav Princess '66 - '94)							
Doug McKeil	TB	1971	D	292*	169' 08"	38' 00"	16' 00"
(Mammoth '71 - '96)							
Dufresne	TB	1944	D	30*	58' 08"	14' 08"	5' 08"
Evans McKeil	TB	1936	D	284*	110' 00"	25' 06"	11' 06"
(Alhajuela '36 - '70, Barbara Ann '70 - '89)							
Flo-Mac	TB	1960	D	18*	40' 00"	13' 00"	6' 00"
Glenbrook	TB	1944	D	91*	81' 00"	21' 00"	9' 00"
Glenevis	TB	1944	D	91*	81' 00"	21' 00"	9' 00"
Glenside	TB	1944	D	91*	81' 00"	21' 00"	9' 00"
Greta V	TB	1951	D	14*	44' 00"	12' 00"	5' 00"
Jerry Newberry	TB	1956	D	244*	98' 00"	28' 00"	14' 00"
(Foundation Victor '56 - '73, Point Victor '73 - '77, Kay Cole '77 - '95)							
John Spence	TB	1972	D	719*	171' 00"	38' 00"	16' 00"
(Mary B. VI '72 - '81, Mary B. '81 - '82, Mary B. VI '82 - '83, Artic Tuktu '83 - '94)							
Kate B.	TB	1950	D	12*	46' 00"	12' 00"	3' 00"
Lac Como	TB	1944	D	65*	65' 00"	16' 06"	7' 09"
Lac Erie	TB	1944	D	65*	65' 00"	16' 06"	7' 09"
Lac Manitoba	TB	1944	D	65*	65' 00"	16' 06"	7' 09"
Lac Vancouver	TB	1943	D	65*	65' 00"	16' 06"	7' 09"
La Malbaie							
McAllister 252	DB	1969	B	2,636*	250' 00"	76' 01"	16' 01"
(Barge 252 '69 - '82, Genmar 252 '82 - '87)							
Niagara II	SC	1930	B	600	182' 06"	35' 03"	13' 00"
(Rideaulite '30 - '47, Imperial Lachine {1} '47 - '54, Niagara {2} '54 - '69, W. M. Edington '69 - '84)							
Ocean Hauler	DB	1943	B	8,500	344' 02"	71' 10"	25' 07"
Offshore Supplier	TB	1979	D	127*	92' 00"	25' 00"	10' 00"
(Elmore M. Misener '79 - '94)							
Otis Wack	TB	1950	D	237*	102' 06"	26' 00"	13' 06"
Paul E. No. 1	TB	1945	D	97*	80' 00"	20' 00"	9' 06"
(E. A. Rockett '46 - '76)							
Robert B. No. 1	TB	1956	D	197*	91' 00"	27' 00"	12' 00"

Fleet No. and Name / Vessel Name	Type of Ship	Year Built	Type of Engine	Cargo Cap. or Gross*	Length	Beam	Depth or Draft*
Stormont	TB	1953	D	108*	74' 00"	20' 00"	8' 00"
Salty Dog No. 1	TK	1945	B	88,735	313' 00"	68' 03"	26' 07"
(Fort Hoskins '45 - '66, Ocean Hauler 10 '66 - '79, ATC 610 '79 - '91)							
Sault au Couchon	DB	1969	B	10,000	422' 11"	74' 10"	25' 07"
Sillery	ER	1963	D	9,384	175' 00"	36' 00"	14' 00"
S.M.T.B. No. 7	ER	1969	B	7,502	150' 00"	33' 00"	14' 00"
Toledo	TK	1962	B	6,388	135' 00"	34' 00"	9' 00"
St. Clair {2}	DB	1927	B	2,770*	400' 00"	53' 00"	22' 00"
(Pere Marquette 12 '27 - '70)							
Scotia II	DB	1915	B	1,854*	300' 00"	48' 03"	18' 02"

REMORQUEURS & BARGES MONTREAL LTEE - DIVISION OF McKEIL MARINE LTD.

Cavalier	TB	1944	D	18*	40' 00"	10' 05"	4' 08"
Connie E.	TB	1974	D	9*	30' 00"	11' 00"	6' 00"
D. C. Everest	CS	1953	B	2,860	259' 00"	43' 06"	21' 00"
(D. C. Everest '53 - '82, Condarrell '82 - '88)							
Dufresne M-58	TB	1944	D	30*	58' 00"	16' 00"	5' 00"
Wilmac	TB	1959	D	16*	40' 00"	13' 00"	5' 08"

M-17 — MCM MARINE, INC., SAULT STE. MARIE, MI

Drummond Islander II	CF	1961	D	97*	65' 00"	36' 00"	9' 00"

M-18 — McMULLEN & PITZ CONSTRUCTION CO., MANITOWOC, WI

Dauntless	TB	1937	D	25*	52' 06"	15' 06"	5' 03"

M-19 — MERCURY CRUISE LINES, CHICAGO, IL

Chicago's First Lady	ES	1991	D		96' 00"	22' 00"	5' 00"
Skyline Princess	ES	1956	D		65' 00"	17' 00"	4' 00"
Skyline Queen	ES	1959	D		66' 00"	17' 08"	4' 09"

M-20 — MILLER BOAT LINE, INC., PUT-IN-BAY, OH

Islander {2}	CF	1983	D	92*	90' 03"	38' 00"	8' 03"
Put-in-Bay {3}	CF	1997	D	95*	96' 00"	38' 06"	14' 02"
South Bass	CF	1989	D	95*	64' 09"	24' 00"	9' 06"
West Shore {2}	CF	1947	D	94*	64' 10"	30' 00"	9' 03"
William M. Miller	CF	1954	D	96*	64' 09"	32' 09"	9' 09"
Wm. Market	CF	1993	D	95*	96' 00"	38' 06"	8' 09"

M-21 — MONTREAL BOATMAN LTD., MONTREAL, PQ

Escorte	TT	1964	D	120*	85' 00"	23' 08"	11' 00"
(USS Menasha (YTB / YTM-773, YTM-761) '64 - '92, Menasha '92 - '95)							

M-22 — MONTREAL HARBOR CRUISES, INC., MONTREAL, PQ

Ville Marie II	PA	1947	R	887*	176' 00"	66' 00"	13' 06"
(Laviolette '47 - '76, Bluewater Belle '76 - '79, Caledonia '79 - '82)							

M-23 — MORTON SALT CO., CHICAGO, IL

Morton Salt 74	DB	1974	B	2,101	195' 00"	35' 00"	12' 00"

M-24 — MUSEUM OF SCIENCE AND INDUSTRY, CHICAGO, IL

U-505	SS	1941	D/DC	1,178*	252' 00"	22' 00"	15' 06"
(Former German Type IX C submarine, captured by the US Navy in the Atlantic ocean off Africa in 1944. Open as a marine museum. See Page 114)							

M-25 — MUSKOKA LAKES NAVIGATION & HOTEL CO., GRAVENHURST, ON

Segwun	PA	1887	R	168*	128' 00"	21' 00"	7' 06"
(Nipissing {2} 1887 - '25)							
Wanda III	ES	1915	R	60*	101' 00"	12' 00"	6' 00"

N-1 — N. M. PATERSON & SONS LTD., MARINE DIVISION, THUNDER BAY, ON

Cartierdoc {2}	BC	1959	D	29,100	730' 00"	75' 09"	40' 02"
(Ems Ore '59 - '76, Montcliffe Hall '76 - '88)							
Comeaudoc	BC	1960	D	26,750	730' 00"	75' 06"	37' 09"
(Murray Bay {2} '60 - '63)							
Mantadoc {2}	BC	1967	D	17,650	607' 09"	62' 00"	36' 00"

Fleet No. and Name Vessel Name	Type of Ship	Year Built	Type of Engine	Cargo Cap. or Gross*	Length	Beam	Depth or Draft*
Paterson {2}	BC	1985	D	32,600	736' 06"	75' 10"	42' 00"
Quedoc {3}	BC	1965	D	28,050	730' 00"	75' 00"	39' 02"

(Beavercliffe Hall '65 - '88)
(Last operated 20 December, 1991 — Currently laid up in Thunder Bay, ON)

Vandoc {2}	BC	1964	D	16,000	605' 00"	62' 00"	33' 10"

(Sir Denys Lowson '64 - '79)
(Last operated 21 December, 1991 — Currently laid up in Thunder Bay, ON)

Windoc {2}	BC	1959	D	29,100	730' 00"	75' 09"	40' 02"

(Rhine Ore '59 - '76, Steelcliffe Hall '76 - '88)

N-2 — NADRO MARINE, PORT DOVER, ON

Miseford	TB	1915	D	116*	85'00	20'00	10'06"
3.Progress	TB	1948	D	123*	86' 00"	21' 00"	10' 00"

(P. J. Murer '48 - '81, Michael D. Misner '81 - '93, Thomas A. Payette '93 - '96)

N-3 — NAUTICAL ADVENTURES, INC., TORONTO, ON

Empire Sandy	ES	1943	SAIL	438*	140' 00"	32' 08"	14' 00"

(Empire Sandy '43 - '48, Ashford '48 - '52, Chris M. '52 - '79)

Wayward Princess	ES	1976	D	325*	92' 00"	26' 00"	10' 00"

(Cayuga II '76 - '82)

N-4 — NAVAL AND SERVICEMAN'S PARK MUSEUM, BUFFALO, NY

Croaker	SS	1942	D/DC	1,526*	311' 09"	27' 00"	15' 03"

(Former US Navy Emergency Program (Gato) class submarine (SS / SSK / AGSS / IXSS-246) stricken 20 December, 1971)

Little Rock	CLG	1945	T	10,000*	610' 01"	66' 04"	25' 00"

(Former US Navy Cleveland class cruiser (CL-92 / CLG-4) stricken 22 November, 1976)

PTF-17	PT	1968	D	85*	80' 04"	24' 06"	6' 09"

(Former US Navy Nasty class fast patrol boat (PTF-17) stricken in 1979)

The Sullivans	DD	1943	T	2,050*	376' 05"	39' 07"	33' 09"

(Former US Navy Fletcher class destroyer (DD-537) stricken 1 December, 1974)
(Above four currently museum vessels in Buffalo, NY. See Page 114

N-5 — NELSON CONSTRUCTION CO., LAPOINTE, WI

Eclipse	TB	1937	D	23*	47' 00"	13' 00"	6' 00"

N-6 — NEUMAN CRUISE & FERRY LINE, SANDUSKY, OH

Commuter	CF	1960	D	13*	64' 06"	33' 00"	9' 00"
Emerald Empress	ES	1994	D	94*	151' 00"	33' 00"	10' 06"
Endeavor	CF	1987	D	98*	101' 00"	34' 06"	10' 00"
Kelley Islander	CF	1969	D	95*	100' 00"	34' 03"	8' 00"

N-7 — NEW JOB CLINIC LTD., TORONTO, ON

Jaguar II	ES	1968	D	142*	95' 03"	20' 00"	9' 00"

N-8 — NICHOLSON TERMINAL & DOCK CO., RIVER ROUGE, MI

Charles E. Jackson	TB	1956	D	12*	35' 00"	10' 06"	5' 01"
Detroit {1}	TF	1904	B22 rail cars		308' 00"	76' 09"	19' 06"

O-1 — OGLEBAY NORTON CO. MARINE TRANSPORTATION, CLEVELAND, OH

Armco	SU	1953	T	25,500	767' 00"	70' 00"	36' 00"
Buckeye {3}	SU	1952	T	22,300	698' 00"	70' 00"	37' 00"

(Sparrows Point '52 - '91)

Columbia Star	SU	1981	D	78,850	1,000' 00"	105' 00"	56' 00"
Courtney Burton	SU	1953	T	22,300	690' 00"	70' 00"	37' 00"

(Ernest T. Weir {2} '53 - '78)

David Z. Norton {3}	SU	1973	D	19,650	630' 00"	68' 00"	36' 11"

(William R. Roesch '73 - '95)

Earl W. Oglebay	SU	1973	D	19,650	630' 00"	68' 00"	36' 11"

(Paul Thayer '73 - '95)

Fred R. White Jr.	SU	1979	D	23,800	636' 00"	68' 00"	40' 00"
Joseph H. Frantz	SU	1925	D	13,600	618' 00"	62' 00"	32' 00"

Fleet No. and Name Vessel Name	Type of Ship	Year Built	Type of Engine	Cargo Cap. or Gross*	Length	Beam	Depth or Draft*
Middletown	SU	1942	T	26,300	730' 00"	75' 00"	39' 03"
(Marquette '42 - '42, USS Neshanic (AO-71) '43 - '47, Gulfoil '47 - '61, Pioneer Challenger '61 - '62)							
Oglebay Norton	SU	1978	D	78,850	1,000' 00"	105' 00"	56' 00"
(Burns Harbor {1} '78 - '78, Lewis Wilson Foy '78 - '91)							
Reserve	SU	1953	T	25,500	767' 00"	70' 00"	36' 00"
Wolverine {4}	SU	1974	D	19,650	630' 00"	68' 00"	36' 11"

O-2 — ONTARIO MINISTRY OF TRANSPORTATION & COMMUNICATION, KINGSTON, ON

Amherst Islander	CF	1955	D	184*	106' 00"	38' 00"	10' 00"
Frontenac II	CF	1962	D	666*	181' 00"	45' 00"	10' 00"
(Charlevoix {2} '62 - '92)							
Glenora	CF	1952	D	209*	127' 00"	33' 00"	9' 00"
(The St. Joseph Islander '52 - '74)							
The Quinte Loyalist	CF	1954	D	209*	127' 00"	32' 00"	8' 00"
Wolfe Islander III	CF	1975	D	985*	205' 00"	68' 00"	6' 00"

O-3 — ONTARIO WATERWAYS CRUISES, INC., ORILLIA, ON

Kawartha Voyager	PA	1983	D	264*	108' 00"	22' 00"	5' 00"

O-4 — ORILLIA BOAT CRUISES, ORILLIA, ON

Lady Belle II	ES	1967	D	89*	65' 00"	19' 00"	5' 00"
(Lady Midland '67 - '82)							
Orillia's Island Princess	ES	1989	D	194*	65' 00"	27' 00"	5' 00"

O-5 — OSBORNE MATERIALS CO., MENTOR, OH

Emmet J. Carey	SC	1948	D	900	114' 00"	23' 00"	11' 00"
(Beatrice Ottinger '48 - '63, James B. Lyons '63 - '88)							
F. M. Osborne {2}	SC	1910	D	500	150' 00"	29' 00"	11' 03"
(Grand Island {1} '10 - '58, Lesco '58 - '75)							

O-6 — OWEN SOUND TRANSPORTATION CO. LTD., OWEN SOUND, ON
PELEE ISLAND TRANSPORTATION SERVICES - DIV. OF OWEN SOUND TRANS. CO. LTD.

Jiimaan	CF	1992	D	2,830*	176' 09"	42' 03"	13' 06"
Pelee Islander	CF	1960	D	334*	145' 00"	32' 00"	10' 00"
Upper Canada	CF	1949	D	165*	143' 00"	36' 00"	11' 00"
(Romeo and Annette '49 - '66)							

ONTARIO NORTHLAND TRANS. COMMISSION - MANAGED BY OWEN SOUND TRANS. CO. LTD.

Chi-Cheemaun	CF	1974	D	6,991*	365' 05"	61' 00"	21' 00"
Nindawayma	CF	1976	D	6,197*	333' 06"	55' 00"	36' 06"
(Monte Cruceta '76 - '77, Monte Castillo '77 - '78, Manx Viking '78 - '87, Manx '87 - '88, Skudenes '88 - '89, Ontario No.1 {2} '89 - '89)							
(Last operated in 1992 — Currently laid up in Owen Sound, ON)							

P-1 — P.& H. SHIPPING, DIV. OF PARRISH & HEIMBECKER LTD., MISSISSAUGA, ON

Mapleglen {2}	BC	1960	T	26,100	715' 03"	75' 00"	37' 09"
(Carol Lake '60 - '87, Algocape {1} '87 - '94)							
Oakglen {2}	BC	1954	T	22,950	714' 06"	70' 03"	37' 03"
(T. R. McLagan '54 - '90)							

P-2 — PENETANG MIDLAND COACH LINE BOAT CRUISES, MIDLAND, ON

Miss Midland	ES	1974	D	123*	68' 07"	19' 04"	6' 04"

P-3 — PENNSYLVANIA HISTORICAL & MUSEUM COMMISSION, ERIE, PA

Niagara	BR	1813	SAIL	493*	119' 00"	30' 00"	9' 00"
(Former US Navy brigantine is currently a museum vessel in Erie, PA. See Page 114)							

P-3A — PETERSEN STEAMSHIP CO., DOUGLAS, MI

Keewatin	PA	1907	Q	3,856*	346' 00"	43' 08"	26' 06"
(Former Canadian Pacific Railway Co. vessel last operated in October, 1965)							
Reiss	TB	1913	R	99*	80' 00"	20' 00"	12' 06"
(Q. A. Gillmore '13 - '32)							
(Former Reiss Steamship Co. vessel last operated in 1969)							
(Above two currently museum vessels in Douglas, MI. See page 115)							

Fleet No. and Name Vessel Name	Type of Ship	Year Built	Type of Engine	Cargo Cap. or Gross*	Length	Beam	Depth or Draft*

P-4 — PICTURED ROCKS CRUISES, INC., MUNISING, MI

Grand Island {2}	ES	1989	D		68' 00"	16' 01"	5' 01"
Miners Castle	ES	1974	D		68' 00"	17' 00"	5' 00"
Miss Munising	ES	1967	D		60' 00"	14' 00"	4' 04"
Miss Superior	ES	1984	D		68' 00"	17' 00"	5' 00"
Pictured Rocks	ES	1972	D		60' 00"	14' 00"	4' 04"

P-5 — PITTS INTERNATIONAL, INC., DON MILLS, ON

Flo Cooper	TB	1962	D	97*	80' 00"	21' 00"	10' 09"

P-6 — PLACE RESOURCES CORP., NANTICOKE, ON

Toni D.	TB	1959	D	15*	50' 00"	16' 00"	5' 00"

P-7 — PLAUNT TRANSPORTATION, CHEYBOGAN, MI

Kristen D.	CF	1988	D	83*	64' 11"	36' 00"	6' 05"

P-8 — PORT CITY PRINCESS, INC., NORTH MUSKEGON, MI

Port City Princess	ES	1966	D	79*	64' 09"	30' 00"	5' 06"
(Island Queen {1} '66 - '87)							

P-9 — PORT DALHOUSIE PIERS, INC., ST. CATHARINES, ON

Normac	PA	1902	D	462*	124' 06"	25' 00"	18' 00"
(James R. Elliot '02 - '31)							

(Owen Sound Transportation Co. vessel last operated in 1968 — Currently a floating restaurant in Port Dalhousie, ON)

P-10 — PRIDE OF WINDSOR CRUISE LINES, WINDSOR, ON

Stella Borealis	ES	1989	D	356*	118 '00"	26' 00"	7' 00"

R-1 — ROCKPORT BOAT LINE (1994) LTD., ROCKPORT, ON

Ida M. II	ES	1973	D	116*	63' 02"	18' 02"	

R-2 — ROEN SALVAGE CO., STURGEON BAY, WI

Chas Asher	TB	1956	D	10*	50' 00"	18' 00"	8' 00"
John R. Asher	TB	1943	D	93*	70' 00"	20' 00"	8' 06"
(US Army ST-71 '43 - '46, Russell 8 '46 - '64, Reid McAllister '64 - '67, Donegal '67 - '85)							
Louie S.	TB	1914	D	43*	37' 00"	12' 00"	5' 00"
Spuds	TB	1946	D	19*	42' 00"	12' 06"	6' 00"
Stephen M. Asher	TB	1954	D	60*	65' 00"	19' 01"	5' 04"
(Captain Bennie '54 - '82, Dumar Scout '82 - '87)							

R-3 — RUSSELL ISLAND TRANSIT CO., ALGONAC, MI

Islander {1}	CF	1982	D		41' 00"	15' 00"	3' 06"

R-4 — RYBA MARINE CONSTRUCTION CO., CHEBOYGAN, MI

Alcona	TB	1957	D	18*	40' 00"	12' 06"	5' 06"
Kathy Lynn	TB	1944	D	140*	85' 00"	24' 00"	9' 06"
(US Army ST-693 '44 - '79, Sea Islander '79 - '91)							
Tonawanda	DB	1935	B	375*	120' 00"	45' 00"	8' 00"
Venture	TB	1922	D	67*	65' 00"	14' 01"	10' 00"

S-1 — SANDUSKY BOAT LINE, SANDUSKY, OH

City of Sandusky	ES	1987	D		110' 00"	26' 00"	6' 00"

S-3 — SEA FOX THOUSAND ISLANDS TOURS, KINGSTON, ON

Sea Fox II	ES	1988	D	55*	39' 08"	20' 00"	2' 00"

S-4 — SEARS OIL CO., INC., ROME, NY

Midstate I	TB	1942	D	106*	86' 00"	24' 00"	12' 00"
Midstate II	TB	1945	D	137*	89' 00"	24' 00"	12' 06"

S-5 — SEAWAY BULK CARRIERS, WINNIPEG, MB
PARTNERSHIP BETWEEN ALGOMA CENTRAL CORP. AND UPPER LAKES GROUP*

ALGOMA CENTRAL CORP.	UPPER LAKES GROUP	
Algocape {2}	Canadian Explorer	Canadian Voyager
Algocen {2}	Canadian Leader	Gordon C. Leitch {2}
Algogulf {2}	Canadian Mariner	Montrealais
Algoisle	Canadian Miner	Quebecois
Algonorth	Canadian Prospector	Seaway Queen
Algontario	Canadian Provider	
Algoriver	Canadian Ranger	*See respective fleets
Algosound	Canadian Trader	for details.
Algowest		

S-6 — SEAWAY SELF-UNLOADERS, ST. CATHARINES, ON
PARTNERSHIP BETWEEN ALGOMA CENTRAL CORP. AND UPPER LAKES GROUP*

ALGOMA CENTRAL CORP.		UPPER LAKES GROUP
Agawa Canyon	Algosoo {2}	Canadian Century
Algobay	Algosteel {2}	Canadian Enterprise
Algolake	Algoville	Canadian Navigator
Algomarine	Algoway {2}	Canadian Olympic
Algoport	Algowood	Canadian Progress
Alogorail {2}	Capt. Henry Jackman	Canadian Transport {2}
	John B. Aird	James Norris

*See respective fleets for details.

Fleet No. and Name Vessel Name	Type of Ship	Year Built	Type of Engine	Cargo Cap. or Gross*	Length	Beam	Depth or Draft*
S-7 — SELVICK MARINE TOWING CORP., STURGEON BAY, WI							
Baldy B.	TB	1932	D	36*	62' 00"	16' 01"	7' 00"
Bonnie G. Selvick	TB	1928	D	95*	86' 00"	21' 00"	12' 00"
(E. James Fucik '28 - '77)							
Carla Anne Selvick	TB	1908	D	191*	96' 00"	23' 00"	11' 02"
Carl William Selvick	TB	1943	D	473*	143' 00"	33' 02"	17' 00"
(USS ATA-172 '43 - '47, Taboga '47 - '75, Daryl C. Hannah {1} '75 - '88)							
Escort I	TB	1955	D		50' 00"	15' 00"	7' 03"
Jimmy L.	TB	1939	D	148*	110' 00"	25' 00"	13' 00"
(USCG Naugatuck (WYTM-92) '39 - '80, Timmy B. '80 - '84)							
John M. Selvick	TB	1898	D	256*	118' 00"	24' 00"	12' 07"
(Illinois {1} 1898 - '41, John Roen III '41 - '74)							
Mary Page Hannah {1}	TB	1949	D	461*	143' 00"	33' 01"	14' 06"
(US Army ATA-230 '49 - '72, G. W. Codrington '72 - '73, William P. Feeley {2} '73 - '73, William W. Stender '73 - '78)							
Sharon M. Selvick	TB	1945	D	28*	45' 06"	13' 00"	7' 01"
William C. Selvick	TB	1944	D	142*	85' 00"	22' 11"	10' 04"
(US Army ST-500 '44 - '49, Sherman H. Serre '49 - '77)							
S-8 — SHELL CANADA PRODUCTS LTD., MONTREAL, PQ							
Horizon Montreal	TK	1958	D	32,900	315' 00"	45' 07"	24' 07"
(Tyee Shell '58 - '69, Arctic Trader '69 - '83, Rivershell {4} '83 - '95)							
S-9 — SHEPLER'S MACKINAC ISLAND FERRY SERVICE, MACKINAW CITY, MI							
Capt. Shepler	PF	1986	D	71*	78' 00"	21' 00"	7' 10"
Felicity	PF	1972	D	84*	65' 00"	18' 01"	8' 03"
Sacre Bleu	PK	1959	D	92*	94' 10"	31' 00"	9' 09"
(Put-In-Bay {2} '59 - '94)							
The Hope	PF	1975	D	87*	77' 00"	20' 00"	8' 03"
The Welcome	PF	1969	D	66*	60' 06"	16' 08"	8' 02"
Wyandot	PF	1979	D	99*	77' 00"	20' 00"	8' 00"
S-10 — SHORELINE MARINE CO., CHICAGO, IL							
Marlyn	ES	1961	D		65' 00"	25' 00"	7' 00"
Shoreline	ES	1953	D		61' 07"	16' 00"	4' 05"

Fleet No. and Name Vessel Name	Type of Ship	Year Built	Type of Engine	Cargo Cap. or Gross*	Length	Beam	Depth or Draft*

S-11 — SIVERTSON'S GRAND PORTAGE - ISLE ROYALE TRANSPORTATION LINES, INC., SUPERIOR, WI

Fleet No. and Name	Type of Ship	Year Built	Type of Engine	Cargo Cap. or Gross*	Length	Beam	Depth or Draft*
A. E. Clifford	ES	1946	D		45' 00"	15' 00"	7' 00"
Hiawatha {1}	ES	1938	D		58' 00"	15' 00"	8' 00"
Provider	ES	1959	D		46' 00"	13' 05"	5' 05"
Voyageur II	ES	1970	D		63' 00"	18' 00"	5' 00"
Wenonah	ES	1960	D		64' 09"	20' 00"	7' 00"

S-12 — SNOW'S EQUIPMENT CO., DETOUR, MI

Albany Bay	TB	1910	D	49*	61' 00"	16' 01"	8' 00"
Katanni	TB	1963	D	52*	51' 06"	19' 04"	7' 00"

S-13 — SOO LOCK BOAT TOURS, SAULT STE. MARIE, MI

Bide-A-Wee {3}	ES	1955	D	99*	64' 07"	23' 00"	7' 11"
Hiawatha {2}	ES	1959	D	99*	64' 07"	23' 00"	7' 11"
Holiday	ES	1957	D	99*	64' 07"	23' 00"	7' 11"
LeVoyageur	ES	1959	D	70*	65' 00"	25' 00"	7' 00"
Nokomis	ES	1959	D	70*	65' 00"	25' 00"	7' 00"

S-14 — SOREL TUG BOATS, INC., SOREL, PQ

Omni Richlieu	TB	1969	D	144*	83' 00"	24' 06"	13' 06"
(Port Alfred II '69 - '82)							
Omni Sorel	TB	1962	D	71*	72' 00"	19' 00"	12' 00"
(Angus M. '62 - '92)							
Omni St. Laurent	TB	1957	D	161*	99' 02"	24' 09"	12' 06"
(Diligent '57 - '89)							

S-15 — SPECIALTY RESTAURANTS CORP., ANAHEIM, CA

Lansdowne	TF	1884	B	1,571*	319' 00"	41' 03"	13' 00"

(Last operated in 1974 — Currently laid up in Lorain, OH)

S-16 — ST. LAWRENCE CRUISE LINES, INC., KINGSTON, ON

Canadian Empress	PA	1981	D	463*	104' 00"	30' 00"	8' 00"

S-17 — ST. LAWRENCE SEAWAY DEVELOPMENT CORP., MASSENA, NY

Eighth Sea	TB	1958	D	17*	40' 00"	12' 06"	4' 00"
Fourth Coast	TB	1957	D	17*	40' 00"	12' 06"	4' 00"
Robinson Bay	TB	1958	D	213*	103' 00"	26' 10"	14' 06"

S-18 — ST. MARY'S CEMENT CO., TORONTO, ON

St. Mary's Cement II	CC	1978	B	18,500	496' 06"	76' 00"	35' 00"
(Velasco '78 - '81, Canmar Shuttle '81 - '90)							
Sea Eagle II	TB	1979	D	560*	132' 00"	35' 00"	19' 00"
(Sea Eagle '79 - '81, Canmar Sea Eagle '81 - '91)							
St. Mary's Cement III	CC	1980	B	4,800	335' 00"	76' 08"	17' 09"
(Bigorange XVI '80 - '84, Says '84 - '85, Al-Sayb-7 '85 - '86, Clarkson Carrier '86 - '94)							

GREAT LAKES INT. TOWING & SALVAGE, INC. - CHARTERED BY ST. MARY'S CEMENT CO.

Petite Forte	TB	1969	D	368*	127' 00"	32' 00"	14' 06"
(E. Bronson Ingram '69 - '70, Jarmac 42 '70 - '73, Scotsman '73 - '81, Al Battal '81 - '86)							

S-19 — ST. MARY'S HOLDINGS, INC., DETROIT, MI

Lewis G. Harriman	CC	1923	R	5,500	350' 00"	55' 00"	28' 00"
(John W. Boardman '23 - '65)							

(Last operated 20 April, 1980 — 5 year survey expires September, 1997 — Currently in use as a non-powered cement storage vessel in Green Bay, WI)

St. Mary's Cement	CC	1986	B	9,400	360' 00"	60' 00"	23' 03"

MERCE TRANSPORTATION CO. - CHARTERED BY ST. MARY'S HOLDING'S, INC.

Triton {2}	TB	1941	D	196*	135' 00"	30' 00"	17' 06"
(USS Tuscarora (AT-77, YT-341, YTB-341, ATA-245) '41 - '79, Challenger {1} '79 - '86)							

S-20 — ST. MARY'S RIVER CENTRE, SAULT STE. MARIE, ON

Norgoma	PA	1950	D	1,477*	188' 00"	37' 06"	22' 06"

(Former Ontario Northland Transportation Comm. vessel last operated in 1974. Currently a museum vessel in Sault Ste. Marie, ON. **See page 115)**

Fleet No. and Name Vessel Name	Type of Ship	Year Built	Type of Engine	Cargo Cap. or Gross*	Length	Beam	Depth or Draft*

S-21 — STAR LINE CORP., CHICAGO, IL

Chicago II	ES	1983	D	42*	123' 03"	28' 06"	7' 00"

(Star of Sandford '83 - '86, Star of Charlevoix {1} '86 - '87, Star of Toronto '87 - '87, Star of Chicago II '87 - '94)

S-22 — STAR LINE MACKINAC ISLAND FERRY, ST. IGNACE, MI

Cadillac {5}	PF	1990	D	73*	64' 07"	20' 00"	7' 07"
Joliet {3}	PF	1993	D	83*	64' 08"	22' 00"	8' 03"
La Salle {4}	PF	1983	D	55*	65' 00"	20' 00"	7' 05"
Marquette {5}	PF	1979	D	55*	62' 03"	22' 00"	7' 01"
Nicolet {2}	PF	1985	D	51*	65' 00"	20' 00"	7' 05"
Radisson {2}	PF	1988	D	97*	80' 00"	23' 06"	7' 00"

S-23— STEAMER COLUMBIA FOUNDATION, DETROIT, MI

Columbia {2}	PA	1902	R	968*	216' 00"	60' 00"	13' 06"

(Last operated 2 September, 1991 — 5 year survey expires January, 1998 — Laid up in Ecorse, MI. See page 108)

S-24 — STEAMER STE. CLAIRE FOUNDATION, DETROIT, MI

Ste. Claire	PA	1910	R	870*	197' 00"	65' 00"	14' 00"

(Last operated 2 September, 1991 — 5 year survey expired May, 1993 — Laid up in Ecorse, MI. See page 108)

S-25 — STEVEN WALLACE, PENETANGUISHENE, ON

Georgian Storm	TB	1931	D	167*	91' 00"	24' 02"	12' 00"

(Capitaine Simard '31 - '57, Renee Simard '57 - '86)

T-1 — TECHNO - NAVIGATION LTEE, SILLERY, PQ

Techno St-Laurent	TB	1944	D	257*	111' 00"	27' 00"	13' 00"
Techno Venture	TB	1939	D	470*	135' 00"	30' 06"	16' 00"

(Dragonet '39 - '61, Foundation Venture '61 - '73, M.I.L. Venture '73 - '79)

T-2 — THE PUT-IN-BAY BOAT LINE CO., PUT-IN-BAY, OH

Jet Express	PC	1989	D	93*	92' 08"	28' 06"	8' 04"
Jet Express II	PC	1992	D	85*	92' 06"	28' 06"	8' 04"

T-3 — THOMAS W. MARSHALL, TORONTO, ON

Still Watch	SV	1960	D	390*	134' 02"	28' 00"	13' 09"

(CCGS Ville Marie '60 - '85, Heavenbound '85 - '95)

T-4 — THUNDER BAY MARINE SERVICE LTD., THUNDER BAY, ON

Agoming	CS	1926	B	155*	100' 00"	34' 00"	9' 00"
Coastal Cruiser	TB	1939	D	29*	65' 00"	18' 00"	12' 00"
Glenada	TB	1944	D	107*	80' 06"	25' 00"	10' 01"
Robert W.	TB	1949	D	48*	60' 00"	16' 00"	8' 06"
Rosalee D.	TB	1943	D	22*	55' 00"	16' 00"	10' 00"

T-5 — THUNDER BAY TUG SERVICES LTD., THUNDER BAY, ON

Valour	TB	1958	D	246*	97' 08"	28' 02"	13' 10"

(Foundation Valour '58 - '83, Point Valour '83 - '92)

T-6 — TOM SHAW CONSTRUCTION, INC., SAULT STE. MARIE, MI

Robert Charles	TB	1966	D	55*	51' 05"	16' 00"	6' 04"

T-7 — TORONTO DRYDOCK CORP., TORONTO, ON

Menier Consol	FD	1962	B	2,575*	304' 07"	49' 06"	25' 06"

T-8 — TOWNSHIP OF ASSIGINACK, MANITOWANING, ON

Norisle	PA	1946	R	1,668*	215' 09"	36' 03"	16' 00"

(Former Ontario Northland Transportation Commission vessel last operated in 1974. Currently a museum vessel in Manitowaning, ON. See page 115)

T-9 — TRANSPORT DESGAGNES, INC., QUEBEC, PQ
CROISIERES NORDIK - DIVISION OF TRANSPORT DESGAGNES, INC.

Nordik Passeur	CF	1962	D	2,371*	285' 04"	62' 00"	20' 01"

(Confederation '62 - '93, Hull 28 '93 - '94)

Fleet No. and Name Vessel Name	Type of Ship	Year Built	Type of Engine	Cargo Cap. or Gross*	Length	Beam	Depth or Draft*
GROUP DESGAGNES - DIVISION OF TRANSPORT DESGAGNES, INC.							
Amelia Desgagnes	CS	1976	D	7,000	355' 00"	49' 00"	30' 06"
(Soodoc {2} '76 - '90)							
Anna Desgagnes	RR	1986	D	17,850			
(Truskavets '86 - '96)							
Catherine Desgagnes	BC	1962	D	8,350	410' 03"	56' 04"	31' 00"
(Gosforth '62 - '72, Thorold {4} '72 - '85)							
Cecelia Desgagnes	BC	1971	D	7,875	374' 10"	54' 10"	34' 06"
(Carl Gorthon '71 - '81, Federal Pioneer '81 - '85)							
Jacques Desgagnes	BC	1960	D	1,250	208' 10"	36' 00"	14' 00"
(Loutre Consol '60 - '77)							
J. A. Z. Desgagnes	BC	1960	D	1,250	208' 10"	36' 00"	14' 00"
(Lievre Consol '60 - '62, Vison Consol '62 - '74)							
Mathilda Desgagnes	BC	1959	D	6,920	360' 00"	51' 00"	30' 02"
(Eskimo '59 - '80)							
Melissa Desgagnes	CS	1975	D	7,000	355' 00"	49' 00"	30' 06"
(Ontadoc {2} '75 - '90)							
Thalassa Desgagnes	TK	1976	D	58,000	441' 05"	56' 07"	32' 10"
(Joasla '76 - '79, Orinoco '79 - '82, Rio Orinoco '82 - '93)							
RELAIS NORDIK - DIVISION OF TRANSPORT DESGAGNES, INC.							
Nordik Express	CF	1974	D				
(Theriot Offshore IV '74 - '77, Scotoil '77 - '79, Tartan Sea '79 - '87)							
T-10 — TRAVERSE TALL SHIP CO., TRAVERSE CITY, MI							
Malabar	PA	1975	SAIL		105' 00"	20' 00"	8' 00"
Manitou {1}	PA	1983	SAIL		114' 00"	21' 00"	9' 00"
T-11 — TROIS RIVIERES REMORQUEURS LTEE., TROIS RIVIERES, PQ							
Andre H.	TB	1963	D	317*	126' 00"	28' 06"	15' 06"
(Foundation Valiant '63 - '73, Point Valiant '73 - '95)							
Duga	TB	1977	D	402*	111' 00"	33' 00"	16' 01"
R. F. Grant	TB	1969	D	78*	71' 00"	17' 00"	8' 00"
Robert H.	TB	1944	D	257*	111' 00"	27' 00"	13' 00"
T-12 — TRUMP CASINO, GARY, IN							
Trump Casino	GC	1996	D		300' 00"	76' 00"	
T-13 — 30,000 ISLANDS CRUISE LINES, INC., PARRY SOUND, ON							
Island Queen V {3}	ES	1990	D	526*	128' 00"	30' 00"	6' 06"
U-1 — UNDERWATER GAS DEVELOPERS, PORT COLBORNE, ON							
C. West Pete	TB	1956	D	29*	63' 00"	17' 03"	5' 06"
Telesis	DV	1957	D	2,099*	259' 00"	43' 11"	22' 06"
(Coniscliffe Hall {2} '57 - '73)							
U-2 — U.S. ARMY CORPS OF ENGINEERS, DETROIT, MI							
Bayfield	TB	1953	D	29*	45' 00"	13' 00"	6' 00"
Buffalo	TB	1953	D	29*	45' 00"	13' 00"	7' 00"
Cheraw	TB	1969	D	356*	109' 00"	30' 06"	16' 06"
Chetek	TB	1973	D	356*	109' 00"	30' 06"	16' 06"
D. L. Billmaier	TB	1970	D	356*	109' 00"	30' 06"	16' 06"
(USS Natchitoches (YTB-799) '70 - '95)							
Duluth	TB	1954	D	82*	70' 00"	20' 00"	8' 06"
Fairchild	TB	1953	D	29*	45' 00"	13' 00"	5' 01"
Forney	TB	1944	D	163*	86' 00"	23' 00"	10' 00"
Hammond Bay	TB	1953	D	29*	45' 00"	13' 00"	6' 00"
Harvey	CS	1961	B		122' 00"	41' 00"	4' 10"
H. J. Schwartz	CS	1995	B		150' 00"	48' 00"	7' 04"
Houghton	TB	1944	D	29*	45' 00"	13' 00"	6' 00"
Huron	CS	1954	B		100' 00"	34' 00"	4' 06"
James M. Bray	SV	1924	D	194*	128' 00"	31' 00"	5' 07"
Kenosha	TB	1954	D	82*	70' 00"	20' 00"	8' 06"

Fleet No. and Name Vessel Name	Type of Ship	Year Built	Type of Engine	Cargo Cap. or Gross*	Length	Beam	Depth or Draft*
Manitowoc	CS	1976	B		132' 00"	44' 00"	8' 00"
McCauley	CS	1948	B		112' 00"	52' 00"	3' 00"
Michigan	CS	1942	B		120' 00"	33' 00"	3' 06"
Nicolet	CS	1971	B		120' 00"	42' 00"	4' 09"
Simonsen	CS	1954	B		142' 00"	58' 00"	5' 00"
Owen M. Frederick	TB	1942	D	56*	65' 00"	17' 00"	7' 00"
Paj	SV	1955	D	151*	120' 06"	34' 02"	6' 05"
Paul Bunyan	GL		B				
Racine	TB	1931	D	61*	66' 03"	18' 05"	7' 08"
Rouge	TB	1954	D	82*	70' 00"	19' 06"	9' 08"
Shelter Bay	TB	1953	D	29*	45' 00"	13' 00"	5' 00"
Stanley	TB	1944	D	163*	86' 00"	23' 00"	10' 04"
Tawas Bay	TB	1953	D	29*	45' 00"	13' 00"	5' 00"
Tonawanda	CS	1935	B		120' 00"	45' 00"	8' 00"
Washington	TB	1952	D	390*	107' 00"	26' 06"	14' 10"
Whitefish Bay	TB	1953	D	29*	45' 00"	13' 00"	5' 00"

U-3 — U.S. COAST GUARD, 9TH COAST GUARD DISTRICT, CLEVELAND, OH

Acacia **(WLB-406)**	BT	1944	D	1,025*	180' 00"	37' 00"	13' 11"*
(Thistle (WAGL-406) '44 - '44)							
Biscayne Bay **(WTGB-104)**	IB	1979	D	662*	140' 00"	37' 06"	12' 00"*
Bramble* **(WLB-392)**	BT	1944	D	1,025*	180' 00"	37' 00"	13' 11"*
Bristol Bay **(WTGB-102)**	IB	1979	D	662*	140' 00"	37' 06"	12' 00"*
Buckthorn **(WLI-642)**	BT	1963	D	200*	100' 00"	24' 00"	4' 08"*
Katmai Bay **(WTGB-101)**	IB	1978	D	662*	140' 00"	37' 06"	12' 00"*
Mackinaw **(WAGB-83)**	IB	1944	D	5,252*	290' 00"	74' 00"	19' 00"*
(Manitowoc (WAG-83) '44 - '44)							
Mobile Bay **(WTGB-103)**	IB	1979	D	662*	140' 00"	37' 06"	12' 00"*
Neah Bay **(WTGB-105)**	IB	1980	D	662*	140' 00"	37' 06"	12' 00"*
Sundew* **(WLB-404)**	BT	1944	D	1,025*	180' 00"	37' 00"	13' 11"*

(*Strengthened for ice breaking.)

U-4 — U.S. DEPT. OF THE INTERIOR, U.S. FISH & WILDLIFE SERVICE, ANN ARBOR, MI

Cisco	RV	1951	D		60' 06"	16' 08"	7' 08"
Grayling	RV	1977	D		75' 00"	22' 00"	9' 10"
Kaho	RV	1961	D		64' 10"	17' 10"	9' 00"
Musky II	RV	1960	D	25*	45' 00"	14' 04"	5' 00"
Siscowet	RV	1946	D	54*	57' 00"	14' 06"	7' 00"

U-5 — U.S. ENVIRONMENTAL PROTECTION AGENCY, WASHINGTON D.C.

Lake Guardian	RV	1989	D	282*	180' 00"	40' 00"	11' 00"
(Marsea Fourteen '81 - '90)							

U-6 — U.S. NATIONAL PARK SERVICE, ISLE ROYALE NATIONAL PARK, HOUGHTON, MI

Beaver	BC	1952	B	550	110' 00"	32' 00"	6' 05"
Charlie Mott	PF	1953	D	28*	56' 00"	14' 00"	4' 07"
Greenstone	TK	1977	B	30	81' 00"	24' 00"	6' 01"
J. E. Colombe	TB	1953	D	25*	45' 00"	12' 05"	5' 03"
Ranger III	PF	1958	D	648*	165' 00"	34' 00"	15' 03"

U-7 — U.S. NAVAL SEA CADET CORPS, WHITE LAKE, MI — 810-666-9359

Pride of Michigan - YP-673	TV	1979	D	70*	80' 06"	7' 08"	5' 03"

U-8 — UNIV. OF MICH. - CENTER FOR GREAT LAKES / AQUATIC SERV., ANN ARBOR, MI

Laurentian	RV		D		80' 00"	21' 06"	8' 09"

U-9 — UPPER CANADA STEAMBOATS, INC., BROCKVILLE, ON

Miss Brockville	ES		D		48' 00"	10' 00"	4' 00"
Miss Brockville IV	ES		D		45' 00"	10' 00"	5' 00"
Miss Brockville V	ES		D		62' 00"	13' 00"	5' 00"
Miss Brockville VI	ES		D		38' 00"	8' 00"	3' 00"

Fleet No. and Name Vessel Name	Type of Ship	Year Built	Type of Engine	Cargo Cap. or Gross*	Length	Beam	Depth or Draft*
Miss Brockville VII	ES		D		66' 00"	15' 00"	5' 00"
Miss Brockville VIII	ES		D		48' 00"	12' 00"	5' 00"

U-10 — UPPER LAKES BARGE LINE, INC., BARK RIVER, MI

McKee Sons	SU	1945	B	19,900	579' 02"	71' 06"	38' 06"
(USNS Marine Angel '45 - '52)							
Olive M. Moore	TB	1928	D	297*	125' 00"	27' 01"	13' 09"
(John F. Cushing '28 - '66, James E. Skelly '66 - '66)							

U-11 — UPPER LAKES GROUP, INC., TORONTO, ON

HAMILTON MARINE & ENGINEERING LTD. - DIVISION OF UPPER LAKES GROUP, INC.

James E. McGrath	TB	1963	D	90*	77' 00"	20' 00"	10' 09"

JACKES SHIPPING, INC. - DIVISION OF UPPER LAKES GROUP, INC.

Canadian Trader	BC	1969	D	28,300	730' 00"	75' 00"	39' 08"
(Ottercliffe Hall '69 - '83, Royalton (2) '83 - '85, Ottercliffe Hall '85 - '88, Peter Misener '88 - '94)							
Canadian Venture	BC	1965	D	28,050	730' 00"	75' 00"	39' 02"
(Lawrencecliffe Hall (2) '65 - '88, David K. Gardiner '88 - '94)							
Gordon C. Leitch (2)	BC	1968	D	29,700	730' 00"	75' 00"	42' 00"
(Ralph Misener '68 - '94)							

PROVMAR FUELS, INC. - DIVISION OF UPPER LAKES GROUP, INC.

Hamilton Energy	TK	1965	D	8,622	201' 05"	34' 01"	14' 09"
(Partington '65 - '79, Shell Scientist '79 - '81, Metro Sun '81 - '85)							
Provmar Terminal	TK	1959	B	60,000	403' 05"	55' 06"	28' 05"
(Varangnes '59 - '70, Tommy Wiborg '70 - '74, Ungava Transport '74 - '85)							
(Last operated in 1984 — Currently in use as a fuel storage barge in Hamilton, ON)							
Provmar Terminal II	TK	1948	B	56,010	408' 08"	53' 00"	26' 00"
(Imperial Sarnia (2) '48 - '87)							
(Last operated 13 December, 1986 — In use as a fuel storage barge in Hamilton, ON)							

ULS CORPORATION - DIVISION OF UPPER LAKES GROUP, INC.

Canadian Century	SU	1967	D	31,600	730' 00"	75' 00"	45' 00"
Canadian Enterprise	SU	1979	D	35,100	730' 00"	75' 08"	46' 06"
Canadian Explorer	BC	1944	D	26,000	730' 00"	75' 00"	39' 03"
((Fore Section) *Verendrye '44 - '47, Edenfield '47 - '61, Northern Venture '61 - '83)*							
((Stern Section) *Cabot '65 - '83)*							
Canadian Leader	BC	1967	T	28,300	730' 00"	75' 00"	39' 08"
(Feux - Follets '67 - '72)							
Canadian Mariner	BC	1963	T	27,700	730' 00"	75' 00"	39' 03"
(Newbrunswicker '63 - '68, Grande Hermine '68 - '72)							
Canadian Miner	BC	1966	D	28,050	730' 00"	75' 00"	39' 01"
(Maplecliffe Hall '66 - '88, Lemoyne (2) '88 - '94)							
Canadian Navigator	SU	1967	D	31,600	729' 10"	75' 10"	40' 06"
(Demeterton '67 - '75, St. Lawrence Navigator '75 - '80)							
Canadian Olympic	SU	1976	D	35,100	730' 00"	75' 00"	46' 06"
Canadian Progress	SU	1968	D	32,700	730' 00"	75' 00"	46' 06"
Canadian Prospector	BC	1964	D	30,500	730' 00"	75' 10"	40' 06"
(Carlton '64 - '75, Federal Wear '75 - '75, St. Lawrence Prospector '75 - '79)							
Canadian Provider	BC	1963	T	27,450	730' 00"	75' 00"	39' 02"
(Murray Bay (3) '63 - '94)							
Canadian Ranger	GU	1943	D	25,900	730' 00"	75' 00"	39' 03"
((Fore Section) *Grande Ronde '43 - '48, Kate N. L. '48 - '61, Hilda Marjanne '61 - '84)*							
((Stern Section) *Chimo '67 - '83)*							
Canadian Transport (2)	SU	1979	D	35,100	730' 00"	75' 08"	46' 06"
Canadian Voyager	BC	1963	T	27,050	730' 00"	75' 00"	39' 02"
(Black Bay '63 - '94)							
Hamilton Transfer	SU	1943	R	15,650	620' 06"	60' 00"	35' 00"
(J. H. Hillman Jr. '43 - '74, Crispin Oglebay (2) '74 - '95)							
(Last operated 29 May, 1991 — 5 year survey expired June, 1994 — Currently in use as a stationary cargo unloading / transfer vessel in Hamilton, ON)							
James Norris	SU	1952	U	18,600	663' 06"	67' 00"	35' 00"

Fleet No. and Name Vessel Name	Type of Ship	Year Built	Type of Engine	Cargo Cap. or Gross*	Length	Beam	Depth or Draft*
Montrealais	BC	1962	T	27,800	730' 00"	75' 00"	39' 00"
(Montrealer '62 - '62)							
Quebecois	BC	1963	T	27,800	730' 00"	75' 00"	39' 00"
Seaway Queen	BC	1959	T	24,300	713' 03"	72' 00"	37' 00"

ULS MARBULK, INC. - DIVISION OF UPPER LAKES GROUP, INC.

Nelvana	SU	1983	D	75,000	797' 00"	106' 00"	65' 00"
Richmond Hill	BC	1981	D	38,000	635' 10"	90' 06"	52' 00"
(Frotacanada '81 - '87, Porthos '87 - '89, Nai Ookkam '89 - '93)							

BARBER SHIP MANAGEMENT - MANAGERS FOR ULS MARBULK, INC.

Ambassador	SU	1983	D	37,800	730' 00"	75' 10"	50' 00"
(Canadian Ambassador '83 - '85)							
Pioneer	SU	1981	D	37,900	730' 00"	75' 10"	50' 00"
(Canadian Pioneer '81 - '86)							
Thornhill	BC	1981	D	38,000	635' 10"	90' 06"	52' 00"
(Frotabrasil '81 - '87, Athos '87 - '89, Chennai Perumai '89 - '93)							

U-12 — UPPER LAKES TOWING, INC., ESCANABA, MI

Joseph H. Thompson	SU	1944	B	21,200	706' 06"	71' 06"	38' 06"
(USNS Marine Robin '44 - '52)							
Joseph H. Thompson Jr.	TB	1990	D	841*	146' 06"	38' 00"	35' 00"
William H. Donner	CS	1914	R	9,400	524' 00"	54' 00"	30' 00"
(Last operated in 1969 — Currently laid up in Menominee, MI)							

U-13 — USS GREAT LAKES FLEET, INC., DULUTH, MN

Arthur M. Anderson	SU	1952	T	25,300	767' 00"	70' 00"	36' 00"
Calcite II	SU	1929	D	12,650	604' 09"	60' 00"	32' 00"
(William G. Clyde '29 - '61)							
Cason J. Callaway	SU	1952	T	25,300	767' 00"	70' 00"	36' 00"
Edgar B. Speer	SU	1980	D	73,700	1,004' 00"	105' 00"	56' 00"
Edwin H. Gott	SU	1979	D	74,100	1,004' 00"	105' 00"	56' 00"
George A. Sloan	SU	1943	D	15,800	620' 06"	60' 00"	35' 00"
(Hill Annex '43 - '43)							
John G. Munson {2}	SU	1952	T	25,550	768' 03"	72' 00"	36' 00"
Myron C. Taylor	SU	1929	D	12,450	603' 09"	60' 00"	32' 00"
Ojibway	SB	1945	D	65*	53' 00"	28' 00"	7' 00"
Philip R. Clarke	SU	1952	T	25,300	767' 00"	70' 00"	36' 00"
Roger Blough	SU	1972	D	43,900	858' 00"	105' 00"	41' 06"

LITTON GREAT LAKES CORP. - MANAGED BY USS GREAT LAKES FLEET, INC.

Presque Isle {2}	TB	1973	D	1,578*	153' 03"	54' 00"	31' 03"
Presque Isle {2}	SU	1973	B	57,500	974' 06"	104' 07"	46' 06"
(Overall Dimensions Together)					1,000' 00"	104' 07"	46' 06"

U-14 — USS SILVERSIDES & MARITIME MUSEUM, MUSKEGON, MI

McLane	WM	1927	D	289*	125' 00"	24' 00"	9' 00"*
(USCG McLane (WSC / WMEC-146) '27 - '70, Manatra II '70 - '93)							
(Former US Coast Guard Buck & A Quarter class medium endurance cutter (WSC / WMEC-146) stricken 31 December 1968)							
Silversides	SS	1941	D/DC	1,525*	312' 00"	27' 00"	33' 09"
(Former US Navy Albacore (Gato) class submarine (SS-236) stricken 30 June, 1969)							
(Above two currently museum vessels in Muskegon, MI. See Page 115)							

V-1 — VERREAULT NAVIGATION, INC., LES MACHINS, PQ

Keta V.	TB	1961	D	236*	98' 00"	26' 00"	12' 06"

V-2 — VOIGHT'S MARINE SERVICES, GILLS ROCK, WI

Bounty	ES	1968	D		40' 00"	14' 00"	3' 03"
Island Clipper {2}	ES	1987	D	149*	65' 00"	20' 00"	5' 00"
Yankee Clipper	ES	1971	D		54' 00"	17' 00"	5' 00"

Fleet No. and Name Vessel Name	Type of Ship	Year Built	Type of Engine	Cargo Cap. or Gross*	Length	Beam	Depth or Draft*

V-3 — VOYAGEURS MARINE CONSTRUCTION CO., VAUDREUIL, PQ

Glenlivet II	TB	1944	D	111*	76' 08"	20' 09"	10' 02"
(HMCS Glenlivet II '44 - '75, Glenlivet II '75 - '77, Canadian Franko '77 - '82)							
Soulanges	TB	1905	D	72*	77' 00"	17' 00"	8' 00"
(Dandy '05 - '39)							

W-1 — WAGNER CHARTER CO., INC., CHICAGO, IL

Trinidad	ES	1926	D		100' 00"	23' 00"	9' 00"

W-2 — WALPOLE - ALGONAC FERRY LINE, PORT LAMBTON, ON

City of Algonac	CF	1990	D	92*	80' 04"	26' 01"	6' 09"
Lowell D.	CF	1946	D	38*	48' 07"	17' 06"	5' 02"
Walpole Islander	CF	1986	D	71*	74' 00"	33' 00"	7' 00"

W-3— WASHINGTON ISLAND FERRY LINE, INC., WASHINGTON ISLAND, WI

C. G. Richter	CF	1950	D	82*	70' 06"	25' 00"	9' 05"
Eyrarbakki	CF	1970	D	95*	87' 00"	36' 00"	7' 06"
Robert Noble	CF	1979	D	97*	90' 04"	36' 00"	8' 03"
Voyager	CF	1960	D	98*	65' 00"	35' 00"	8' 00"
Washington (2)	CF	1989	D	93*	100' 00"	37' 00"	9' 00"

W-4 — WATERMAN'S SERVICES LTD., TORONTO, ON

Colinette	TB	1943	D	64*	65' 00"	16' 00"	7' 00"
(Ottawa (1) '43 - '57, Lac Ottawa '57 - '66)							
Duchess V	TB	1955	D	18*	55' 00"	16' 00"	6' 08"

W-5 — WENDELLA SIGHTSEEING CO., CHICAGO, IL

Queen of Andersonville	ES	1962	D		40' 00"	5' 00"	3' 05"
Wendella Clipper	ES	1958	D		67' 00"	20' 00"	4' 00"
Wendella Limited	ES	1992	D		68' 00"	20' 00"	4' 09"
Wendella Sunliner	ES	1961	D		68' 00"	17' 00"	5' 00"

W-6 — WINDSOR CASINO LTD., WINDSOR, ON

Northern Belle	GC		B				

W-7 — WISCONSIN & MICHIGAN STEAMSHIP CO., DETROIT, MI

Highway 16	AC	1942	D	190 cars	328' 00"	50' 00"	25' 00"
(USS LST-393 '42 - '48)							

(Last operated 31 July, 1973. Currently laid up in Muskegon, MI)

W-8 — WISCONSIN MARITIME MUSEUM, MANITOWOC, WI

Cobia	SS	1943	D/DC	1,500*	312' 00"	27' 00"	15' 00"

(Former US Navy Emergency Program (Gato) class submarine (SS / AGSS-245) stricken 1 July, 1970. Currently a museum vessel in Manitowoc, WI. See Page 115)

The pilothouse of the William Clay Ford is on display at Dossin Great Lakes Museum in Detroit. See page 111.

INTERNATIONAL VESSELS

This list as completely as possible reflects the ships of the world which regularly call on the lakes and Seaway. Information on many of these vessels is elusive and changes rapidly. All available data has been included.

Trident Mariner (above) at the Welland Canal, 19 August, 1996

Fleet No. and Name Vessel Name	Type of Ship	Year Built	Type of Engine	Cargo Cap. or Gross*	Length	Beam	Depth or Draft*
A-1 — A. P. MOLLER, COPENHAGEN, DENMARK							
Ras Maersk	TK	1986	D	120,000	557' 09"	75' 11"	50' 05"
Rasmine Maersk	TK	1986	D	120,000	557' 09"	75' 11"	50' 05"
Romo Maersk	TK	1986	D	120,000	557' 09"	75' 11"	50' 05"
IA-2 — A/S THOR DAHL SHIPPING, SANDEFFJORD, NORWAY							
Thor I	BC	1978	D	14,795	541' 08"	75' 02"	48' 03"
Thorscape	BC	1977	D	14,794	541' 08"	75' 02"	48' 03"
IA-3 — ALALMA SHIPPING CO.							
Ithaki	BC	1977	D	27,541	600' 06"	74' 08"	47' 01"
IA-4 — ALL TRUST SHIPPING CORP. S.A.							
Aghia Marina	BC	1975	D	10,178	426' 05"	60' 00"	32' 06'
IA-5 — ALTAIR OCEAN CORP.							
Golden Shield	TK	1982	D	80,000	416' 08"	65' 08"	36' 09"
IA-6 — AMERICAN CANADIAN CARIBBEAN LINE, INC., WARREN, RI							
Grande Prince	PA	1997	D	99*	182' 00"	39' 00"	9' 08"
Mayan Prince	PA	1992	D	683*	169' 07"	37' 06"	9' 08"
Niagara Prince	PA	1994	D	687*	174' 00"	40' 00"	14' 00"
IA-7 — ANANGEL SHIPPING ENTERPRISES S.A., PIRAEUS, GREECE							
Amilla	BC	1972	D	13,631	542' 01"	75' 05"	44' 08"
Anangel Ares	BC	1980	D	16,883	477' 04"	68' 11"	43' 00"
Anangel Atlas	BC	1984	D	16,978	477' 04"	68' 11"	43' 00"
Anangel Endeavour	BC	1978	D	23,202	539' 02"	75' 00"	44' 06"
Anangel Fidelity	BC	1979	D	23,198	539' 02"	75' 00"	44' 06"
Anangel Honesty	BC	1983	D	31,272	598' 07"	77' 05"	50' 06"
Anangel Honour	BC	1976	D	22,313	539' 02"	75' 00"	44' 06"
Anangel Hope	BC	1974	D	22,313	539' 02"	75' 00"	44' 06"
Anangel Horizon	BC	1977	D	25,822	584' 00"	76' 00"	47' 00"
Anangel Liberty	BC	1976	D	22,313	539' 02"	75' 00"	44' 06"
Anangel Might	BC	1978	D	23,131	539' 02"	75' 00"	44' 06"
Anangel Prosperity	BC	1976	D	22,313	539' 02"	75' 00"	44' 06"
Anangel Prudence	BC	1984	D	17,024	477' 04"	68' 11"	43' 00"
Anangel Sky	BC	1979	D	16,927	477' 04"	68' 11"	43' 00"
Anangel Spirit	BC	1978	D	23,202	539' 02"	75' 00"	44' 06"
Anangel Triumph	BC	1976	D	22,313	539' 02"	75' 00"	44' 06"
Anangel Victory	BC	1979	D	16,918	477' 04"	68' 11"	44' 06"
IA-8 — ANCORA INVESTMENT TRUST, INC.							
Wind	BC	1979	D	15,844	472' 10"	70' 05"	40' 00"
IA-9 — ANDEAN SHIP MANAGEMENT LTD.							
Pride of Donegal	BC	1982	D	17,330	518' 06"	75' 08"	44' 00"
IA-10 — ANDREADIS UK LTD., LONDON, ENGLAND							
Ira	BC	1979	D	26,854	591' 02"	75' 10"	45' 08"
Ivi	BC	1979	D	26,854	591' 04"	75' 10"	45' 08"
IA-11 — ANGLO-GEORGIAN SHIPPING CO. LTD.							
Uznadze	TK	1988	D	101,000	496' 05"	73' 07"	39' 10"
Vekua	TK	1987	D	101,000	496' 05"	73' 07"	39' 10"
IA-12 — ANT SEACLIPPER LTD.							
Alexis {ii}	BC	1984	D	26,795	599' 05"	73' 09"	46' 08"
IA-13 — ANTHONY NAVIGATION CO. LTD.							
Anthony	BC	1981	D	15,863			
IA-14 — ATLANTIS MANAGEMENT, INC.							
Atlantis Spirit	BC	1977	D	19,020	497' 10"	75' 00"	42' 00"
IA-15 — ATLANTSKA PLOVIDBA, DUBROVNIK,							
Cvijeta Zuzoric	BC	1974	D	15,398	599' 05"	73' 09"	46' 07"

Fleet No. and Name Vessel Name	Type of Ship	Year Built	Type of Engine	Cargo Cap. or Gross*	Length	Beam	Depth or Draft*
Hercegovina	BC	1977	D	18,426	644' 11"	75' 04"	47' 06"
Mljet	BC	1983	D	29,651	622' 01"	74' 11"	49' 10"
Petka	BC	1986	D	15,938	728' 09"	75' 11"	48' 05"
Plitvice	BC	1979	D	1,591	266' 05"	48' 09"	21' 08"
Ruder Boskovic	BC	1974	D	15,398	599' 05"	73' 09"	46' 07"

IA-16 — ATRIUM SHIPPING CO.

Aurora Topaz	BC	1982	D	29,268	639' 09"	75' 10"	46' 11"

IA-17 — AZOV SEA SHIPPING CO., MARIUPOL, UKRAINE

Avdeevka	BC	1977	D	16,576	570' 11"	75' 03"	47' 07"
Dobrush	BC	1982	D	28,136	644' 06"	75' 10"	46' 11"
Fatezh	BC	1981	D	7,805	399' 08"	57' 09"	32' 06"
General Blazhevich	BC	1981	D	7,805	399' 08"	57' 09"	32' 06"
Komsomolets	BC	1970	D	8,230	423' 05"	58' 06"	32' 03"
Kramatorsk	BC	1980	D	7,805	399' 08"	57' 09"	32' 06"
Makeevka	BC	1982	D	28,136	644' 06"	75' 07"	46' 11"
Mekhanik Aniskin	BC	1973	D	8,264	426' 04"	58' 06"	32' 03"
Sumy	BC	1978	D	28,321	539' 11"	75' 00"	44' 10"

IB-1 — B &N, BYLOCK & NORDSJOFRAKT AB

Bergon	BC	1978	D	3,380*	330' 10"	54' 02"	26' 03"
Bremon	BC	1976	D	7,806	393' 10"	54' 06"	33' 04"
Nordon	BC	1977	D	7,884			
Storon	BC	1975	D	7,301	470' 02"	61' 00"	33' 04"
Tofton	BC	1980	D	14,883			
Weston	BC	1979	D	14,938			

IB-2 — BLACK SEA SHIPPING CO., FLORIANA, MALTA

Donetskiy Komsomoltes	BC	1969	D	8,160	427' 00"	59' 00"	32' 00"
Kaleli Ana	BC	1976	D	8,307	349' 07"	53' 06"	27' 05"
Lynx	BC	1978	D	29,536	599' 09"	75' 11"	48' 07"
Petr Emtsov	BC	1975	D	13,541	532' 06"	72' 11"	43' 11"
Valeria Barsova	BC	1982	D	15,855			

IB-3 — BLACK STAR LINE LTD., TEMA, GHANA

Keta Lagoon	BC	1980	D	16,687	552' 00"	75' 05"	42' 09"
Sissili River	BC	1980	D	16,687	552' 00"	75' 05"	42' 09"
Tano River	BC	1980	D	16,687	552' 00"	75' 05"	42' 09"
Volta River	BC	1980	D	16,687	552' 00"	75' 05"	42' 09"

IB-4 — BRIDEN SHIPPING CO.

Blue Bill	BC	1977	D	30,242	621' 06"	75' 00"	47' 11"

IB-5 — BULKVANG A/S

Stalvang	BC	1970	D	950	251' 01"	40' 07"	13' 07"

IB-6 — BURMA NAVIGATION CORP.

Great Laker	BC	1987	D	28,358	590' 07"	75' 10"	48' 07"

IB-7 — BURSALIOGLU SANAYII VE TICARET LTD. SIRKETI

Turkay B.	BC	1975	D	5,194	386' 10"	59' 04"	29' 07"

IB-8 — BYZANTINE MARITIME CORP., PIRAEUS, GREECE

Barbara H	BC	1976	D	30,242	621' 08"	75' 00"	47' 11"
Ellie	BC	1979	D	26,984	622' 00"	75' 00"	49' 10"
Stella	BC	1974	D	21,712	510' 10"	75' 00"	44' 08"

IC-1 — C. VENINGA EN ZN. C.V.

Eemshorn	BC	1995	D	4,250	294' 00"	43' 03"	23' 04"

IC-2 — CAPELLE CHARTERING EN TRADING B.V.

Alecto	BC	1984	D	5,050			

IC-3 — CARSTEN REHDER (GMBH & CO.), HAMBURG, GERMANY

Astra Lift	BC	1977	D	3,861	307' 00"	54' 06"	26' 06"

Fleet No. and Name Vessel Name	Type of Ship	Year Built	Type of Engine	Cargo Cap. or Gross*	Length	Beam	Depth or Draft*
IC-4 — CERE HELLENIC SHIPPING ENTERPRISES, PIRAEUS, GREECE							
Agios Georgios	BC	1970	D	3,015	214' 10"	50' 02"	21' 08"
Catherine L.	BC	1970	D	16,285	600' 00"	75' 05"	48' 05"
George L.	BC	1975	D	14,786	597' 01"	75' 02"	48' 03"
Grace L.	BC	1971	D	16,306	600' 00"	75' 05"	48' 05"
Kalliopi L.	BC	1974	D	15,938	580' 04"	75' 09"	47' 08"
Larry L.	BC	1970	D	16,306	600' 00"	75' 05"	48' 05"
Maria G L	BC	1974	D	15,938	580' 04"	75' 09"	47' 08"
Marka L.	BC	1975	D	14,784	597' 01"	75' 02"	48' 03"
Pantazis L.	BC	1975	D	14,790	597' 02"	75' 02"	48' 03"
Patricia L.	BC	1971	D	16,306	600' 00"	75' 07"	48' 05"
Tatiana L.	BC	1975	D	16,306	597' 01"	74' 11"	48' 03"
IC-5 — CHARTWORLD SHIPPING CORP.							
Golden Sky	BC	1975	D	17,355	625' 06"	75' 00"	47' 11"
IC-6 — CLIPPER CRUISE LINES, INC., ST. LOUIS, MO							
Nantucket Clipper	PA	1984	D	96*	172' 06"	37' 00"	11' 06"
Yorktown Clipper	PA	1988	D	97*	224' 00"	40' 00"	12' 05"
IC-7 — COMPAGNIE TUNISIENNE DE NAVIGATION S.A.							
El Kef	BC	1982	D	26,965	599' 10"	75' 08"	46' 00"
IC-8 — CONTINENTAL COMMERCIAL ENTERPRISES, INC., MONROVIA, LIBERIA							
Trident Mariner	BC	1984	D	25,650	590' 03"	75' 04"	47' 07"
IC-9 — COSCO (HONG KONG) GROUP LTD., HONG KONG							
Aptmariner	BC	1979	D	31,000	619' 03"	75' 11"	47' 07"
Jing Hong Hai	BC	1976	D	28,863	594' 01"	76' 01"	47' 07"
Seadaniel	BC	1976	D	16,169	580' 10"	75' 00"	46' 04"
Rong Cheng	BC	1977	D	11,363	484' 07"	75' 06"	42' 08"
Yick Hua	BC	1984	D	28,086	584' 08"	75' 11"	48' 05"
IC-10 — CZECHOSLOVAK OCEAN SHIPPING INTERNATIONAL JOINST STOCK CO.							
Slapy	BC	1981	D	15,236	477' 06"	71' 00"	41' 00"
ID-1 — DALEX SHIPPING CO. S.A., PIRAEUS, GREECE							
Indian Express	BC	1982	D	17,279	509' 03"	74' 10"	43' 04"
ID-2 — DEN GULDING SOL (PANAMA) S.A.							
Inge	TK	1981	D	46,500	355' 10"	54' 02"	26' 11"
ID-3 — DENSAN SHIPPING CO. LTD.							
Gunay-A	BC	1981	D	30,900	617' 04"	76' 00"	47' 07"
Necat-A	BC	1981	D	28,645	655' 06"	75' 09"	45' 11"
ID-4 — DEXTON OVERSEAS S.A.							
Pauline Olivieri	BC	1976	D	20,950	521' 08"	75' 06"	44' 03"
ID-5 — DIANA SHIPPING AGENCIES S.A., PIRAEUS, GREECE							
M. Hass	BC	1977	D	25,364	532' 05"	74' 00"	43' 04"
Maple	BC	1977	D	19,020	497' 10"	75' 01"	42' 00"
Oak	BC	1981	D	21,951	509' 03"	75' 01"	44' 07"
Sea Laurel	BC	1977	D	25,364	532' 02"	75' 00"	43' 11"
ID-6 — DIXIE CARRIERS, INC., HARVEY, LA							
Dixie Avenger	TB	1941	D	199*	135' 00"	34' 00"	17' 00"
Dixie Commander	TB	1941	D	197*	120' 04"	35' 00"	22' 03"
Dixie Progress	TB	1968	D	164*	105' 11"	30' 00"	15' 11"
Courageous	TB	1982	D	161*	127' 00"	40' 00"	19' 07"
Invincible	TB	1979	D	180*	100' 00"	34' 10"	22' 06"
Louis Howland	DB	1978	B	21,524	462' 00"	82' 00"	30' 00"
Mary Cecilia	DB	1985	B	20,254	452' 06"	76' 00"	36' 00"
Mickie Birdsall	DB	1982	B	21,524	462' 00"	82' 00"	30' 00"
Miss Dott-O	DB	1979	B	21,524	462' 00"	82' 00"	30' 00"
Reliance	TB	1979	D	161*	127' 00"	40' 00"	19' 06"

Fleet No. and Name Vessel Name	Type of Ship	Year Built	Type of Engine	Cargo Cap. or Gross*	Length	Beam	Depth or Draft*
Resolute	TB	1982	D	161*	127' 00"	40' 00"	19' 06"
Vigilant	TB	1981	D	197*	109' 08"	33' 00"	15' 11"

IE-1 — EASTERN CANADA TOWING LTD., HALIFAX, NS

Point Carroll	TB	1973	D	366*	127' 00"	30' 05"	14' 05"
Point Chebucto	TT	1992	D	412*	110' 00"	33' 00"	17' 00"
Pointe Aux Basques	TB	1972	D	396*	105' 00"	33' 06"	19' 06"
Pointe Comeau	TT	1976	D	391*	104' 00"	40' 00"	19' 00"
Pointe Sept Iles	TB	1980	D	424*	105' 00"	34' 06"	19' 06"
Point Halifax	TT	1986	D	417*	110' 00"	36' 00"	19' 00"
Point Vibert	TB	1961	D	236*	96' 03"	28' 00"	14' 06"
Point Vigour	TB	1962	D	207*	98' 05"	26' 10"	13' 05"
Point Vim	TB	1962	D	207*	98' 05"	26' 10"	13' 05"

IE-2 — EGON OLDENDORFF (HONG KONG) LTD., LUBECK, GERMANY

Erna Oldendorff	BC	1994	D	18,355			
Helena Oldendorff	BC	1984	D	28,136	644' 06"	75' 10"	46' 11"
Regina Oldendorff	BC	1986	D	29,268	639' 09"	75' 10"	46' 11"
Rixta Oldendorff	BC	1984	D	29,268	639' 09"	75' 10"	46' 11"

IF-1 — FAR EASTERN SHIPPING CO.

Argut	BC	1990	D	3,600	311' 08"	51' 10"	25' 07"
Kapitan Milovzorov	BC	1975	D	14,204	497' 10"	69' 01"	38' 00"

IF-2 — FEDICIA INVESTMENTS LTD.

NST Challenge	BC	1984	D	29,192	593' 03"	75' 10"	47' 07"

IF-3 — FEDNAV INTERNATIONAL LTD., MONTREAL, PQ

Arctic	BC	1978	D	28,000	692' 04"	75' 05"	49' 05"
Arctic Ivik	TB		D	1,565*			
Arctic Nanook	TB	1982	D	841*	154' 07"	41' 03"	17' 04"
Arctic Nutsukpok	TB	1982	D	841*	154' 07"	41' 03"	17' 04"
ASL Sanderling	RR		D	14,689			
Cabot	RR		D	7,089			
Cicero	RR		D	7,132			
Cavallo	BC	1979	D	5,108	485' 07"	74' 02"	46' 02"
Cicero	RR		D	7,132			
Consensus Manitou	BC	1983	D	28,192	584' 08"	75' 11"	48' 05"
Federal Aalesund	BC	1984	D	30,674	589' 11"	75' 10"	50' 11"
Federal Agno	BC	1985	D	29,643	599' 09"	75' 11"	48' 07"
Federal Baffin	BC	1995	D	44,000			
Federal Bergen	BC	1984	D	29,159	593' 00"	76' 00"	47' 00"
Federal Calumet	BC	1996	D	41,500	656' 00"	77' 00"	
Federal Calliope	BC	1978	D	29,531	622' 07"	76' 05"	47' 05"
Federal Dora	BC	1978	D	29,531	622' 07"	76' 05"	47' 05"
Federal Franklin	BC	1995	D	44,000			
Federal Fraser	BC	1983	D	36,248	730' 00"	75' 09"	48' 00"
(Selkirk Settler '83-'91, Federal St. Louis '91-'91							
Federal Fuji	BC	1986	D	29,531	599' 09"	75' 11"	48' 07"
Federal Huron	BC	1978	D	18,818	659' 03"	76' 02"	46' 02"
Federal Kumano	BC		D	45,750			
Federal Maas	BC	1996	D	41,500	656' 00"	77' 00"	
Federal Mackenzie	BC	1983	D	36,248	730' 00"	75' 09"	48' 00"
(Canada Marquis '83-'91, Federal Richelieu '91-'91)							
Federal Matane	BC	1984	D	28,214	585' 00"	75' 10"	48' 05"
Federal Nord	BC	1981	D	29,466	589' 11"	76' 00"	47' 00"
Federal Oslo	BC	1985	D	29,462	601' 00"	76' 00"	48' 11"
Federal Pescadores	BC		D	40,864			
Federal Polaris	BC	1985	D	29,536	599' 09"	75' 11"	48' 07"
Federal Saguenay	BC	1996	D	41,500	656' 00"	77' 00"	
Federal St. Clair	BC	1978	D	38,450	734' 02"	76' 08"	47' 05"
Federal St. Laurent	BC	1996	D	41,500	656' 00"	77' 00"	

Golden Sky in the St. Clair River off Harsen's Island. (Willilam H. Merritt)

Maltese-registered Malinska upbound for Lake Superior. (Roger LeLievre)

Fleet No. and Name / Vessel Name	Type of Ship	Year Built	Type of Engine	Cargo Cap. or Gross*	Length	Beam	Depth or Draft*
Federal Vibeke	BC	1981	D	30,900	617' 04"	76' 00"	47' 07"
Federal Vigra	BC	1984	D	30,674	589' 11"	75' 10"	50' 11"
Handy Laker	BC	1984	D	17,065	584' 08"	75' 11"	48' 05"
Handymariner	BC	1978	D	31,000	619' 03"	75' 11"	47' 07"
Jeannie	BC	1977	D	27,541	600' 06"	74' 08"	47' 01"
Kalisti	BC	1977	D	26,620	600' 06"	75' 00"	47' 01"
Kalvik	IB	1983	D	4,391*	288' 00"		33' 00"
Lady Hamilton	BC	1983	D	34,500	730' 00"	75' 09"	48' 00"
(Saskatchewan Pioneer '83-'95							
Lake Carling	BC	1992	D	26,264	591' 01"	75' 09"	45' 07"
Lake Champlain	BC	1992	D	26,264	591' 01"	75' 09"	45' 07"
Lake Charles	BC	1990	D	26,209	591' 01"	75' 09"	45' 07"
Lake Erie	BC	1980	D	38,294	729' 11"	76' 02"	47' 01"
Lake Michigan	BC	1981	D	38,294	729' 11"	76' 03"	47' 01"
Lake Ontario	BC	1980	D	38,294	729' 11"	76' 03"	47' 01"
Lake Superior	BC	1981	D	38,294	729' 11"	76' 03"	47' 01"
Mosdeep	BC		D	49,000			
Trias	BC	1977	D	38,568	729' 11"	76' 00"	47' 00"
Mosdeep	BC		D	49,000			
Seaglory	BC	1977	D	29,212	593' 03"	75' 11"	47' 07"

IF-4 — FG SHIPPING OY AB, HELSINKI, FINLAND

Finnfighter	BC	1978	D				
Lotila	BC	1977	D	12,407			
Varjakka	BC	1979	D	12,385	522' 02"	70' 03"	41' 04"

IF-5 — FISA LTD.

Carl Metz	BC	1980	D	24,516	417' 05"	58' 11"	32' 00"

IF-6 — FLAMINGO BAY SHIPPING LTD.

Nea Doxa	BC	1984	D	30,900	617' 03"	76' 00"	47' 07"
Nea Elpis	BC	1978	D	29,300	593' 03"	76' 00"	47' 07"
Nea Tyhi	BC	1978	D	29,300	593' 03"	76' 00"	47' 07"

IF-7 — FOCAL SHIPPING CO.

Lyra	BC	1976	D	26,713	579' 11"	75' 00"	46' 03"

IF-8 — FRANCO COMPANIA NAVIERA S.A., ATHENS, GREECE

Odysseas I	BC	1974	D	26,952	583' 10"	75' 02"	48' 03"
Rhea	BC	1978	D	29,300	593' 10"	76' 00"	47' 07"

IF-9 — FREJA TANKERS A/S

Freja Nordic	TK	1980	D	81,000	406' 10"	60' 00"	35' 00"
Freja Scandic	TK	1981	D	82,500	405' 07"	59' 09"	32' 02"

IG-1 — GAJAH NAVIGATION SENDIRIAN BERHAD

Gajah Borneo	BC	1978	D	5,076	327' 05"	59' 02"	32' 00"

IG-2 — GODBY SHIPPING A/B

Julia	BC	1993	D	5,314	345' 04"	55' 11"	27' 00"

IG-3 — GOOD FAITH SHIPPING CO. S.A., PIRAEUS, GREECE

Amitie	AC	1970	D	20,139	485' 07"	74' 10"	44' 03"
Encouragement	BC	1974	D	27,004	537' 02"	75' 00"	47' 03"
Enterprise I	BC	1974	D	27,004	537' 02"	75' 00"	47' 03"
Epos	BC	1975	D	24,482	608' 04"	74' 10"	46' 04"
Euroreefer	BC	1982	D	5,862	302' 06"	53' 02"	22' 06"
Krissa	BC	1979	D	25,432	521' 00"	74' 02"	43' 08"
Mana	BC	1978	D	22,608	505' 03"	72' 10"	41' 02"
Ocean Grace	BC	1976	D	26,365	521' 08"	74' 10"	44' 04"
Ocean Lake	BC	1976	D	26,365	521' 08"	74' 10"	44' 04"
Sila	BC	1977	D	18,816	470' 06"	65' 00"	40' 06"

IG-4 — GORSE DOWN TANKERS, BARBADOS

Le Chene No. 1	TK	1961	D	64,580	430' 07"	52' 00"	28' 00"
J. Edouard Simard '61-76, Edouard Simard '67-'82							

Fleet No. and Name Vessel Name	Type of Ship	Year Built	Type of Engine	Cargo Cap. or Gross*	Length	Beam	Depth or Draft*
L' Orme No. 1	TK	1974	D	68,000	432' 09"	60' 00"	28' 00"
Leon Simard '74-'82							
Le Saule No. 1	TK	1970	D	63,000	412' 06"	52' 00"	28' 00"
Ludger Simard '70-'83							

IG-5 — GOURDOMICHALIS MARITIME S.A., PIRAEUS, GREECE

Kavo Alexandros	BC	1977	D	32,842	538' 01"	74' 10"	48' 05"
Kavo Mangalia	BC	1976	D	31,967	607' 08"	74' 10"	46' 05"
Kavo Sidero	BC	1976	D	32,959	592' 10"	75' 02"	47' 06"
Kavo Yerakas	BC	1981	D	25,845	585' 00"	75' 08"	45' 11"

IG-6 — GREAT CIRCLE SHIPPING AGENCY LTD.

Chada Naree	BC	1981	D	18,668	479' 03"	75' 01"	41' 04"
Fujisan Maru	BC	1976	D	16,883	481' 03"	75' 02"	40' 00"
Wana Naree	BC	1980	D	26,977	566' 00"	75' 11"	48' 05"

IH-1 — H.S.S. HOLLAND SHIP SERVICE B.V.

Alidon	BC	1978	D	6,110	274' 07"	56' 01"	33' 03"
Alsydon	BC	1979	D	6,110	274' 07"	56' 01"	33' 03"
Andrealon	BC	1978	D	6,110	274' 07"	56' 01"	33' 03"
Anita 1	BC	1979	D	7,800			
Cecilia I	BC	1982	D	6,110	276' 02"	56' 01"	33' 04"

IH-2 — HALCOUSSIS, Z. & G. CO. LTD., PIRAEUS, GREECE

Akti	BC	1977	D	29,300	593' 10"	76' 00"	47' 07"
Alexandria	BC	1981	D	29,466	589' 11"	76' 00"	47' 00"

IH-3 — HAPAG LLOYD, HAMBURG, GERMANY

Columbus	PA	1997	D	14,000*	492' 00"	70' 06"	

IH-4 — HARBOR BRANCH FOUNDATION, INC., FORT PIERCE, FL

Edwin Link	RV	1982	D	292*	168' 00"	38' 01"	14' 03"
Johnson Sea-Link I	SS	1971	D/DC	1,200*	23' 07"	8' 03"	7' 06"
Johnson Sea-Link II	SS	1971	D/DC	1,200*	23' 07"	8' 03"	7' 06"
Sea Diver	RV	1959	D	162*	100' 01"	22' 06"	9' 01"
Seaward Johnson	RV	1984	D	299*	175' 09"	36' 00"	16' 00"

IH-5 — HELLENIC STAR SHIPPING

Winter Star	BC	1978	D	25,984	655' 06"	75' 09"	46' 00"

IH-6 — HERMAN BUSS K.G.

Altair	BC	1985	D	2,814	322' 07"	44' 04"	23' 00"
Edda	BC	1985	D	2,812	322' 07"	44' 04"	23' 00"

II-1 — IMPERIAL OIL LTD., ESSO PETROLEUM CANADA DIVISION, DARTMOUTH, NS

A. G. Farquharson	TK	1969	D	53,000	400' 06"	54' 02"	26' 05"
(Texaco Chief {2} '69-'87							
Imperial Acadia	TK	1966	D	84,000	440' 00"	60' 00"	31' 00"
Imperial Bedford	TK	1969	D	118,000	485' 05"	70' 02"	33' 03"
Imperial Dartmouth	TK	1970	D	15,265	205' 06"	40' 00"	16' 00"
Imperial Lachine {2}	TK	1963	D	9,385	175' 00"	36' 00"	14' 00"
Imperial St. Clair	TK	1974	D	106,000	435' 00"	74' 00"	32' 00"
Imperial St. Lawrence {2}	TK	1977	D	78,000	431' 05"	65' 07"	35' 05"
Texaco Brave {2} '77-'86, Le Brave '86-'96							

II-2 — INTERMOTION SHIPPING LTD.

Diana	BC	1971	D	28,855	593' 02"	75' 11"	47' 07"

II-3 — IONIA SHIPPING & TRADING CORP., PIRAEUS, GREECE

Arma	BC	1981	D	15,721	472' 10"	70' 05"	40' 01"

II-4 — IRVINGDALE SHIPPING LTD., SAINT JOHN, NB

Atlantic Cedar	TB	1974	D	492*	151' 01"	35' 06"	17' 08"
Irving Cedar '74-'96							
Atlantic Fir	TB	1995	D	290*	101' 00"	36' 06"	17' 00"
Irving Fir '95-'96							
Atlantic Hemlock	TB	1996	D	290*	101' 00"	36' 06"	12' 06"
Irving Hemlock '96-'96							
Atlantic Spruce	TB	1994	D	290*	101' 00"	36' 06"	12' 06"

Fleet No. and Name Vessel Name	Type of Ship	Year Built	Type of Engine	Cargo Cap. or Gross*	Length	Beam	Depth or Draft*
Irving Spruce '94-'96							
Irving Beech	TB	1983	D	294*	104' 02"	30' 03"	13' 02"
Irving Birch	TT	1967	D	827*	162' 03"	38' 02"	19' 08"
Irving Elm	TB	1980	D	427*	116' 01"	31' 06"	18' 08"
Irving Maple	TB	1966	D	487*	126' 03"	32' 06"	17' 04"
Irving Timber	RR	1978	D	7,087	415' 00"	66' 03"	38' 05"
Wellington Kent	TK	1980	D	48,741	433' 11"	67' 04"	30' 04"
Irving Nordic '80-'94							

IJ-1 — JADROPLOV INTERNATIONAL MARITIME TRANSPORT, SPLIT, CROATIA

Botic	BC	1976	D	20,927	521' 08"	74' 10"	44' 04"
Marul	BC		D				
Ciovo	BC	1977	D	9,912	479' 03"	73' 02"	40' 10"
Hope I	BC	1982	D	30,900	617' 03"	76' 00"	47' 07"
Solta	BC	1984	D	29,651	622' 01"	74' 11"	49' 10"

IJ-2 — JAN WIND SHIPPING LTD.

Lida	BC	1974	D	1,448	214' 03"	35' 05"	16' 01"

IJ-3 — JEBSENS SHIP MANAGEMENT (BERGEN) AS

Brunto	BC	1977	D	7,972	478' 07"	64' 04"	35' 00"
Finnsnes	BC	1978	D	8,098	441' 04"	67' 11"	37' 09"
Frines	BC	1978	D	8,098	441' 04"	67' 11"	37' 09"
Fullnes	BC	1978	D	8,116	441' 04"	68' 00"	37' 09"
Furunes	BC	1979	D	8,116	441' 04"	68' 00"	37' 09"
General Cabal	BC	1976	D	7,952	477' 04"	64' 03"	34' 11"

IK-1 — KISHINCHAAND CHELLARAM MARITIME AGENCIES LTD.

Darya Kamal	BC	1983	D	30,900	617' 04"	76' 00"	47' 07"
Darya Ma	BC	1983	D	30,900	617' 04"	76' 00"	47' 00"

IK-2 — KNUD I LARSEN

Barbara E.	BC	1982	D	4,499	336' 04"	57' 07"	29' 07"

IK-3 — KNUTSEN O.A.S. SHIPPING A.S.

Sidsel Knutsen	TK	1993	D	112,000	533' 02"	75' 06"	48' 07"
Torill Knutsen	TK	1990	D	112,000	533' 02"	75' 06"	48' 07"
Turid Knutsen	TK	1993	D	112,000	533' 02"	75' 06"	48' 07"

IL-1 — LARSEN & TOUBRO LTD.

Holck-Larson	BC	1981	D	16,069	627' 07"	75' 03"	44' 03"
LT Argosy	BC	1984	D	17,825	606' 11"	75' 11"	48' 01"
LT Odyssey	BC	1984	D	17,825	606' 11"	75' 11"	48' 01"
Mangal Desai	BC	1983	D				
Soren Toubro	BC	1981	D	15,708	627' 07"	75' 03"	44' 03"

IL-2 — LATVIAN SHIPPING CO.

Juris Avots	RR	1983	D	9,749	501' 00"	63' 01"	43' 00"

IL-3 — LAURIN MARITIME (AMERICA), INC.

Aurum	TK	1982	D	135,000	445' 04"	62' 05"	33' 02"
Mountain Blossom	TK	1986	D	160,000	527' 07"	74' 11"	39' 04"
Nordic Blossom	TK	1981	D	151,580	505' 03"	74' 07"	45' 04"
Sunny Blossom	TK	1986	D	160,000	527' 07"	74' 11"	39' 05"

IL-4 — LEONHARDT & BLUMBERG, HAMBURG, GERMANY

Hans Leonhardt	BC	1977	D	12,010	424' 01"	64' 05"	34' 06"

IL-5 — LINK LINE LTD., PIREAUS, GREECE

Beluga	BC	1977	D	23,725	585' 02"	74' 04"	44' 02"

IL-6 — LITHUANIAN SHIPPING CO.

Kapitonas A. Lucka	BC	1980	D	14,550	479' 08"	67' 09"	42' 04"
Kapitonas Andzejauskas	BC	1978	D	14,550	479' 08"	67' 09"	42' 04"
Kapitonas Chromcov	BC	1976	D	14,550	479' 08"	67' 09"	42' 04"
Kapitonas Domerika	BC	1979	D	14,550	479' 08"	67' 09"	42' 04"
Kapitonas Duagirdis	BC	1976	D	14,550	479' 08"	67' 09"	42' 04"

Fleet No. and Name Vessel Name	Type of Ship	Year Built	Type of Engine	Cargo Cap. or Gross*	Length	Beam	Depth or Draft*
Kapitonas Kaminskas	BC	1978	D	14,550	479' 08"	67' 09"	42' 04"
Kapitonas Marcinkus	BC	1977	D	14,550	479' 08"	67' 09"	42' 04"
Kapitonas Sevcenko	BC	1977	D	14,320	479' 08"	67' 09"	42' 04"
Kapitonas Stulov	BC	1980	D	14,550	479' 08"	67' 09"	42' 04"
Kapitonas Stulpinas	BC	1981	D	14,550	479' 08"	67' 09"	42' 04"

IL-7 — LOGISTEC NAVIGATION, INC., MONTREAL, PQ

Lucien Paquin	BC	1969	D	26,158	459' 05"	70' 06"	42' 01"

IL-8 — LYNX SHIPPING CO.

Island Gem	BC	1984	D	28,192	584' 08"	76' 02"	48' 05"

IM-1 — MALTA CROSS SHIPPING CO. LTD., FLOARIANA, REPUBLIC OF MALTA

Karlobag	BC	1980	D	32,656	634' 04"	75' 01"	46' 05"
Slavonija	BC	1980	D	32,656	634' 04"	75' 02"	46' 05"
Malinska	BC	1987	D	23,306	729' 00"	75' 11"	48' 05"
Omisalj	BC	1987	D	23,306	729' 00"	75' 11"	48' 05"

IM-2 — MAMMOET SHIPPING (NETH. ANT.) B.V.

Project Americas	RR	1979	D	9,768	455' 10"	70' 08"	42' 08"
Project Europa	RR	1983	D	9,857	456' 02"	75' 02"	42' 08"
Titan Scan	RR	1982	D	6,902	404' 08"	67' 11"	33' 10"

IM-3 — MANILA SEALINK CORP.

Rubin Hawk	BC	1995	D	18,315	487' 11"	74' 10"	40' 00"

IM-4 — MARINE ATLANTIC, INC., MONCTON, NB

Abegweit	CF	1982	D	13,483	403' 09"	71' 02"	20' 04"
Atlantic Freighter	CF	1978	D	12,162	498' 03"	71' 06"	24' 00"
Blue Nose	CF	1973	D	6,419	412' 01"	77' 02"	18' 01"
Caribou	CF	1986	D	13,000	590' 07"	84' 04"	21' 05"
Holiday Island	CF	1971	D	3,037	323' 00"	68' 06"	16' 05"
John Hamilton Gray	CF	1968	D	11,260	402' 09"	69' 06"	20' 04"
Joseph & Clara Smallwood	CF	1990	D	13,000	590' 07"	84' 04"	21' 05"
Marine Evangeline	CF	1974	D	2,794	363' 04"	57' 09"	40' 06"
Princess of Acadia	CF	1971	D	10,051	482' 07"	66' 01"	15' 01"
Sir Robert Bond	CF	1975	D	10,433	446' 06"	71' 06"	16' 08"
Taverner	BC	1962	D	1,135	189' 05"	38' 09"	12' 05"
Vacationland	CF	1971	D	3,037	323' 00"	68' 06"	16' 05"

IM-5 — MARINE MANAGEMENT SERVICES LTD., PIRAEUS, GREECE

Gonio	TK	1983	D	120,152	496' 05"	73' 07"	39' 11"
Kobuleti	TK	1985	D	120,152	496' 05"	73' 07"	39' 11"

IM-6 — MARMARAS NAVIGATION LTD.

Proussa	BC	1979	D	18,739	504' 07"	75' 00"	41' 01"
Redestos	BC	1977	D	19,020	520' 00"	73' 06"	43' 00"

IM-7 — MEDITERRANEA DI NAVIGAZIONE S.R.L.

Snark	TK	1981	D	135,850	425' 03"	63' 08"	28' 09"

IM-8 — MELADON SHIPPING, INC.

Kreon	BC	1970	D	30,781	645' 01"	75' 05"	47' 06"

IM-9 — METRON SHIPPING & AGENCIES S.A.

Pontokratis	BC	1981	D	29,466	590' 02"	75' 11"	47' 07"
Pontoporos	BC	1984	D	29,261	580' 09"	75' 02"	47' 06"

IM-10 — MID MED SHIPPING LTD.

Margaret John	BC	1977	D	7,583	379' 01"	57' 02"	28' 06"

IM-11 — MTO MARITIME S.A.

Astral Ocean	BC	1985	D	28,214	584' 08"	75' 11"	48' 05"

IM-12 — MURMANSK SHIPPING CO.

Admiral Ushakov	BC	1979	D	13,752	531' 07"	75' 01"	44' 05"
Dmitriy Donskoy	BC	1977	D	13,567	531' 10"	75' 02"	44' 05"
Dmitriy Pozharskiy	BC	1977	D	13,567	531' 10"	75' 02"	44' 05"
Fastov	BC	1979	D	7,810	399' 08"	57' 09"	32' 06"

Fleet No. and Name Vessel Name	Type of Ship	Year Built	Type of Engine	Cargo Cap. or Gross*	Length	Beam	Depth or Draft*
Ivan Bogun	BC	1981	D	13,522	531' 10"	75' 02"	44' 04"
Kapitan Bochek	BC	1982	D	13,522	531' 10"	75' 02"	44' 04"
Kapitan Chukhchin	BC	1981	D	13,522	531' 10"	75' 02"	44' 04"
Kapitan Kudley	BC	1983	D	13,522	531' 10"	75' 02"	44' 04"
Mikhail Kutuzov	BC	1979	D	13,572	531' 10"	75' 02"	44' 05"
Stepan Razin	BC	1980	D	13,572	531' 10"	75' 02"	44' 05"

IN-1 — NAVIERA POSEIDON

Areito	BC	1977	D	10,057	485' 07"	67' 07"	41' 01"
South Islands	BC	1986	D	9,112	472' 05"	67' 02"	38' 07"

IN-2 — NAVIGATION MARITIME BULGARE, VARNA, BULGARIA

Balkan	BC	1975	D	24,386	607' 07"	74' 10"	46' 05"
Milan Kamak	BC	1979	D	24,482	607' 04"	75' 00"	46' 04"

IN-3 — NAVRON SHIPPING CO.

Hagieni	BC	1982	D	8,750			
Razboieni	BC	1982	D	15,555	520' 08"	73' 10"	43' 04"
Zarnesti	BC	1983	D	4,620	347' 10"	48' 08"	27' 11"

IN-4 — NEABULK SHIPPING CO. LTD.

Seapearl II	BC	1974	D	26,641	580' 09"	75' 03"	47' 06"
Tim Buck	BC	1983	D	14,009	531' 10"	75' 02"	44' 04"

IN-5 — NOMADIC SHIPPING A/S, MINDE, NORWAY

Nomadic Patria	BC	1978	D	17,160	511' 06"	73' 11"	45' 10"

IN-6 — NORDBULK SHIPPING CO. LTD., LIMASOL, CYPRUS

Nordmark	BC	1975	D	4,616	385' 09"	59' 03"	29' 06"

IN-7 — NORTH ISLAND SHIPPING CO.

North Islands	BC	1987	D	15,136	472' 06"	67' 02"	38' 07"

IN-8 — NORTHERN SHIPPING CO.

Kapitan Alekseyev	BC		D				
Kapitan Lazarev	BC		D				
Kapitan Zamyatin	BC	1976	D	14,200	497' 10"	69' 01"	38' 00"
Vasiliy Musinskiy	BC	1974	D	14,200	497' 10"	69' 01"	38' 00"

IN-9 — NORTHUMBERLAND FERRIES LTD., CHARLOTTETOWN, PEI

Lord Selkirk	CF	1958	D	1,834	260' 07"	54' 07"	18' 01"
Prince Edward	CF	1972	D	1,772	250' 04"	55' 04"	18' 01"
Prince Nova	CF	1964	D	1,765	250' 01"	55' 04"	18' 01"

IO-1 — OCEAN BEAUTY NAVIGATION CORP.

Ocean Priti	BC	1982	D	26,795	599' 05"	73' 09"	46' 08"

IO-2 — OCEAN VIEW SHIPPING CORP., MONROVIA, LIBERIA

Beta Fortune	BC	1976	D	24,516	559' 06"	75' 00"	45' 04"
Beta Luck	BC	1976	D	24,130	559' 06"	75' 00"	45' 03"

IO-3 — OCEANFREE MARINE CO. LTD.

Hellenic Confidence	BC	1977	D	17,694	479' 00"	73' 03"	40' 10"

IO-4 — OLYMPIC MARITIME S.A., MONTE CARLO, MONACO

Calliroe Patronicola	BC	1985	D	29,643	599' 09"	75' 11"	48' 07"
Olympic Harmony	BC	1973	D	15,278	603' 04"	74' 04"	46' 09"
Olympic Hope	BC	1973	D	15,478	603' 04"	74' 04"	46' 09"
Olympic Melody	BC	1984	D	17,879	599' 09"	75' 11"	48' 07"
Olympic Mentor	BC	1984	D	29,643	599' 09"	75' 11"	48' 07"
Olympic Merit	BC	1985	D	29,643	599' 09"	75' 11"	48' 07"
Olympic Miracle	BC	1984	D	29,643	599' 09"	75' 11"	48' 07"
Olympic Palm	BC	1965	D	15,577	576' 01"	75' 02"	36' 00"
Olympic Peace	BC	1969	D	15,688	576' 01"	75' 02"	36' 00"
Olympic Pearl	BC	1965	D	15,671	576' 01"	75' 02"	36' 00"
Olympic Pegasus	BC	1965	D	15,577	576' 01"	75' 02"	36' 00"
Olympic Phaeton	BC	1965	D	15,179	576' 01"	75' 02"	36' 00"
Olympic Pioneer	BC	1966	D	15,625	576' 01"	75' 02"	36' 00"
Olympic Power	BC	1968	D	15,809	576' 01"	75' 02"	36' 00"

Fleet No. and Name Vessel Name	Type of Ship	Year Built	Type of Engine	Cargo Cap. or Gross*	Length	Beam	Depth or Draft*
Olympic Prestige	BC	1969	D	15,808	576' 01"	75' 02"	36' 00"
Olympic Pride	BC	1967	D	15,697	576' 01"	75' 02"	36' 00"
Olympic Progress	BC	1969	D	15,688	576' 01"	75' 02"	36' 00"

IP-1 — PACC SHIP MANAGERS PTE. LTD., SINGAPORE, MALAYSIA

Ikan Selayang	BC	1981	D	29,466	590' 02"	76' 00"	47' 07"
Ikan Sepat	BC	1984	D	25,650	590' 03"	75' 04"	47' 07"
Ikan Tamban	BC	1980	D	21,239	477' 04"	68' 11"	43' 00"
Ulloa	BC	1983	D	28,126	584' 08"	75' 11"	48' 05"
Union	BC	1984	D	28,192	584' 08"	75' 11"	48' 05"

IP-2 — PACIFIC SHIP MANAGERS SENDIRIAN BERHAD, SELANGOR DARUL EHSAN, MALAYSIA

Alam Sejahtera	BC	1985	D	29,223	599' 09"	75' 10"	48' 07"
Alam Sempurna	BC	1984	D	27,650	584' 08"	75' 11"	48' 05"
Alam Senang	BC	1984	D	27,654	584' 08"	75' 11"	48' 05"
Alam Tenteram	BC	1979	D	16,902	477' 04"	68' 11"	43' 00"
Alam United	BC	1984	D	26,793	584' 08"	75' 11"	48' 05"

IP-3 — PAPHIAN SHIPPING CO. LTD.

Serenade	BC	1972	D	6,341	317' 09"	52' 07"	30' 03"

IP-4 — PARAKOU SHIPPING LTD.

Steel Flower	BC	1977	D	35,910	729' 11"	76' 00"	47' 00"

IP-5 — PEARLBOAT MARINE CO. LTD.

Europegasus	BC	1972	D	19,515	558' 11"	74' 11"	46' 06"

IP-6 — PERGAMOS SHIPPING CO. S.A., PIRAEUS, GREECE

Adventure	AC	1971	D	14,938	466' 09"	65' 00"	40' 06"
Akadan Bulk	BC	1978	D	26,795	599' 05"	73' 09"	46' 08"

IP-7 — POLISH STEAMSHIP CO., SZCZECIN, POLAND

Odranes	BC	1992	D	13,790	470' 07"	67' 07"	37' 03"
Pomorze Zachodnie	BC	1985	D	28,552	591' 04"	75' 11"	45' 08"
Wislanes	BC	1992	D	13,790	470' 07"	67' 07"	37' 03"
Ziemia Bialostocka	BC	1972	D	24,482	607' 04"	75' 00"	46' 04"
Ziemia Chelminska	BC	1984	D	28,350	591' 04"	75' 11"	45' 08"
Ziemia Gnieznienska	BC	1985	D	28,552	591' 04"	75' 11"	45' 08"
Ziemia Krakowska	BC	1971	D	26,874	617' 07"	75' 09"	46' 02"
Ziemia Olsztynska	BC	1973	D	24,482	607' 04"	75' 00"	46' 04"
Ziemia Suwalska	BC	1984	D	28,350	591' 04"	75' 11"	45' 08"
Ziemia Tarnowska	BC	1985	D	28,552	591' 04"	75' 11"	45' 08"
Ziemia Zamojska	BC	1984	D	28,350	591' 04"	75' 11"	45' 08"

IP-8 — POLSTEAM S.A.

Fjordnes	BC	1978	D	16,500	490' 03"	75' 06"	39' 08"
Fossnes	BC	1995	D	16,500			

IP-9 — PRESENT SHIPPING LTD.

Laserbeam	BC	1974	D	26,795	599' 05"	73' 09"	46' 08"

IP-10 — PRIME ORIENT SHIPPING S.A.

Luna Verde	BC	1986	D	28,350	591' 06"	75' 10"	48' 07"

IP-11 — PROJECT SHIPPING

Marinik G.	BC	1972	D	25,635	591' 06"	75' 02"	45' 01"

IP-12 — PROSPERITY BAY SHIPPING CO.

Anna {2}	BC	1976	D	27,541	600' 06"	74' 08"	47' 01"

IP-13 — PYRSOS MANAGING CO.

Anax	BC	1979	D	29,609	622' 00"	74' 10"	49' 10"
Anemi	BC	1978	D	14,840	469' 02"	65' 00"	40' 06"
Anemone	BC	1979	D	16,909	477' 04"	68' 11"	43' 00"
Clipper Amaryllis	BC	1983	D	23,441	510' 00"	75' 00"	46' 05"
Clipper Amethyst	BC	1978	D	23,165	539' 02"	75' 00"	46' 05"

IR-1 — RAMILU TRANSPORTES S.A.

Maisi	BC	1977	D	15,193	485' 07"	67' 09"	41' 01"

Federal Bergen at Port Huron in August, 1996. The Blue Water Bridge's new span can be seen at right. (David Maize)

Fleet No. and Name Vessel Name	Type of Ship	Year Built	Type of Engine	Cargo Cap. or Gross*	Length	Beam	Depth or Draft*
IR-2 — RAMSES MARINE LTD.							
Kathrin	BC	1981	D	11,122	392' 01"	65' 09"	33' 00"
IR-3 — REDERI DONSOTANK A/B							
Credo	BC	1978	D	6,917	449' 02"	56' 00"	36' 01"
IR-4 — REINAUER TRANSPORTATION CO., STATEN ISLAND, NY							
Bert Reinauer II	TK	1938	D	85,000	286' 07"	43' 01"	17' 04"
BFT No. 50	TK	1972	B	89,524	290' 00"	60' 00"	19' 04"
Dace Reinauer	TB	1968	D	84*	108' 10"	30' 06"	14' 06"
Franklin Reinauer	TB	1983	D	96*	85' 00"	28' 00"	12' 00"
Fulton	TK	1969	B	87,654	242' 07"	43' 05"	14' 10"
George Morris	TK	1982	B	96,524	325' 00"	60' 00"	22' 00"
Joanne Reinauer III	TB	1970	D	160*	96' 02"	27' 00"	13' 09"
John Reinauer	TB	1969	D	144*	92' 02"	27' 06"	12' 03"
Morgan Reinaver	TB	1981	D	184*	126' 00"	34' 00"	16' 00"
Peter R. Hearne	TK	1971	B	98,762	227' 00"	43' 00"	14' 09"
Richmond	TK	1975	B	97,685	251' 06"	60' 00"	17' 00"
Rockland	TK	1975	B	97,364	316' 06"	59' 05"	26' 02"
Stephan Reinauer	TB	1970	D	151*	110' 00"	31' 00"	16' 00"
Stephan Scott	TB	1967	D	188*	96' 03"	27' 01"	13' 10"
Westchester	TK	1975	B	97,364	316' 06"	59' 05"	26' 02"
Zachery Reinauer	TB	1971	D	271*	100' 00"	28' 00"	14' 11"
IR-5 — RIGEL SCHIFFAHRTS GMBH & CO. KG							
Ledastern	TK	1993	D	110,500	405' 11"	58' 01"	34' 09"
Diamond Star	TK	1992	D	110,500	405' 11"	58' 01"	34' 09"
Emerald Star	TK	1992	D	110,500	405' 11"	58' 01"	34' 09"
Jade Star	TK	1993	D	110,500	405' 11"	58' 01"	34' 09"
IR-6 — RISING STAR SHIPPING S.A.							
Lake Challenger	BC	1985	D	28,192	584' 08"	75' 11"	48' 05"
IS-1 — S. FRANGOULIS SHIP MANAGEMENT LTD.							
Kostantis F.	BC	1977	D	15,202	472' 05"	69' 08"	40' 07"
IS-2 — SCIO SHIPPING, INC., NEW YORK, NY							
Island Skipper	BC	1984	D	28,192	584' 08"	76' 02"	48' 05"
Island Sky	BC	1976	D	24,188	512' 06"	74' 02"	42' 04"
IS-3 — SEAARLAND SHIPPING MANAGEMENT G.M.B.H., VILLACH, AUSTRIA							
Allegra	TK	1986	D	135,025	536' 06"	75' 06"	37' 09"
Conny	TK	1984	D	135,025	536' 06"	75' 06"	37' 09"
Giacinta	TK	1984	D	135,025	536' 06"	75' 06"	37' 09"
Grazia	TK	1987	D	135,025	536' 06"	75' 06"	37' 09"
Peonia	BC	1983	D	28,136	647' 08"	75' 10"	46' 11"
Punica	BC	1983	D	28,136	647' 08"	75' 10"	46' 11"
IS-4 — SEACOT SHIPTRADING LTD.							
Nyanza	BC	1978	D	16,923	497' 10"	71' 08"	40' 09"
IS-5 — SEASTAR NAVIGATION CO. LTD.							
Polydefkis	BC	1976	D	30,244	621' 06"	75' 00"	47' 11"
Praxitelis	BC	1976	D	30,242	621' 06"	75' 00"	47' 11"
IS-6 — SEATRANS ANS							
Trans Arctic	TK	1991	D	101,500	383' 02"	57' 05"	31' 06"
IS-7 — SHINWA MARINE CORP.							
Liberty Sky	BC	1985	D	28,192	584' 08"	75' 11"	48' 05"
IS-8 — SIDEMAR TRASPORTI COSTIERI S.P.A., GENOA, ITALY							
Aquarius	BC	1978	D	6,227	397' 00"	59' 00"	32' 10"
Cygnus	BC	1987	D	28,907	610' 03"	75' 11"	46' 11"
Galassia	BC	1987	D	35,734	610' 05"	75' 11"	46' 11"
Gemini	BC	1986	D	35,734	610' 05"	75' 11"	46' 11"
Sagittarius	BC	1987	D	35,734	610' 03"	75' 06"	45' 11"

Fleet No. and Name Vessel Name	Type of Ship	Year Built	Type of Engine	Cargo Cap. or Gross*	Length	Beam	Depth or Draft*
IS-9 — SILVER SHIPPING LTD.							
Concorde	TK	1975	D	44,185	319' 11"	52' 06"	24' 11"
IS-10 — SOCIETA PER LA MOVIMENTAZIONE DEL CARBONE							
C. Martin	BC	1978	D	16,711	537' 11"	75' 03"	38' 09"
IS-11 — SOCIETE ANONYME MONEGASQUE D' ADMINISTRATION MARITIME ET AERIENNE							
Alpha	BC	1976	D	16,139	580' 00"	75' 02"	47' 11"
Haight	BC	1977	D	16,008	580' 10"	75' 04"	47' 07"
Hydra	BC	1977	D	16,278	567' 08"	74' 10"	48' 05"
IS-12 — SOCIETE NAT. DE TRANS. MARITIME. & COMPAGNIE NAT. ALGERIENNE DE NAV. MAR.							
Nememcha	BC	1978	D	26,854	565' 02"	75' 11"	47' 01"
IS-13 — SOHTORIK DENIZCILIK VE TICARET A.S., ISTANBUL, TURKEY							
Duden	BC	1981	D	26,975	567' 07"	74' 11"	48' 05"
Eber	BC	1978	D	18,739	504' 07"	75' 01"	41' 00"
Med Transporter	BC	1973	D	12,982	513' 01"	75' 05"	44' 02"
IS-14 — SPACEWAY SHIPPING LTD.							
Trust	BC	1976	D	25,635	581' 04"	74' 11"	47' 11"
IS-15 — SPETSAI SHIPPING CO. LTD.							
Clipper Majestic	BC	1979	D	17,154	477' 04"	68' 11"	43' 00"
IS-16 — SPHINX NAVIGATION LTD.							
Elikon	BC	1980	D	16,106	582' 00"	75' 02"	44' 04"
IS-17 — SPLIETHOFF'S BEVACHTINGGSKANTOR B.V.							
Bickersgracht	BC	1981	D	3,488	263' 02"	52' 10"	34' 06"
Bontegracht	BC	1981	D	3,437	263' 02"	52' 10"	34' 06"
Parkgracht	BC	1986	D	9,656	371' 02"	62' 03"	37' 01"
Poolgracht	BC	1986	D	9,673	371' 02"	62' 03"	37' 01"
IS-18 — STAR SHIPPING CORP.							
Gur Master	BC	1978	D	15,720	492' 00"	69' 00"	40' 03"
IS-19 — STARAI SHIPPING S.A.							
Liski	BC	1983	D	5,869	392' 01"	60' 09"	31' 03"
IS-20 — STARLADY MARINE LTD.							
Coral	BC	1981	D	24,482	605' 08"	75' 00"	46' 04"
IS-21 — STEPHENSON CLARKE SHIPPING LTD.							
Durrington	BC	1981	D	11,990	451' 05"	61' 03"	35' 01"
IS-22 — STEVNSLAND SCHIFFSBETRIEB G.M.B.H. & CO. K.G.							
Stevnsland	BC	1972	D	2,510	290' 04"	45' 05"	26' 03"
IS-23 — STOLT NIELSON TANKERS, INC., GREENWICH, CA							
Stolt Alliance	TK	1985	D	84,500	404' 06"	65' 08"	36' 09"
Stolt Aspiration	TK	1987	D	84,000	422' 11"	66' 04"	36' 01"
Stolt Taurus	TK	1985	D	84,500	404' 06"	67' 04"	36' 09"
IS-24 — STREAM CLIPPER SHIPPING CO. LTD.							
Riomar	BC	1982	D	7,073	446' 09"	63' 02"	35' 10"
IS-25 — SUNNY SHORE SHIPPING FINANCE							
Lady Emily	BC	1988	D	16,916	520' 11"	74' 11"	44' 00"
IS-26 — SURRENDRA OVERSEAS LTD., BOMBAY, INDIA							
APJ Angad	BC		D				
APJ Anjli	BC	1982	D	27,890	577' 05"	75' 10"	47' 11"
APJ Priti	BC	1976	D	16,745	470' 05"	71' 10"	40' 01"
APJ Sushma	BC	1983	D	27,890	577' 05"	75' 10"	47' 11"
IT-1 — TALENT MARINE CORP.							
Fuji Braves	TK	1983	D	82,500	405' 07"	59' 09"	32' 02"

Fleet No. and Name Vessel Name	Type of Ship	Year Built	Type of Engine	Cargo Cap. or Gross*	Length	Beam	Depth or Draft*
IT-2 — TANKER TRANSPORT SERVICES N.V.							
Crestar	TK	1981	D	42,000	265' 04"	42' 08"	24' 01"
IT-3 — TARGET MARINE S.A., PIRAEUS, GREECE							
Corithian Trader	BC	1973	D	26,965	599' 10"	73' 06"	46' 07"
Ranger	BC	1976	D	26,620	600' 06"	75' 00"	47' 01"
IT-4 — TEO SHIPPING CORP.							
Antalina	BC	1984	D	28,192	584' 08"	75' 11"	48' 05"
Erikousa Wave	BC	1986	D	28,082	600' 08"	73' 08"	46' 08"
Marilis T.	BC	1984	D	28,192	584' 08"	75' 11"	48' 05"
Sevilla Wave	BC	1986	D	28,082	600' 08"	73' 08"	46' 08"
Vamand Wave	BC	1985	D	28,082	600' 08"	73' 08"	46' 08"
IT-5 — THAUMAS SHIPPING CO. S.A.							
Roubini	BC	1982	D	18,494	481' 04"	75' 01"	41' 04"
IT-6 — THE SHIPPING CORP. OF INDIA LTD., BOMBAY, INDIA							
Jhulelal	TK	1981	D	151,580	505' 03"	74' 06"	45' 03"
Lok Maheshwari	BC	1986	D	33,587	605' 03"	75' 01"	47' 03"
Lok Prakash	BC	1989	D	26,716	606' 11"	75' 04"	47' 03"
Lok Pratap	BC	1993	D	26,450	605' 09"	75' 04"	47' 04"
Lok Rajeshwari	BC	1988	D	26,639	605' 01"	75' 04"	47' 03"
State of Haryana	BC	1983	D	22,332	465' 06"	74' 10"	47' 03"
IT-7 — THENAMARIS SHIPS MANAGEMENT, INC., ATHENS, GREECE							
Baronia	BC	1982	D	29,368	646' 10"	75' 10"	46' 11"
Seachampion	BC	1973	D	22,278	502' 08"	77' 05"	58' 00"
Sealane II	BC	1973	D	25,100	586' 09"	76' 02"	44' 11"
Sea Monarch	BC	1984	D	29,268	639' 09"	75' 10"	46' 11"
Searanger II	BC	1976	D	29,300	594' 01"	76' 00"	47' 07"
IT-8 — THIEN & HEYENGA BEREEDERUNGS-UND BREFRACHTUNGSGESELLSCHAFT MBH							
Rantum	TK	1978	D	43,550	300' 00"	46' 09"	28' 03"
IT-9 — TOLANI BULK CARRIERS LTD., BOMBAY, INDIA							
Prabhu Daya	BC	1987	D	26,716	608' 11"	75' 04"	47' 03"
Prabhu Gopal	BC	1969	D	24,531	503' 07"	78' 00"	41' 01"
IT-10 — TOMONGO SHIPPING CO. LTD.							
Arosa	BC	1975	D	17,355	625' 06"	75' 00"	47' 10"
IT-11 — TORKEL ALENDAL REDERI A.S.							
Spirit Trader	TK	1975	D	44,125	317' 08"	39' 06"	23' 11"
IT-12 — TRANSMAN SHIPPING ENTERPRISE							
Luckyman	BC	1980	D	28,192	584' 08"	75' 10"	48' 05"
IT-13 — TRANSPORT IGLOOLIK, INC., MONTREAL, PQ							
Aivik	RR	1980	D	7,048*	359' 08"	63' 08"	38' 10"
IU-1 — UNICOM MANAGEMENT SERVICES (CYPRUS) LTD.							
Socofl Wave	BC	1992	D	6,273	365' 02"	59' 03"	24' 11"
IU-2 — UNIVAN SHIP MANAGEMENT LTD., HONG KONG							
Bergen Bay	BC	1977	D	16,736	579' 11"	75' 02"	48' 03"
Bergen Luna	BC		D				
Bergen Sea	BC	1977	D	16,736	579' 11"	75' 02"	48' 03"
Rover	BC	1979	D	24,274	579' 01"	75' 02"	45' 11"
Stormy Annie	BC	1975	D	20,950	521' 08"	75' 06"	44' 04"
Ucka	BC	1979	D	11,155	500' 04"	74' 04"	38' 05"
IV-1 — VALE DO RIO DOCE NAVEGACAO S.A., RIO DE JANEIRO, BRAZIL							
Docegulf	BC	1979	D	17,861	674' 03"	75' 08"	47' 07"
Helio Ferraz	TB	1973	D	208*	90' 08"	28' 03"	13' 02"
Itabira	TB	1963	D	149*	78' 00"	24' 00"	10' 04"
Tubarao	TB	1974	D	228*	82' 00"	28' 02"	11' 06"
IV-2 — VIKEN SHIPPING CO. A/S							
Utviken	BC	1985	D	30,052	621' 05"	75' 01"	47' 11"

EXTRA TONNAGE ...

Stewart J. Cort fights ice at the Soo Locks in April, 1996.   (Alan Jewell)

LOCATIONS OF MAJOR GREAT LAKES SHIPWRECKS

SEAWAY SHIPWRECKS
5, 7, 11

LAKE HURON
Exact Location Unknown
23, 53

LAKE SUPERIOR
Exact Location Unknown
22, 26, 30, 38, 51, 56, 95

LAKE MICHIGAN
Exact Location Unknown
46

St Lawrence Seaway

Lake Ontario

Buffalo

Toronto

Collingwood

Hamilton

Welland Canal

Lake Erie

Erie
Conneaut
Ashtabula
Cleveland
Sandusky

Goderich

Sault Ste. Marie, ON

Lake Huron

Sarnia
Port Huron
Detroit
Toledo

Alpena

Bay City

Sault Ste. Marie, MI
(Soo Locks)

Marquette

Lake Superior

Thunder Bay

Two Harbors
Duluth
Superior

Isle Royale

Ludington

Muskegon

Green Bay

Sheboygan

Milwaukee

Kenosha

Chicago

Lake Michigan

SHIPWRECK KEY

The first 15 shipwrecks are listed chronologically; the remainder alphabetically. Listing includes only those vessels declared a total loss ... those salvaged and returned to service are not listed. Please match the shipwreck's number to its location on the map on previous page (locations are approximate). Casualties, where known, are listed after reason lost (no entry means no lives known lost). An asterisk indicates the ship was lost in the **Great Storm of Nov. 11-13, 1913.**

Vessel	Date lost	Reason lost, location, # of casualties
1. **Jupiter**	9-1990	Exploded, burned at Bay City (1 lost)
2. **Mesquite (WLB-305)**	12-1989	Stranded, (later sunk as underwater preserve) off the Keweenaw Peninsula
3. **Edmund Fitzgerald**	11-1975	Foundered, cause unknown, on Lake Superior (29 lost)
4. **Jennifer**	12-1974	Foundered, heavy seas, off Milwaukee
5. **Roy A. Jodrey**	11-1974	Hit obstruction, sank, in St. Lawrence Seaway
6. **Sidney E. Smith Jr.**	06-1972	In collision with Str. Parker Evans at Port Huron
7. **Eastcliffe Hall**	07-1970	Hit obstruction, sank in St. Lawrence River (9 lost)
8. **Nordmeer**	11-1966	Stranded in gale *(superstructure still visible)* off Alpena
9. **Daniel J. Morrell**	11-1966	Foundered, heavy seas, off Harbor Beach (28 lost)
10. **Cedarville**	05-1965	Hit in fog by M/V Topdalsfjord in Straits of Mackinac (10 lost)
11. **Leecliffe Hall**	09-1964	Collision with M/V Appolonia, St. Lawrence River (3 lost)
12. **Francisco Morazon**	11-1960	Stranded on S. Manitou Island
13. **Carl D. Bradley**	11-1958	Foundered in gale near Beaver Island (33 lost)
14. **Scotiadoc**	06-1953	Hit in fog by Str. Burlington off Thunder Bay (1 lost)
15. **Henry Steinbrenner**	05-1953	Foundered in heavy seas off Isle Royale (17 lost)
16. **Admiral** (tug)	12-1942	Foundered in heavy seas off Cleveland (7 lost)
17. **Altadoc**	12-1927	Stranded, Keweenaw Point, Lake Superior
18. **Andaste**	09-1929	Foundered, Lake Michigan (25 lost)
19. **Argus***	11-1913	Foundered, Lake Huron (25 lost)
20. **Arlington**	05-1940	Foundered, Lake Superior (1 lost)
21. **Asia**	09-1882	Foundered, Georgian Bay (123 lost)
22. **Bannockburn**	11-1902	Disappeared on Lake Superior (21 lost)
23. **Kate L. Bruce**	11-1877	Disappered on Lake Huron (8 lost)
24. **Marshall F. Butters**	10-1916	Foundered in heavy seas in Lake Erie
25. **James Carruthers***	11-1913	Foundered in heavy seas in Lake Huron (25 lost)
26. **Cerisoler** (minesweeper)	11-1918	Disappeared on Lake Superior (39 lost)
27. **Chicora**	01-1895	Disappeared in heavy seas on Lake Michigan (24 lost)
28. **City of Bangor**	11-1926	Stranded, Keweenaw Point, Lake Superior
29. **Clarion**	12-1909	Stranded, burned on Lake Erie. (15 lost, approx.)
30. **D.M. Clemson**	11-1908	Disappeared, Lake Superior (24 lost)
31. **Cleveco** (barge)	12-1942	Foundered in heavy seas, Lake Erie (11 lost)
32. **Clifton**	09-1924	Foundered in heavy seas, Lake Huron (27 lost)
33. **Dewitt Clinton**	10-1839	Sank off Milwaukee (5 lost)
34. **James B. Colgate**	10-1916	Foundered in Lake Erie (24 lost)
35. **Omar D. Conger**	04-1922	Exploded at Port Huron (4 lost)
36. **John B. Cowle**	07-1909	Hit in fog by Str. Issac M. Scott, Whitefish Bay (14 lost)
37. **George M. Cox**	05-1933	Stranded, sank off Isle Royale
38. **Cyprus**	09-1907	Foundered, heavy seas, Lake Superior (21 lost)

Con't on Page 94

39. **William B. Davock** . . . . .11-1940 . . . . . . .Foundered off Pentwater, Lake Michigan (33 lost)
40. **L.R. Doty** . . . . .10-1898 . . . . . . .Sank in heavy seas, Lake Michigan (17 lost)
41. **David Dows** . . . . .11-1889 . . . . .Lost in Lake Michigan gale
42. **Eastland** . . . . .07-1915 . . . . . .Capsized at Chicago pier (835 lost)
43. **Emperor** . . . . .06-1947 . . . . . .Ran aground, Canoe Rocks off Isle Royale (12 lost)
44. **Erie** . . . . .08-1841 . . . . . .Exploded and burned on namesake lake (175 lost)
45. **D.L. Filer** . . . . .10-1916 . . . . . .Sank in heavy seas in western Lake Erie (6 lost)
46. **W. H. Gilcher** . . . . .11-1892 . . . . . .Foundered in Lake Michigan gale (21 lost)
47. **Hamonic** . . . . .07-1945 . . . . . .Burned at Sarnia, Ont.
48. **D.R. Hanna** . . . . .05-1919 . . . . . .In collision with Str. Quincy A. Shaw off Alpena
49. **Hydrus*** . . . . .11-1913 . . . . . .Foundered in Lake Huron (28 lost)
50. **Independence** . . . . .11-1853 . . . . . .Exploded at the Soo (4 lost)
51. **Inkerman** (minesweeper) . . . .11-1918 . . . . . .Disappeared on Lake Superior (39 lost)
52. **Iosco** . . . . .09-1905 . . . . . .Sank in Lake Superior storm (19 lost)
53. **Kaliyuga** . . . . .10-1905 . . . . . .Vanished on Lake Huron (16 lost)
54. **Kamloops** . . . . .12-1927 . . . . . .Lost off Isle Royale in gale (22 lost)
55. **Lady Elgin** . . . . .09-1860 . . . . . .Sank after collision on Lake Michigan, (297 lost)
56. **Lambton** . . . . .04-1922 . . . . . .Lighthouse tender vanished on Lake Superior (22 lost)
57. **Leafield *** . . . . .11-1913 . . . . . .Grounded, sank on Lake Superior (18 lost)
58. **John B. Lyon** . . . . .09-1900 . . . . . .Lost in Lake Erie gale (11 lost)
59. **Marquette-Bessemer No. 2** . . .12-1909 . . . . . .Carferry vanished on Lake Erie (36 lost)
60. **Seldon E. Marvin** . . . . .11-1914 . . . . . .Sank in Lake Superior gale (all hands)
61. **John A. McGean*** . . . . .11-1913 . . . . . .Foundered in Lake Huron (28 lost)
62. **Merida** . . . . .10-1916 . . . . . .Foundered in Lake Erie during a gale (23 lost)
63. **Milwaukee** . . . . .10-1929 . . . . . .Carferry vanished on Lake Michigan (all hands lost)
64. **Anna C. Minch** . . . . .11-1940 . . . . . .Foundered in Lake Michigan gale (24 lost)
65. **Myron** . . . . .11-1919 . . . . . .Foundered off Whitefish Point (17 lost)
66. **Alex. Nimick** . . . . .09-1907 . . . . . .Hit shoal, sank near Duluth (6 lost)
67. **Benjamin Noble** . . . . .04-1914 . . . . . .Disappeared off Two Harbors (21 lost)
68. **Noronic** . . . . .09-1949 . . . . . .Burned at dock in Toronto (139 lost)
69. **Novadoc** . . . . .11-1940 . . . . . .Sank in a Lake Michigan gale off Pentwater (2 lost)
70. **Onoko** . . . . .09-1915 . . . . . .Exploded, sank on Lake Superior
71. **Orinoco** . . . . .05-1923 . . . . . .Foundered in heavy seas near the Soo (5 lost)
72. **Our Son** . . . . .09-1930 . . . . . .Schooner foundered in Lake Michigan gale
73. **Ira H. Owen** . . . . .11-1905 . . . . . .Foundered, Lake Superior (19 lost)
74. **John Owen** . . . . .11-1919 . . . . . .Foundered, Lake Superior (22 lost)
75. **William Peacock** . . . . .09-1830 . . . . . .Boiler blew up at Buffalo (casualties unknown)
76. **Pewabic** . . . . .08-1865 . . . . . .Collided with Str. Meteor off Alpena (75-100)
77. **Pere Marquette No. 18** . . . . . .09-1910 . . . . . .Swamped in Lake Michigan gale (25 lost)
78. **Anna M. Peterson** . . . . .11-1914 . . . . . .Lost in Lake Superior gale (9 lost)
79. **Phoenix** . . . . .11-1847 . . . . . .Burned off Sheboygan (200)
80. **Plymouth** (barge)* . . . . .11-1913 . . . . . .Foundered in Lake Michigan (9 lost)
81. **Charles S. Price*** . . . . .11-1913 . . . . . .Overcome by seas on Lake Huron (28 lost)
82. **Prindoc** . . . . .06-1943 . . . . . .Sank after collision with Str. Battleford off Isle Royale
83. **Quedoc** . . . . .12-1927 . . . . . .Foundered in Lake Superior blow
84. **Regina*** . . . . .11-1913 . . . . . .Foundered in Lake Huron gale
85. **H.E. Runnells** . . . . .11-1919 . . . . . .Grounded, broke up near Grand Marais
86. **Sagamore** . . . . .07-1901 . . . . . .Sank, Lake Superior, after collision (3 lost)
87. **Sand Merchant** . . . . .10-1936 . . . . . .Foundered near Cleveland (19 lost)
88. **Saturn** . . . . .11-1872 . . . . . .Went down in gale west of Whitefish Point (7 lost)
89. **William F. Sauber** . . . . .10-1903 . . . . . .Sank in storm near Manitou Island (1 lost)
90. **Issac M. Scott *** . . . . .11-1913 . . . . . .Foundered in high seas on Lake Huron (28 lost)
91. **Ferdinand Schlesinger** . . . . . .05-1919 . . . . . .Sank in heavy weather near Isle Royale

92. Senator	10-1929	Collision with Str. Marquette on Lake Michigan (20 lost)
93. Sevona	.09-1905	Foundered, Lake Superior (7 lost)
94. Rouse Simmons	11-1913	Foundered, Lake Michigan (17 lost)
95. Henry B. Smith*	11-1913	Foundered in heavy seas, Lake Superior (25 lost)
96. Steel Vendor	.09-1942	Capsized in rough weather, Lake Superior (1 lost)
97. Sunbeam	.08-1863	Sank in heavy seas, Lake Superior (28 lost)
98. Superior City	08-1920	Collision with Willis L. King in Whitefish Bay (29 lost)
99. Wexford *	11-1913	Foundered, Lake Huron (17 lost)
100. Western Reserve	.08-1892	Sank in Lake Superior (26 lost)

EMPEROR'S REIGN ENDED IN 1947

(Tom Manse)

The 525-foot Canada Steamship Lines' bulk carrier **Emperor** fell victim to Canoe Rocks off Lake Superior's Isle Royale on June 4, 1947 - 50 years ago this year. Twenty-one survivors were picked up by the U.S. Coast Guard cutter **Kimball,** which happened to be in the area, but 12 crewmembers were lost in the disaster.

BIGGEST BLOWS

Besides the *"Great Storm of 1913,"* three other major cataclysms have earned proper names for their power and devastation: the Nov. 30 *"1905 Blow,"* which particularly crippled shipping on Lake Superior; what became known as the *"Black Friday Storm"* of Oct. 20, 1916, which hit particularly hard on Lake Erie; and the Nov. 11,1940 *"Armistice Day Storm,"* which focused mainly on Lake Michigan.

*The author acknowledges the invaluable help of "**Shipwreck**" by David D. Swayze, Harbor House Publishers, in preparing this reference.*

THREE BROTHERS DISCOVERED

With a bit of assistance from Mother Nature, the remains of the 162-foot steamer **Three Brothers** was discovered in April, 1996, near South Manitou Island in Lake Michigan. The wooden vessel sank during a storm 23 September, 1911. All 13 crew members were saved, but marine historians assumed the ship sank without a trace. However, sometime during the winter of '96, a large portion of beach and underwater sand bar washed away, exposing the nearly intact ship. The find was made by U.S. Park Service employees preparing the island for the tourist season.

The Three Brothers rests in 45 feet of water only about 50 feet from the southeast corner of South Manitou, in the Manitou Passage Underwater Preserve. Although recreational divers may explore the site, nothing may be taken off the ship. Looting a wreck protected by state law is a felony punishable by a $5,000 fine; nevertheless some items have already been reported missing.

Built in 1888, the Three Brothers hauled lumber and other cargos between Great Lakes ports. Her name paid tribute to William, James and Thomas White, siblings who operated the William H. White lumber concern in Boyne City, MI.

Nearly 1,200 divers visited the Three Brothers in 1996.

Three Brothers.   *(Courtesy Great Lakes Historical Society)*

GOING, GOING ... GONE

The 71-foot tug **Steven M. Selvick** was deliberately scuttled in 71 feet of water the first week of June, 1996. The vessel, sunk as a dive site, is now part of the Alger Underwater Shipwreck Preserve in Lake Superior, off Munising, MI. Built in 1915 in Lorain, OH, she was used during the construction of the Mackinac Bridge.

(Photos by John C. Meyland)

FOLLOWING THE FLEET

Here's some information to help track that elusive vessel.

BY PHONE

Try calling these pre-recorded messages to keep abreast of vessel movements.

COMPANY	PHONE #	COVERAGE
Algoma Central Marine	905-708-3873	Vessel movements
Boatwatcher's Hotline	218-722-6489	Superior,WI, Duluth, Two Harbors, Taconite Harbor and Silver Bay, MN
CSX Coal Docks/Torco Dock	419-697-2304	Toledo, OH arrivals
DMIR Ore Dock	218-628-4590	Duluth, MN arrivals
DMIR Ore Dock	218-834-8190	Two Harbors, MN arrivals
Eisenhower Lock	315-769-2422	Vessel Movements
Inland Lakes Management	517-354-4400	ILM Fleet movements
Michigan Limestone Docks	517-734-2117	Rogers City / Cedarville, MI arrivals
Oglebay Norton Co.	800-861-8760	Vessel movements
Presque Isle Corp.	517-595-6611	Stoneport, MI arrivals
Sarnia Traffic Center	519-337-6221	Vessel movements, St. Clair River
Seaway Traffic Center (Canada only)	800-465-9107	Vessel movements
Soo Control	906-635-3224	Previous day's traffic - St. Mary's River
Superior Midwest Energy Terminal	715-395-3559	Superior, WI arrivals
Thunder Bay Port Authority	807-345-1256	Thunder Bay, ON arrivals
USS Great Lakes Fleet	218-628-4389	USS Fleet movements
ULS Group	905-688-5878	Vessel movements
Welland Canal	905-688-6462	Vessel movements

ON THE RADIO

With a VHF scanner, you can tune to ship-to-shore traffic, using the following guide.

Bridge to Bridge Communications	**Ch. 13**	(156.650 Mhz)	Commercial vessels only
Calling / Distress ONLY	**Ch. 16**	(156.800 Mhz)	Calling / Distress ONLY
Working Channel	**Ch. 06**	(156.300 Mhz)	Commercial vessels only
Working Channel	**Ch. 08**	(156.400 Mhz)	Commercial vessels only
Soo Supply Warehouse	**Ch. 08**	(156.400 Mhz)	Supply boat at Soo
Sarnia Traffic - Sector 1	**Ch. 11**	(156.550 Mhz)	Detour Reef to Lake St. Clair Light
Sarnia Traffic - Sector 2	**Ch. 12**	(156.600 Mhz)	Long Point Light to Lake St. Clair Light
Seaway Beauharnois - Sector 1	**Ch. 14**	(156.700 Mhz)	Montreal to about mid-Lake St. Francis
Seaway Eisenhower - Sector 2	**Ch. 12**	(156.600 Mhz)	Mid-Lake St. Francis to Bradford Island
Seaway Iroquois - Sector 3	**Ch. 11**	(156.550 Mhz)	Bradford Island to Crossover Island
Seaway Clayton - Sector 4	**Ch. 13**	(156.650 Mhz)	Crossover Island to Cape Vincent
St. Lawrence River portion			
Seaway Sodus - Sector 4	**Ch. 13**	(156.650 Mhz)	Cape Vincent to Mid-Lake Ontario
Lake Ontario portion			

Seaway Newcastle - Sector 5	**Ch. 11** (156.550 Mhz)	Mid-Lake Ontario to Welland Canal
Seaway Welland - Sector 6	**Ch. 14** (156.700 Mhz)	Welland Canal
Seaway Long Point - Sector 7	**Ch. 11** (156.550 Mhz)	Welland Canal to Long Point Light Lake Erie
Soo Control	**Ch. 12** (156.600 Mhz)	St. Mary's River Traffic Service
Soo Lockmaster (call WUD-31)	**Ch. 14** (156.700 Mhz)	Lockmaster, Soo Locks
United States Coast Guard	**Ch. 21** (157.050 Mhz)	
	Ch. 22 (157.100 Mhz)	
	Ch. 23 (157.150 Mhz)	
J. W. Westcott II	**Ch. 10** (156.500 Mhz)	U. S. Mailboat, Detroit, MI

ALL THE NEWS THAT FITS

To track vessel news, information and rumors, try joining one or more of the marine societies around the lakes (send a stamped, self-addressed envelope to Marine Publishing Co., Inc. for a free list), or subscribe to *Great Lakes Log,* 221 Water St., Boyne City, MI. 49712. On-line? Turn to page 100.

Roger LeLievre

Canada Steamship Lines' Tadoussac below Welland Canal Lock 1.

ADRIFT ON THE INTERNET

Newsgroups of Great Lakes Interest
(chat, information exchange, ask questions)
alt.great-lakes
misc.transport.marine

Lakes/Seaway Web Pages
http://www.oakland.edu/boatnerd
The largest Great Lakes home page offers the following categories: Photo Gallery, Museums and Where to Buy; Vessel Passages (Duluth, Soo Locks, Detroit, Welland Canal, Toledo and the St. Lawrence Seaway); Facts & Figures; Calendar of Events; News & Rumor; Information Search; U.S. Mailboat *J.W. Westcott II*; Marine Historical Society of Detroit and other Internet links.

Great Lakes Museum/Maritime Societies

http://little.nhlink.net/wgm/glmh/glmh.html Ass'n for Great Lakes Maritime History
http://sparky.nce.usace.army.mil/behind/excencan.html Canal Park &Museum
http://www.ais.org/~lsa/grtlakes.html Great Lakes Lighthouse Keepers' Assn.
http://www.lssu.edu/shipwreck The Great Lakes Shipwreck Historical Society
http://www.bgsu.edu/colleges/library/iglr/iglr.html Inst. for Great Lakes Research
http://www.oakland.edu/boatnerd/museums/columbia Str. Columbia Foundation
http://www.oakland.edu/boatnerd/mhsd Marine Historical Society of Detroit
http://www.artcom.com/museums/nv/mr/49090-05.htm Mich. Maritime Museum
http://www.sscl.uwo.ca/assoc/sos/ Save Ontario Shipwrecks
http://sparky.nce.usace.army.mil/behind/excensoo.html Corps of Engineers
http://www.execpc.com/~bbaillod/wmhs.html Wisconsin Marine Hist. Society

Vessel Museums

http://stauffer.queensu.ca/marmus/ Alexander Henry
http://pwp.usa.pipeline.com/~tholecek/tabirv.htm William A. Irvin
http://little.nhlink.net/wgm/wgmhome.html William G. Mather
http://www.ncinter.net/~niagara/index.shtml The flagship Niagara
http://www.oakland.edu/boatnerd/museums/clipper/ Milwaukee Clipper
http://www.oakland.edu/boatnerd/museums/spcm/ City of Milwaukee
http://www.artcom.com/museums/nv/sz/49443.htm U.S.S. Silversides
http://execpc.com/~abuelow/ferry.html Great Lakes carferry page
http://www.webpay.com/canadiana.html Str. Canadiana

Locks & Canals

http://sparky.nce.usace.army.mil/SOO/soohmpg.html The Soo Locks
http://www.dot.gov/dotinfo/slsdc/index.htm St. Lawrence Seaway Development Corporation
http://www.seaway.ca/english/english.html St. Lawrence Seaway System
http://badger.ac.brocku.ca/~lp94bs/ships.html Welland Canal Page

(Cont'd on Page 101)

Shipwrecks

http://www.execpc.com/~bbaillod/ Shipwreck Research and Diving Warehouse
http://icity.kosone.com/scuba/wrecksa.html Kingston Shipwrecks
http://www.rtd.com/~fzr1000/index.five.html Lake Erie Shipwrecks
http://scuba.uwsuper.edu/scuba/sites.html Lake Superior Diving
http://www.solutions.net/aqualand/royale.html Shipwrecks, Isle Royal
http://www.mnhs.org/prepast/mnshpo/ship/ship.html Lake Superior Shipwrecks
http://www.seagrant.wisc.edu/Communications/Shipwrecks/shipwrecks.html
   Lake Superior Shipwrecks, Wisconsin Sea Grant
http://www.onramp.ca/~adb/ontdive/ Ontario SCUBA Diving
http://www.sscl.uwo.ca/assoc/sos/ Save Ontario Shipwrecks
http://www.rust.net/Architext/people/haggard/shipwrecked/index.htm
   Shipwrecked on the Internet
http://www.cris.com/~linleysa/ Submerged World Great Lakes shipwreck site
http://supernova.uwindsor.ca/people/drexle2/wrecks/wrecks.html Wreck of the
   Week Archive

Edmund Fitzgerald

EDMUND FITZGERALD

1958-1975

http://www.ships-service.com/fitz/index.html (highly recommended)
http://www.oakland.edu/boatnerd/mhsd/glswr.fitz.htm Edmund Fitzgerald
   From the Marine Historical Society of Detroit's "Great Lakes Ships We
   Remember Volume I"
http://cp.duluth.mn.us/~knewhams/edfitzpics.html Fitzgerald Pictures
http://www.oakland.edu/~awesley/edm-fitz.html Fitzgerald history
http://www.haja.com/fitz.html Fitzgerald Interactive Explorer CD-ROM
http://oldthunder.ssec.wisc.edu/wxwise/fitz.html Sinking of the Fitzgerald
http://home.earthlink.net/~margott/edmund.html Wreck of The Fitzgerald

*For more complete listings, send a stamped, self-addressed envelope to **Marine
Publishing Co., Inc**, 317 S. Division St. #8, Ann Arbor, MI 48104.*

Canadian Venture, 8 August, 1996
(Roger LeLievre)

Courtney Burton, 10 July, 1996.
(Roger LeLievre)

TALKING LIGHTS

RANGE LIGHTS

SIDELIGHTS

STARBOARD - Green

PORT - Red
(Shown here but normally unseen from this angle)

MASTHEAD LIGHT (White) Masthead light means a white light placed over the fore and aft centerline of the vessel showing an unbroken light over an arc of the horizon of 225 degrees and so fixed as to show the light from right ahead to 22.5 degrees abaft the beam on either side of the vessel.

ALL-ROUND LIGHT (White) All-round light means a light showing over an arc of the horizon of 360 degrees.

STERNLIGHT (White) Sternlight means a white light placed as nearly as practicable at the stern showing an unbroken light over an arc of the horizon of 135 degrees and so-fixed as to show the light 67.5 degrees from right aft on each side of the vessel.

SIDELIGHTS (Green/Red) Sidelight means a green light on the starboard side and a red light on the port side, each showing an unbroken light over an arc of the horizon of 112.5 degrees and so-fixed as to show the light from right ahead to 22.5 degrees abaft the beam on its respective side.

As a vessel changes course, it will look as if her all-round light is swinging and her masthead light is standing still. This is literally correct, as it is her stern that is swinging, pivoting on the bow. As the lights move apart the "range is opening." As they come closer together, the "range is closing." ***Be alert for course changes, indicated by the lights changing position.*** Remember, large cargo vessels have a hard time maneuvering so allow plenty of room. If necessary, contact them on VHF Ch. 16 (156.800 Mhz).

WHISTLE LIGHTS

Most Great Lakes vessels carry a whistle light atop the foremast in addition to the masthead light. It is often the capital letter initial of the owner, and is white. The light, an additional safety device, comes on when the whistle is blown, and stays on for the duration of each blast. On lakers with all superstructure located aft, the whistle light is atop the after mast and is usually amber.

PASSING

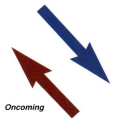

Oncoming

Oncoming vessel is directing her course to the right (starboard) for a port to port passing.

"Bows on" - a collision course. Change course to the right (starboard) if possible.

Oncoming

Oncoming vessel is directing her course to the left (port) for a starboard to starboard passing.

CARGO RECORDS

Cargo	Vessel	Net Tons	Gross Tons	Year
Cement	**Integrity**	16,889	15,080	1996
Eastern Coal *(Seaway)*				
	J.W. McGiffin	31,028	27,509	1972
Eastern Coal *(Soo)*				
	Indiana Harbor	60,578	53,708	1994
Iron ore				
Lake Ontario	**Simcoe**	29,114	25,995	1972
Great Lakes	**Lewis Wilson Foy**	81,033	72,351	1986
Seaway	**Paterson**	31,922	28,502	1986
Soo	**Burns Harbor**	72,167	64,435	1996
Limestone	**Oglebay Norton**	59,078	52,749	1992
Mixed Grain				
Oats	**Saguenay**	1,446,727	bushels	1964
Rye	**Senneville**	1,026,983	bushels	1975
Western Coal *(Lake Superior)*				
	Indiana Harbor	71,369	63,276	1993
Western Coal *(Soo)*				
	Columbia Star	70,706	62,688	1986

GREAT LAKES TRIVIA

The Largest Bulk Carrier

The **Paul R. Tregurtha**, built in 1981 and measuring 1,013' 06" x 105' 6" x 56' 00", is operated by Interlake Steamship Co. of Cleveland, OH.

Newest / Oldest Bulk Carriers

Both are cement carriers operated by the same interests. The newest, the barge **Integrity** (propelled by the pusher tug **Jacklyn M**), entered service in 1996 for Lafarge Cement. The Integrity is the first major construction on the lakes since the **Paterson** and **Atlantic Erie** were built in 1985. The vintage steamer **E.M. Ford**, built in 1898, sailed under her own power until 1995. Most recently, she has been used for dry cement storage at Saginaw, MI.

The First 1,000-Footer

Constructed in 1972, Bethlehem Steel's motor vessel **Stewart J. Cort** proudly wears the #1 designation painted on her aft deckhouse.

The Most Powerful Bulk Carrier

The 1979-built 1,000-footer **Edwin H. Gott** packs a powerful 19,500 HP.

Cement carrier J. A. W. Iglehart, seen from the Blue Water Bridge at Port Huron/Sarnia. (Richard t Weiss)

PLIMSOLL MARKINGS

The Plimsoll Mark is a load line on the side of a ship's hull. It shows how much cargo the ship can carry safely under different conditions. The position of the marking depends on the type and size of the vessel. A ship "loaded down to her marks" carries capacity cargo - any more would lessen the chance of a safe voyage. Load lines on American ships were established by the American Bureau of Shipping, provided by the Load Line Act of 1929, and apply to deep sea vessels of 150 tons or more. The distance between the Plimsoll Mark and the deck is the ship's "freeboard." Special markings were established in 1935 for Great Lakes /Atlantic/Pacific coast voyages.

Plimsoll Mark - Great Lakes-Seaway

The letters **AB** signify American Bureau of Shipping
The letters **LR** signify Lloyd's Registry of Shipping
The letters **FW** signify load line in fresh water
The letters **SW** signify load line in salt water*
The letters **MS** signify midsummer load (May 1- Sept. 15)
The letter **S** signifies summer load line (April 26-30 and Sept. 16-30)
The letter **I** signifies intermediate load line (April 1-15 and Oct. 1-31)
The letter **W** signifies winter load line (Nov.1 to March 31)

*The salt water marks are assigned only to vessels intending to load in salt water of the St. Lawrence River.

(U.S. Flag)

A   B

(Canadian Flag)

L   R

SW	FW	MS
MS		S
S		I
I		W
W		

Additional Plimsoll Markings Seen on Saltwater Vessels

The letters **LL** signify Lloyd's of London
The letter **T** signifies load line in tropical waters
The letters **TF** signify load line in tropical fresh water
The letters **WNA** apply to winter, North Atlantic load line

L—Ⓞ—L

Indicates a vessel has a bulbous bow that may be hidden beneath the waterline.

Indicates a bow or stern thruster directly below and beneath the waterline. Use caution.

*Federal Mackenzie inbound at Toledo.
Note the bowthruster and bulbous bow
warnings on her bow.* (Jim Hoffman)

ABANDONED SHIPS ...

These old Great Lakes hulls are awaiting new careers as historic vessels. Here's an update.

Aquarama - Built during World War II as the U.S. troop carrier *Marine Star*, the Aquarama saw limited success carrying passengers between Detroit and Cleveland in the late '50s and early '60s. Since 1963, she has been laid up at various ports, including Muskegon and Windsor, awaiting whatever fate has in store. In 1995, her original name Marine Star restored, the vessel was towed to Buffalo for a $30 million refit to convert her into a casino/gaming ship. Work has yet to begin on the project, which would see the majestic, seven story, 521-foot vessel returned to active service. She is now moored in Lackawanna, NY.

Canadiana - The S.S. Canadiana Preservation Society, Inc. continues its effort to bring this 215-foot passenger ship back to Buffalo, where she was built in the early 1900s, for restoration and operation. Her deteriorated hull lies at Port Colborne, ON. To find out more, write the S.S.C.P.S. at 17 Delray Drive, Cheektowaga, N.Y. 14225.

Columbia & Ste. Claire - These passenger steamers (built in 1902 and 1911)

sailed the Detroit River, ferrying passengers to and from the Bob Lo Island Amusement Park until 1990. In 1991 the park filed for bankruptcy and the boats were laid up at the Nicholson dock in Ecorse. The vessels are now owned by the non-profit Steamer Columbia and Steamer St. Claire foundations of Detroit. Efforts continue to raise money to restore the Columbia to service for charters, excursions and other special events. Restoration of the Ste. Claire is hoped for at a later date. To help, write P.O. Box 43232, Detroit, MI 48243.

Milwaukee Clipper - Built in 1905 as the passenger steamer *Juniata*, the Clipper, laid up and for sale near Chicago, faces a very uncertain future. Extensively rebuilt in 1941, the Clipper ran a popular, cross-Lake Michigan service from Muskegon until 1970. After her lay-up, the vessel kicked around various Lake Michigan ports until she was bought by the Hammond (IN) Port Authority and brought to that city in hopes of making it a floating convention center and visitor attraction. She was pushed aside in 1996 by a glitzy new gaming vessel, the *Empress III*. A visit in July, 1996, found her run down but sound, with her original quadruple expansion engine, wheel and bell still in place. Coal barges bustle busily around her while the Clipper waits patiently for a new port to call her own.

Niagara - 100-year-old, former Great Lakes sandsucker, which was operated by the Erie Sand Steamship Co. until 1985, awaits conversion to a museum at Erie, PA. The vessel had actually been sold to Marine Salvage Co. for scrap when she was bought by a group of Erie investors hoping to preserve her as a museum piece. Vandals have since stripped the vessel of some of her equipment, and preservation efforts appear to be at a standstill.

IN PROGRESS

City of Milwaukee - Owned by the non-profit Society For the Preservation of the S.S. City of Milwaukee, this former Lake Michigan rail and passenger ferry, built in 1931, is now being converted to a museum at Elberta, near Frankfort, MI. She is open to members by special arrangement for work activities, fireworks and other events. To join, write to S.P.C.M., P.O. Box 506, Beulah, MI 49617 or e-mail sscitymilw @ aol.com for details.

(4 July, 1996 - Richard I. Weiss)

Voyage Into History ...

Sault Ste. Marie's museum ship *Valley Camp* has been open for public tours since 1968, Inside her three vast cargo holds, photos, paintings, artifacts, aquariums and other memorabilia - including two lifeboats from the *Edmund Fitzgerald* (inset) - help interpret the history of the Great Lakes and Sault Ste. Marie regions. Call *906-632-3658*, or see listing on page 114 for details on touring this vintage steamer.

MARINE MUSEUMS

A-Admission fee; T-Tours; G-Gift Shop

(Information subject to change; museum hours can vary. Please phone ahead.)

Bernier Maritime Museum *(55 rue des Pionniers Est., L'Islet-Sur-Mer, PQ)*
Museum explores the history of navigation on the St. Lawrence River. The icebreaker ***Ernest Lapointe*** *is on display.* **418-247-5001 - A -** *Open year 'round.*

Canal Park Marine Museum *(Port of Duluth, MN)*
Operating steam engine, full-size replicas of cabins as found on Great Lakes ships, and numerous hands-on exhibits. **218-727-2497 - *Operated by the U.S. Army Corps of Engineers, - Free -*** *Open year 'round.*

City of Port Huron Museum of Arts & History *(Pine Grove Park, Port Huron, MI)*
The lightship ***Huron***, built in 1920 and the last of its kind, guided mariners into lower Lake Huron for 50 years, until replaced by lighted buoys in 1970. The museum was established in 1990. **810-985-7101 - A,T -** *Mid-May-Sept.*

City of Toledo, OH *(International Park)*
The museum ship ***Willis B. Boyer*** was built in 1911 as ***Col. James M. Schoonmaker*** for the now-defunct Shenango Furnace Co. fleet. The vessel was chartered to Republic Steel Co. in 1969, when it was given its current name. Bought by the Cleveland Cliffs Iron Co. in 1972 and retired after the 1980 season, the Boyer opened as a museum in 1987. **419-936-3070 - A,T,G -** *Year' 'round (call for winter hours). -* **Volunteers needed**

Willis B. Boyer

Collingwood Marine Museum *(Memorial Park, Collingwood, ON)*
More than 100 years of shipbuilding, illustrated with models, photos and videos. **705-445-4811 - A,G -** *Open year 'round.*

Door County Maritime Museum *(Sunset Park, Sturgeon, Bay, WI)*
Located in the former offices of the Roen Steamship Co., exhibits portray the role shipbuilding has played in the Door Peninsula. Refurbished pilothouse on display. **414-743-8139 - A (donations) -** *Memorial Day-mid-Oct.*

Dossin Great Lakes Museum *(100 The Strand, Belle Isle, Detroit, MI)*
Ship models, photographs, interpretive displays, the smoking room from the 1912 passenger steamer ***City of Detroit III,*** an anchor from the ***Edmund Fitzgerald*** and the working pilothouse from the steamer ***William Clay Ford*** are just a few of the museum's attractions. **313-852-4051 - A (donations),G -** *Open year 'round.*

Duluth & Area Convention Center *(Port of Duluth, MN)*
The steamer ***William A. Irvin***, former flagship of the U.S. Steel fleet, last sailed in 1978. Her museum career began in 1986. Also displayed: the Corps of Engineers' tug ***Lake Superior***, added in 1996. **218-722-7876 - A,T,G -** *Late spring-fall.*

(Con't on Page 112)

Fathom Five National Marine Park *(Tobermory, ON)*
Underwater maritime park encompasses 19 of the area's 26 shipwrecks, two of which can be seen from a glass-bottom boat. *519-596-2233 - **A** - April-mid-Nov.*

Government of Ontario, *(Ontario Place, Toronto, ON)*
The World War II-era destroyer HMCS **Haida** participated in the destruction of 14 enemy ships. The vessel was designated a marine museum in 1965. ***416-314-9900 -A,T,G-** May 21-Oct. 14.*

Great Lakes Historical Society *(480 Main St., Vermilion, OH)*
Extensive museum tells the story of the Great Lakes through ship models, paintings, exhibits and artifacts, including engines and other machinery. Pilothouse of retired laker **Canopus** and a replica of the Vermilion lighthouse are also on display. *216-967-3467 - **A,G** - museum open year 'round. An affiliated operation is the **USS Cod**, a World War II submarine open to the public in Cleveland harbor. May 1-Labor Day.-. tour restrictions may apply - call **216-566-8770** for details. - **A,T,G***

Great Lakes Marine & U.S. Coast Guard Memorial Museum
(1071-73 Walnut Blvd., Ashtabula, OH)
Housed in 1898-built former lighthouse keepers' residence, the museum includes models, paintings, artifacts, photos, the world's only working scale model of a Hulett ore unloading machine and the pilothouse from the steamer **Thomas Walters**. *216-964-6847 - **A** (donations) - **T,G** - Memorial Day-Oct. 31.*

Great Lakes Shipwreck Historical Museum *(Whitefish Point, MI)*
Located next to the Whitefish Point lighthouse, the museum houses lighthouse and shipwreck artifacts, a shipwreck video theater and an **Edmund Fitzgerald** display that includes the ship's bell. *906- 635-1742 -**A,G** - May 15-Oct. 15.*

H. Lee White Marine Museum *(Foot of West First St., Oswego, NY)*
The former U.S. Army Corps of Engineers tug **Nash** , her original name, **LT-5** restored in 1996, is the only known surviving such vessel associated with D-Day. Also on display: **Derrick Barge No. 8**. *315-342-0480 - **A,G- (guided tours by appointment)** - Call for hours.*

Harbor Heritage Society *(E. Ninth Street pier, Cleveland, OH)*
The steamer **William G. Mather**, former flagship of the Cleveland-Cliffs Iron Co. fleet, was donated to the city of Cleveland for use as a marine museum in 1987. Her hull may soon receive a colorful new paint scheme. ***Adjacent to the Rock and Roll Hall of Fame; 216-574-6262 - A,T,G** - May-Oct.*

Head of the Lakes Maritime Society *(Barker's Island, Superior, WI)*
The historic **Meteor** , built in 1898 as the bulk carrier **Frank Rockefeller**, was renamed **South Park** in 1927 and converted for use in the sand and gravel business. In 1936, she was altered to carry autos and grain. Rebuilt as a tanker and given her present name in 1943, she was retired in 1969. Brought to Superior for use as a museum in 1973, the Meteor is the last surviving example of the "whaleback" vessel design popular on the lakes a century ago. Also on display is the dipper dredge **Col. D.D. Gaillard**. ***715-392-5742 or 715-392-1083. - A,T,G -** May-mid-Oct.*

(Con't on Page 114)

Norisle at Manitowaning, ON. — (Tom Manse)

Lake County Historical Society *(Two Harbors, MN)*
Steam tug **Edna G** served the Duluth, Missabe & Iron Range Railway for almost 100 years. Refurbished in 1994 and opened to the public in 1996. **218-834-4898 - A**- Seasonal.

Le Sault de Sainte Marie Historic Sites *(foot of Johnston Street, Sault Ste. Marie, MI)*
The 1917-built steamer **Valley Camp**, which last sailed in 1966 for the Republic Steel Co., is home to an extensive marine museum. Dedicated in 1968, her cargo holds house artifacts, ship models, aquariums, photos and other memorabilia, as well as a tribute to the **Edmund Fitzgerald** that includes the ill-fated vessel's lifeboats. Historic Sites also operates the nearby, 21-story **Tower of History** viewing platform and museum. **906-632-3658 - A,T,G** - May 15-Oct.15.

Marine Museum of the Great Lakes at Kingston *(Kingston, ON)*
The 1959-built Canadian Coast Guard icebreaker, **Alexander Henry**, retired from service in 1985, is open for tours and as a bed and breakfast. **613-542-2261 - A,T,G** - May-Sept.

Marine Museum of Upper Canada *(Exhibition Place, Toronto, ON)*
Exhibits detail the development of the shipping industry on the Great Lakes and St. Lawrence Seaway. The 79-foot steam tug **Ned Hanlan**, built in 1932, is also on display. **416-392-1765 - A,G** - Year 'round.

Marquette Maritime Museum *(East Ridge & Lakeshore Dr., Marquette, MI)*
Contained in an 1890s waterworks building, the museum recreates the offices of the first commercial fishing and passenger freight companies. Displays also include charts, photos, models and maritime artifacts. **906-226-2006 - A** - May 31-Sept. 30.

Michigan Maritime Museum *(off I-196 at Dyckman Ave., South Haven, MI)*
Exhibits are dedicated to the U.S. Lifesaving Service and U.S. Coast Guard. Displays tell the story of various kinds of boats and their uses on the Great Lakes. **616-637-8078 - A,G** - Open year 'round.

Museum of Science & Industry *(57th Street & Lakeshore Dr., Chicago, IL)*
The museum houses the German submarine **U-505**, captured in the Atlantic Ocean in 1944. **312-684-1414 - T** - Open year 'round.

Naval and Serviceman's Park Museum *(Naval Park Cove, Buffalo, NY)*
On display are the guided missile cruiser **USS Little Rock**, the WW2 destroyer **USS The Sullivans** and the WW2 submarine **USS Croaker**. Museum displays include models, armed service artifacts and aircraft. **716-847-1773 - A,T,G** - April-Nov.

Old Mariners' Church *(170 E. Jefferson Ave., Detroit, MI)*
Church was built in 1849 on Woodward Avenue, but was moved in 1955 to make way for a civic center. The blessing of the Great Lakes fleet and a memorial service for those who have died at sea takes place on the second Sunday of March. A memorial service is held for the crew of the **Edmund Fitzgerald** the Sunday closest to Nov. 10. Normal services are held every Sunday at 11 a.m. The annual blessing of the fleet is held in March. **313-259-2206 - T (reservations required), A (donation)**

(Con't on Page 115)

Pennsylvania Historical & Museum Commission *(Port of Erie, PA)*

The brig **Niagara**, Commodore Oliver Hazard Perry's flagship, has been rebuilt and opened to the public. From the Niagara's decks, Perry proclaimed "We have met the enemy and they are ours," during the War of 1812's Battle of Lake Erie. **814-452-2744 - A,T -** *(phone ahead to make sure ship is in port).*

Petersen Steamship Co. *(Blue Star Highway, Douglas, MI)*

The 1907-built passenger steamer **Keewatin,** which sailed for the Canadian Pacific Railway from 1907 until 1965, opened as a museum in 1968. Also on display is the historic steam tug **Reiss. 616-857-2464 or 616-857-2107 - A,T,G -** *Memorial Day-Labor Day.*

Port Colborne Historical & Marine Museum *(Port Colborne, ON)*

Wheelhouse from the steam tug **Yvonne Dupre Jr.,** anchor from the propeller ship **Raleigh**, and a lifeboat from the steamer **Hochelaga** are among the museum's displays. **905-834-7604 - Free -** *May-Dec.*

River of History Museum *(209 E. Portage Ave., Sault Ste. Marie, MI)*

Interpretive display explores 8,000 years of history of the St. Mary's River Valley, from glacial origins to Native American occupation, the French fur trade, British expansion and the U.S. creation of a state. **906-632-1999 - A,G -** *Seasonal.*

St. Mary's River Marine Centre *(Bondar Park, Sault Ste. Marie, ON)*

Built in 1950 for the Owen Sound Transportation Co., the museum ship **Norgoma** served the Georgian Bay-Sault Ste. Marie area in freight and passenger service until its retirement in 1974. **705-256-7447 - A,T,G -** *Mid-April - Oct.*

Township of Assiginak *(Manitowaning, ON)*

The **Norisle**, a former Georgian Bay-area passenger and freight carrier operated by the Owen Sound Transportation Co., was retired from service in 1974. **705-859-3977 - A,T -** *June 1-Labor Day.*

U.S. Army Corps of Engineers Museum *(inside the Soo Locks Visitor Center, Sault Ste. Marie, MI)*

Exhibits include a working model of the Soo Locks, photos, and a 25-minute film. Also, three observation decks adjacent to the MacArthur Lock provide an up-close view of ships locking through. **909-632-3311- Free -** *May-Nov. Check at the information desk for a list of vessels expected at the locks.*

USS Silversides & Marine Museum *(Port of Muskegon, MI)*

The former U.S. Navy submarine **Silversides** and the high endurance cutter **McLane** are open for public viewing. **616-755-1230 - A,T-** *April-October.*

Welland Canal Visitor Center *(At Lock 3, Welland Canal, Thorold, ON)*

Museum traces the development of the Welland Canal. The pilothouse of the former package freighter **Fort Henry** is also on site. **905-685-3711 - G -** *Museum open year 'round. Observation deck open during the navigation season. Check at the information desk for vessels expected at Lock 3.*

Wisconsin Maritime Museum *(75 Maritime Dr., Manitowoc, WI)*

Displays explore the history of area shipbuilding, and also honor submariners and submarines built in Manitowoc during World War 2. The submarine **USS Cobia,** built in 1943, is open for tours. **414-684-0218 - A,G,T -** *open year 'round.*

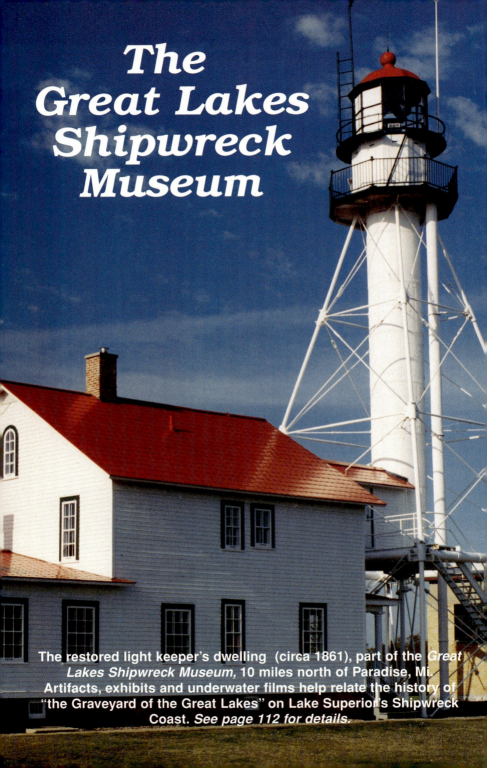

The Great Lakes Shipwreck Museum

The restored light keeper's dwelling (circa 1861), part of the *Great Lakes Shipwreck Museum,* 10 miles north of Paradise, Mi. Artifacts, exhibits and underwater films help relate the history of "the Graveyard of the Great Lakes" on Lake Superior's Shipwreck Coast. *See page 112 for details.*

Colors of the Great Lakes & Seaway Smokestacks

Algoma Central Marine Navigation Sonamar Sault Ste. Marie, ON

American Steamship Co. Williamsville, NY

American Tug & Transit Co. Bay City, MI

Andrie, Inc. Muskegon, MI

Arnold Transit Co. Mackinac Island, MI

B+B Dredging Corp. Crystal River, FL

Beaver Island Transit Co. Charlevoix, MI

Bethlehem Steel Corp. Chesterton, IN

Bigane Vessel Fueling Co. Chicago, IL

Black Creek Shipping Co. Lower Lakes Towing Port Dover, ON

Buchanan Forest Products Thunder Bay, ON

Buffalo Fire Department Buffalo, NY

Canada Steamship Lines, Inc. Montreal, PQ

Canadian Coast Guard Ottawa, ON

Canadian Dredge & Dock Inc. Don Mills, ON

Canadian Forest Navigation Co. Ltd. Montreal, PQ

Chicago Fire Department Chicago, IL

Cleveland Fire Department Cleveland, OH

Cleveland Tankers, Inc. Cleveland, OH

Coastwise Trading Co. East Chicago, IN

Dean Construction Co. Belle River, ON

Diamond Jack River Tours Detroit, MI

Duluth - Superior Excursions Duluth, MN

Durocher Dock & Dredge, Inc. Cheboygan, MI

Eastern Canada Towing Ltd. Halifax, NS

Enerchem Transport, Inc. Montreal, PQ

Erie Navigation Co. Erie Sand & Gravel Co. Erie, PA

Erie Sand Steamship Co. Erie, PA

Essroc Canada Inc. Toronto, ON

Fednav International Ltd. Montreal, PQ

Fraser Shipyards, Inc. Superior, WI

Gaelic Tug Boat Co. Grosse Ile, MI

Goodtime Transit Boats, Inc. Cleveland, OH

Great Lakes Dredge & Dock Co. Oak Brook, IL

Great Lakes International Towing & Salvage Ltd. Burlington, ON

Great Lakes Maritime Academy Northwestern Michigan College Traverse City, MI

Great Lakes Towing Co. Cleveland, OH

Hannah Marine Corp. Lemont, IL

Imperial Oil Ltd. Esso Petroleum Canada Div. Dartmouth, NS

Inland Lakes Management, Inc. Alpena, MI

LaFarge Canada, Inc. Canada Steamship Lines - Mgr. Montreal, PQ

MacDonald Marine Ltd. Goderich, ON

Merca Transportation Co. Sylvania, OH

P & H Shipping Div. of Parrish & Heimbecker Ltd. Mississauga, ON

Roen Salvage Co. Sturgeon Bay, WI

Knudsen Shipping Haugesund, Norway

Luedtke Engineering Co. Frankfort, MI

Medusa Cement Co. Division of Medusa Corp. Cleveland, OH

Ontario Northland Transportation Commission Owen Sound, ON

Rideau St. Lawrence Cruise Ships, Inc. Kingston, ON

Kinsman Lines, Inc. Cleveland, OH

Look Tours Canada Sault Ste. Marie, ON

McKeil Marine Ltd. Hamilton, ON

Ontario Ministry of Transportation & Communication Kingston, ON

Quebec Tugs Ltd. Quebec, PQ

King Construction Co. Holland, MI

Litton Great Lakes Corp. USS Great Lakes Fleet - Mgr. Erie, PA

McAllister Towing & Salvage, Inc. Montreal, PQ

Oglebay Norton Co. Cleveland, OH

J. W. Purvis Marine Ltd. Sault Ste. Marie, ON

Kent Line Ltd Saint John, NB

Lee Marine, Ltd. Port Lambton, ON

Marine Fueling Co. St. Paul, MN

Neuman Boat Line, Inc. Sandusky, OH

Provmar Fuels, Inc. Div. of ULS Corporation Toronto, ON

Kellstone, Inc. Cleveland, OH

Lake Michigan Contractors, Inc. Holland, MI

Malcom Marine St. Clair, MI

Nadro Marine Services Port Dover, ON

Polish Steamship Co. Szczecin, Poland

The Interlake Steamship Co. Lakes Shipping Co. Cleveland, OH

Lake Michigan Carferry Service, Inc. Ludington, MI

Maid of the Mist Steamboat Co., Ltd. Niagara Falls, ON

Muskoka Lakes Navigation & Hotel Co. Gravenhurst, ON

Pelee Island Transportation Services Pelee Island, ON

Inland Steel Co. East Chicago, IN

Lafarge Cement Corp. Andrie, Inc. - Mgr. Alpena, MI

Madeline Island Ferry Line, Inc. LaPoint, WI

Miller Boat Line, Inc. Put - In - Bay, OH

N.M. Paterson & Sons Ltd. Thunder Bay, ON

St. Lawrence Seaway Authority
Cornwall, ON

Soo Locks Boat Tours
Sault Ste. Marie, MI

Soo Locks Boat Tours
Sault Ste. Marie, MI

Socanav, Inc.
Montreal, PQ

Shepler's Mackinac
Island Ferry Services
Mackinaw City, MI

MUSEUM SHIPS

Museum Ships
Willis B. Boyer (Toledo)
William G. Mather (Cleveland)

Museum Ship
Valley Camp
Sault Ste. Marie, MI

Museum Ship
Keewatin
Douglas, MI

Museum Ship
City of Milwaukee
Elberta, MI

Museum Ships
Norgoma (Sault Ste. Marie)
Norisle (Manitowaning)

Museum Ship
USCGE Nash
Oswego, NY

Museum Ship
William A. Irvin
Duluth, MN

Museum Ship
CCGC Alexander Henry
Kingston, ON

Museum Ship
USCGC Lightship 103
"Huron"
Port Huron, MI

Museum Ship
Meteor
Superior, WI

Museum Ships
USS Little Rock
USS The Sullivans
Buffalo, NY

Museum Ship
HMCS Haida
Toronto, ON

Shell Canada Products Ltd.
Montreal, PQ

Star Line Fleet
St. Ignace, MI

Upper Lakes Group
Jackes Shipping, Inc.
ULS Marbulk, Inc.
Ottawa, ON

United States
Environmental Protection Agency
Bay City, MI

Upper Lakes Towing Company, Inc.
Escanaba, MI

Selvick Marine Towing Corp.
Sturgeon Bay, WI

St. Mary's Cement Co.
Toronto, ON

Transport Desgagnes, Inc.
Quebec, PQ

United States Coast Guard
9th Coast Guard District
Cleveland, OH

University of Michigan
Center for Great Lakes
& Aquatic Sciences
Ann Arbor, MI

Sandusky Boat Line
Sandusky, OH

St. Lawrence Seaway
Development Corp.
Massena, NY

Stott Nielsen Tankers
Greenwich, CT

United States Army -
Great Lakes - Corps of Engineers
Detroit, MI

USS Great Lakes Fleet, Inc.
Duluth, MN

House Flags of Great Lakes & Seaway Fleets

Algoma Central
Marine

American
Steamship Co.

Atlantic Towing
Ltd.
Kent Line Ltd.

Bethlehem Steel
Corp.

Canada
Steamship Lines,
Inc.

Cleveland
Tankers, Inc.

Enerchem
Transport, Inc.

Erie Navigation
Co.; Erie Sand &
Gravel

Gaelic Tug Boat
Co.

Great Lakes
Towing Co.

Imperial Oil Ltd.
Esso Petroleum
Canada Div.

Inland Steel Co.

Interlake Steamship
Co.
Lakes Shipping Co.

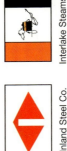

Kinsman Lines,
Inc.

Oglebay Norton
Co.

P. & H. Shipping

Inland Lakes
Management, Inc.

N.M. Paterson
& Sons Ltd.

Seaway Bulk Carriers

USS Great Lakes
Fleet, Inc.

Seaway Self
Unloaders

Socanav, Inc.

Transport
Desgagnes, Inc.

Upper Lakes
Group, Inc.

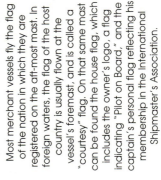

Most merchant vessels fly the flag
of the nation in which they are
registered on the aft-most mast. In
foreign waters, the flag of the host
country is usually flown at the
vessel's foremast, and is called a
"courtesy" flag. On that same mast
can be found the house flag, which
includes the owner's logo, a flag
indicating "Pilot on Board," and the
captain's personal flag reflecting his
membership in the International
Shipmaster's Association.

Flags of Nations in the Marine Trade

United States

Bermuda
Chile
Cyprus
Equatorial Guinea
Gabon

Benin
Cape Verde
Cuba
El Salvador
French Polynesia

Belize
Cameroon
Croatia
Egypt
France

Antigua & Barbuda
Azerbaijan
Belgium
Cambodia
Cote D'Ivoire
Ecuador
Finland

Angola
Austria
Barbados
Bulgaria
Costa Rica
Dominican Republic
Fiji

Algeria
Australia
Bangladesh
Brunei
Congo
Djibouti
Ethiopia

Albania
Armenia
Bahrain
Brazil
Colombia
Denmark
Estonia

Afghanistan
Argentina
Bahamas
Bosnia & Herzegovina
China
Czech Republic
Eritrea

International Code Flags & Pennants

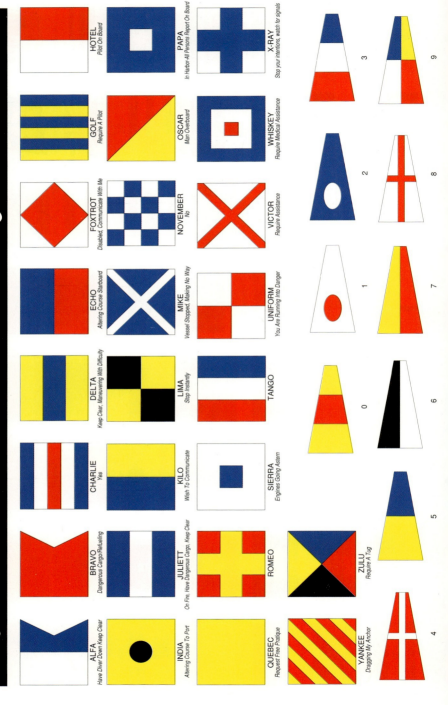

ALFA
Have Diver Down Keep Clear

BRAVO
Dangerous Cargo/Refueling

CHARLIE
Yes

DELTA
Keep Clear, Maneuvering With Difficulty

ECHO
Altering Course Starboard

FOXTROT
Disabled, Communicate With Me

GOLF
Require A Pilot

HOTEL
Pilot On Board

INDIA
Altering Course To Port

JULIETT
On Fire, Have Dangerous Cargo, Keep Clear

KILO
Wish To Communicate

LIMA
Stop Instantly

MIKE
Vessel Stopped, Making No Way

NOVEMBER
No

OSCAR
Man Overboard

PAPA
In Harbor-All Persons Report On Board

QUEBEC
Request Free Pratique

ROMEO

SIERRA
Engines Going Astern

TANGO

UNIFORM
You Are Running Into Danger

VICTOR
Require Assistance

WHISKEY
Require Medical Assistance

X-RAY
Stop your intentions, watch for signals

YANKEE
Dragging My Anchor

ZULU
Require A Tug

0 1 2 3 4 5 6 7 8 9

LOG NOTES

Country: ....

Ship: ....
Company: ....

Country: ....

Ship: ....
Company: ....

....
....
....

The information in this book was obtained from the United States Coast Pilot (Vol. 6), the St. Lawrence Seaway Authority, the Lake Carriers Association, Farwell's Rules of the Nautical Road, the Institute for Great Lakes Research, the Great Lakes Commission, Jane's Merchant Ships, the American Merchant Seaman's Manual, the U.S. Army Corps of Engineers and other sources.

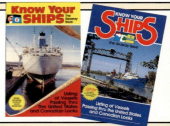

Canadian bulk carrier Meaford, downbound in the lower St.Mary's River near Lime Island on 15 August, 1973. The Meaford was scrapped in Spain in 1980 after ending her career under the name Pierson Independent.

(Roger LeLievre)

Seadaniel in the lower St. Mary's River near the Soo Locks. (Roger LeLievre)